D0623359

SHIBA KŌKAN

Studies of the East Asian Institute, Columbia University

Frontispiece. Self-portrait. *Ink and light color on paper. Courtesy of the Tenri Library, Nara prefecture.*

SHIBA KŌKAN

ARTIST, INNOVATOR, AND PIONEER IN THE WESTERNIZATION OF JAPAN

by CALVIN L. FRENCH

New York • WEATHERHILL • Tokyo

THE EAST ASIAN INSTITUTE OF COLUMBIA UNIVERSITY

The East Asian Institute of Columbia University was established in 1949 to prepare graduate students for careers dealing with East Asia and to aid research and publication on East Asia during the modern period. The faculty of the Institute are grateful to the Ford Foundation and the Rockefeller Foundation for their financial assistance.

The Studies of the East Asian Institute were inaugurated in 1962 to bring to a wider public the results of significant new research on modern and contemporary East Asia. For a complete list of Studies, see the end of this book.

First edition, 1974

Published by John Weatherhill, Inc., 149 Madison Avenue, New York, New York 10016, with editorial offices at 7-6-13 Roppongi, Minato-ku, Tokyo 106, Japan. Printed and first published in Japan.

LCC Card Number 74-76104 ISBN 0-8348-0098-5

To my Mother and Father
whose patience and assistance
reach over many years

CONTENTS

LIST OF PLATES

UNLESS OTHERWISE INDICATED, ALL WORKS ILLUSTRATED ARE BY SHIBA KŌKAN

Color Portfolio

Monochrome Plates

PREFACE

MANY AUTHORS AND SCHOLARS have focused attention on the cross-cultural influences affecting Japanese society during the three hundred years from the European discovery of Japan in the mid-sixteenth century to the Japanese acceptance of Europe in the mid-nineteenth. During the Tokugawa era and its period of self-imposed isolation from 1639 to 1854, a bewildering complex of intellectual, political, and economic forces existed within and without the closed society; ultimately, these forces contributed to the collapse of traditional standards, to the opening of the country, and to the rise of Japan as a modern nation. The rapidity with which Japan has been able in modern times to assume status as a leading economic and cultural force in international affairs has been due at least in part to the earlier activities of a group of enlightened scholars of Western learning working within the confines of a society officially closed to the outside world. Though sometimes naive and occasionally misguided in their interpretations of Western methods, in the main their outlook was remarkably sure and they worked with impressive determination. The actions and writings of these men show progressive attitudes, open-minded investigations of foreign ideas, and eagerness to advance their nation's social and economic status by incorporating into Japanese culture what they deemed the best aspects of European society.

Shiba Kōkan, besides sharing these interests and aims, also was an artist working both in traditional Far Eastern styles and in the European manner. The diversity of his activities—he was at once a scholar of significance, a painter and engraver of marked originality, and an exceedingly successful disseminator of knowledge—reflects the complexity of the society that his biography elucidates. A further dimension of his appeal lies in his colorful personality, for he was—to a greater degree than were any of his peers—unorthodox, iconoclastic, controversial, and unpredictable. His astonishing range of interests, his many accomplishments, and his individuality distinguish him as an uncommon man among those uncommon men who created the intellectual foundations of modern Japan.

Reproductions in the text have been selected as a representative sampling of Shiba Kōkan's diverse interests and his artistic style in various media. They are not intended to represent the only extant works by him; others that might equally well support the arguments presented are omitted if they add no further understanding of the man or his artistic style. Detailed information on the works included appears in the List of Plates; dated paintings are noted in the Chronology, Appendix I. To present a complete compendium of the works by Shiba Kōkan, however, would be presumptuous and inevitably inconclusive. The problem of authentication is immense, complicated by the long tradition of Japanese excellence in forgery and by the fact that style and technique in the "oil" medium used in Tokugawa times are especially easy to copy. Kōkan had many imitators during his lifetime, and after his death, particularly during the Meiji era (1868–1912), a great many forgeries of his work were executed. In distinguishing imitator from imitated, as well as in unraveling the confused web of little-known minor artists all working in the same manner, one ultimately must rely on one's own critical judgment. After studying several hundred paintings by or attributed to Shiba Kōkan, I have a fairly firm conviction of what constitutes Kōkan's style—and have learned there always is room for re-evaluation. Only when further research has been carried out on the extant body of Japanese oil paintings in the Western manner, and when individual styles have been more precisely investigated, can we hope to enumerate and critically evaluate Kōkan's total *oeuvre*.

The terms "naturalism" and "realism" as they appear in this text are not to be taken as definitive aesthetic categories; rather, they are used in reference to the type of European art admired by Kōkan and his contemporaries for its photographic accuracy. Kōkan himself termed such art *shasei:* a true representation of reality or living nature.

Names of Japanese historical personages throughout the text are given in Japanese order, surname first.

It is a privilege to express my sincere appreciation for assistance received in the compilation of this manuscript.

To Professor Donald Keene, whose superb translations and literary productions on so many diverse aspects of Far Eastern culture are the foundations and touchstones for anyone involved in Japanese studies, I owe a major debt of gratitude. It was he who introduced me to Far Eastern studies, and from him I received my training. His outstanding research on the topic of Western influences in Japan first aroused my own interest, and his patient hours of personal guidance gave shape and direction to the data I assembled both in the United States and during a four-year residence in Japan.

Funds for study in Japan were made available by the Foreign Area Fellowship Program and a Traveling Fellowship in Chinese and Japanese from Columbia University. A Horace H. Rackham Fellowship and Grant from the University of Michigan, as well as funds from the Center for Japanese Studies, under the directorships of professors Robert Ward and Roger Hackett, also aided immeasurably.

Anyone interested in the study of early Western-influenced Japanese art would do well to begin at the Kobe City Museum of Namban Art, which houses the outstanding collection assembled by Mr. Hajime Ikenaga (1891–1955). For his generosity in permitting me time to study and photograph the works in that collection, I am deeply grateful to the Curator, Dr. Tadashi Sugase.

To the following persons I express appreciation for invaluable aid and many acts of kindness: Dr. Jane Gaston-Mahler of Columbia University; Dr. Tōru Haga of Tokyo University; the late Dr. Chibiki Okamura of Waseda University; Mr. John Powers; Dr. John M. Rosenfield of Harvard University; Dr. Harold P. Stern, Director of the Freer Gallery of Art; Dr. Egon Verheyen of Johns Hopkins University; Ms. Grace Vlam; Mr.

Meredith Weatherby, President of John Weatherhill, Inc.; and Dr. Herschel Webb of Columbia University.

Ms. Toni Graeber and Ms. Judy Hopkins gave most generously of their time and energy in preparing the final stages of the manuscript.

I should like to extend special appreciation to Mr. Dana Levy for his personal kindness in photographing many of the works reproduced in this book, and to Ms. Becky Davis, firm friend and editor, for her final word of taste.

Lastly and with special warmth, it is a pleasure to acknowledge those friends who have remained friends in spite of Shiba Kōkan. They have read and commented on countless drafts, checked translations, and given willingly of their time, interest, and patience. A debt of personal gratitude to Ms. Gail C. Weigl, Professor James Redfern of Louisiana State University, Professor Niel Sir of the University of New Hampshire, Professor Zino Song of the University of Hawaii, and Mr. Takashi Takahashi of Asia Library at the University of Michigan.

For errors and oversights I alone am responsible.

C. L. F.

ANN ARBOR
1971

SHIBA KŌKAN

CHAPTER ONE

INTRODUCTION

WRITING AT THE AGE of sixty-four, near the end of a long life, Shiba Kōkan summed up the conflict of his own nature in these words:

> Everyone, whatever his station in life, enjoys pictures, and if pictures are distinguished by color, even persons who know nothing about art will admire them. Today's styles of painting, both Chinese and Japanese, originated in China. . . . Japan has never invented anything. . . .
>
> The excellence of a painting lies in the fact that one can see immediately things that could not otherwise be seen; therefore, if pictures do not portray objects accurately, they are neither admirable nor useful. . . . Dutch paintings are not judged by the methods, spirit, or force of the brush as are Japanese and Chinese paintings. . . . They never illustrate imaginary landscapes, . . . nor are they ever executed before noblemen at official banquets. The art of painting, like that of writing, is not a frivolous pastime, but a national asset.
>
> The people of our country have no interest in investigating natural laws of the universe and ignore such studies as astronomy and geography. They are shallow and lack wisdom.
>
> I live in Japan, however, and in trying to be different from my countrymen, I have made a great mistake.[1]

In other words, he was on the one hand a Japanese and a product of Japanese culture and, on the other, a heretic dissatisfied with the values and mores of his own society and committed to expanding the dimensions of Japanese thought. Hence he was peculiarly qualified to play the role of gadfly in Tokugawa Japan.

To be different was to be subversive in that insular society. His government had chosen to exclude the nation from the rest of the known world. Kōkan, whose every interest centered on some aspect of the world beyond the confines of Japan, inevitably divorced himself from the mainstream of Tokugawa life. Everything to which he dedicated himself mirrors his concern with a new order of things. All his attempts to classify, to categorize, are pieces of the vast system offered to him by Western artists and scientists. He preferred to think of himself as a man of urgent scientific inquiry and concentrated his efforts on geography and astronomy—sciences he considered most beneficial to Japan as an island nation. Art, however, was his vocation. He was the first outstanding Japanese exponent of painting in the European manner, and among the earliest to paint in oils. Moreover, he introduced the technique of copperplate etching, a contribution of major importance to the development of Japanese graphic arts. The advances he achieved in the world of art were revolutionary; the paintings and etchings he produced, significant pioneer endeavors.

At the same time, the European knowledge and techniques transmitted by Kōkan to Japan were filtered through a thoroughly Japanese imagination. In no sense, of course, was he competing with his European contemporaries; what he chose of the West to value, his means of expression, the products of his creativity, his very misconceptions of Europe were affected by his national heritage.

Even in Tokugawa Japan Kōkan's enthusiasm and respect for European cultural and scientific achievements was not unique, and in a larger historical context, his admiration was part of a tradition of interest dating back to the earliest contacts of Japan with Western nations. If interest in the West was considered unorthodox during Kōkan's lifetime, it had not always been so. Others before him had looked favorably on European civilization, contrasting what they saw—or thought they saw—with their own nation, questioning and censuring established ideas and customs of their country.

Conflicts in eighteenth-century Japan over whether to accept, reject, or try to assimilate Western ideas and technology were the result of some two hundred years of sporadic contacts with Europeans. The reception accorded the early Europeans was eminently cordial, and Japanese had at first displayed no hostility toward imports from European nations.

The first representatives of the West to reach Japan were Portuguese seamen, blown off course by a typhoon in 1542. They landed on the island of Tanegashima off the southern coast of Kyushu, carrying with them the first firearms the Japanese had ever seen. The excitement these weapons aroused among the Japanese, caught in the throes of warfare that was to last more than a century, can easily be imagined. Of equal wonder were the exotic strangers who came from some distant continent beyond the reaches of China.

The foreigners, for their part, saw Japan as a new land for possible economic exploitation and, almost concurrently, another area for missionary activity. In 1549 the Jesuit Francis Xavier, "Apostle of the Indies," arrived and inaugurated the first era of active contact between Japan and the West. Christianity made strong headway among the Japanese during the fifty years of comparatively free cultural intercourse that followed. Trading missions were established by the Spanish, Portuguese, Dutch, and English, and great interest in Western objects and learning was evinced by Japanese of all classes. In Nagasaki a Jesuit press, set up in 1591, printed instructional and devotional manuals of Christianity both in roman letters and Japanese writing, as well as Japanese grammars and dictionaries. Contact between Europeans and Japanese was unrestricted; some missionaries learned Japanese, and the Japanese, particularly the lay brothers who worked in close association with their Jesuit mentors, made progress in learning Latin, as well as Portuguese, the lingua franca of trade. As part of their proselytizing activity, the Jesuits were instrumental in introducing Western art to Japan, printing religious pictures and providing instruction in oil painting, chiefly in copying religious subjects from European works.

At the same time that Christian converts were adopting Western techniques for the imitation of European religious paintings and engravings, artists associated with such traditional schools of painting as the Kanō were incorporating foreign subject matter of a nonreligious nature in otherwise indigenous works of art. Their paintings, usually executed on large folding screens, depicted the missionaries and Portuguese traders, the great foreign ships and the strange plants, animals, and inventions brought from abroad. Both the Christian-influenced paintings executed in Western techniques and those in native style depicting foreigners were known as *namban-ga,* or "southern-barbarian pictures," since the Portuguese "barbarians" arrived in Japan by ships from the south.

The Dutch traders, too, brought pictures, though generally in the form of small book illustrations. Japanese paintings inspired by these works, as well as representations of the Hollanders and their possessions, were known as *kōmō-ga,* or "red-hair pictures," a name borrowed from the Chinese (*hung-mao*), derived from the Oriental belief that all Dutchmen, like demons, had red hair. Thus, both Portuguese and Dutch influences were present during the early Tokugawa period; although the names of many foreign-style artists have been preserved in the records of Nagasaki painters,[2] it is not always possible to ascertain whether a particular artist painted Portuguese-influenced *namban-ga* or Dutch-influenced *kōmō-ga.*

Among the curiosities introduced by the early Europeans in Japan, maps and globes proved especially exciting. Although well-acquainted with their own coastline, the Japanese had little notion of the geography of the rest of the world and eagerly adopted European cartography. World maps by Japanese often were painted in lavish style on large decorative screens of two, four, or six panels. A companion screen frequently depicted a map of Japan, or illustrated male and female specimens from the forty traditionally distinguished races. These "races" included what seem to be representatives from Europe, Asia, Africa, and America, but only a few—such as the Japanese, Chinese, American Indian, Portuguese, and Dutch couples—can be identified. The depiction of foreigners suffered from the absence of real-life models; they were either based on imported Dutch pictures or derived from imaginary beings of Japanese or Chinese mythology. Great attention was devoted to costume, but comparatively little to distinguishing characteristics of personal appearance.

Besides a knowledge of world geography, information on navigation, mathematics, and such natural phenomena as comets and meteors was also gathered from the Westerners. The study and absorption of European culture might have made rapid and steady progress during the succeeding centuries had not other forces altered completely the manner of contact between Japan and the West.

With the increased influx of Westerners—Jesuits, Spanish Franciscans and traders, and later Dutch and English merchants—distrust of their real motives arose, in part because of bickering among the foreigners themselves. The first edict repressing the activities of the Jesuits was promulgated in 1587; though of little immediate effect, it was a portent of things to come. Ten years later, persecutions and repressions of Christians became severe and continued thereafter to increase in frequency and ferocity, resulting in widespread martyrdoms among converts. These culminated, in 1638–39, in the wholesale slaughter of thousands of Japanese Christians who had joined in a rebellion in the Shimabara Peninsula area, not far from Nagasaki. The Japanese government was intent upon preventing a repetition of the pattern of proselytizing and conquest they observed as the common outcome of European interest in the East. They probably feared less a direct invasion by a European power than an uprising of native converts, fomented and aided by Europeans.

By the time of the Shimabara Rebellion, the Jesuit printing press in Nagasaki had already been dismantled and removed (circa 1614), the English trading station had failed (1623), and the Spanish had been forbidden access to the country (1624). Any publications of the Jesuit press uncovered by government officials were confiscated and destroyed, along with other works preaching Christian doctrine.

In 1639 all Portuguese traders were expelled from Japan. The only Europeans remaining, the nonproselytizing Dutch merchants, were moved two years later from their original port on the island of Hirado in northern Kyushu to the small manmade island of Deshima in Nagasaki Bay; here, their activities could be more carefully scrutinized and controlled by Japanese officials. Thus ended the era of unrestricted intercourse between East and West, and the progress that had been made by the Japanese in their studies of Western art and science was virtually halted. During the century that followed, the few men who studied Western scholarship worked in secret.

The Tokugawa era was the longest period of peace Japan has ever known. From 1603 to 1868 the Japanese government sought to maintain peace indefinitely by preserving the status quo within the country; from 1638 the policy of seclusion was enforced to prevent all but Dutch and Chinese merchants from entering Japanese ports and outside nations from interfering in national affairs. While Europe was awakening to new discoveries of science, to mechanization, to social and economic progress, Japanese rulers sought nothing more than the preservation of traditional patterns and the right to be left alone.

Japan, they felt, had already taken the best of Chinese culture and incorporated it into the national scheme of government. Morality was based on neo-Confucianism, and the Japanese believed there could be no nobler or more workable system of ethical behavior. No contribution to the Japanese social order was expected from the Western barbarians who sought adventure and material gain. While they possessed certain medicines, fabrics, and practical inventions of value to the Japanese nation, these could be obtained through Nagasaki. Imported articles were reserved almost exclusively for the ruling class. Foreign books were severely censored, and any unorthodox ideas that might upset the political balance were at once suppressed.

The Dutch merchants who replaced the Christian missionaries as representatives of the West in Japan had neither the inclination nor the ability to instruct interested Japanese in European culture. Their own interest was solely in the profit to be gained through commerce. Instead of religion, they had cotton cloth, liquors, woolens, and other commodities for sale; in return they sought primarily copper and other metals. Among the Dutch traders, few evinced any interest whatever in Japanese customs and culture.

There were some exceptions, although these were generally men of other nationalities employed by the Dutch East India trading company. The German physician Engelbert Kaempfer, who arrived in Japan in 1690, was deeply interested in all aspects of Japanese life; from research during two years of residency he published an illustrated history of the country. Foreigners in Japan generally were received with suspicion and distrust, but Kaempfer was rewarded for his good faith by kind treatment and assistance from Japanese associates:

> I must beg leave to observe, that besides the several things hitherto mention'd, which travellers usually carry along with them in their journies, I had for my own private use a very large Javan box, which I had brought with me from Batavia. In this box I privately kept a large mariner's compass, in order to measure the directions of the roads, mountains, and coasts but openly, and exposed to every body's view, was an inkhorn, and I usually fill'd it with plants, flowers, and branches of trees, which I figur'd and described, (nay

under this pretext, whatever occur'd to me remarkable:) Doing this, as I did it free and unhindred, to every bodies knowledge, I should be wrongly accus'd to have done any thing which might have proved disadvantageous to the company's trade in this country, or to have thereby thrown any ill suspicion upon our conduct from so jealous and circumspect a nation. Nay, far from it, I must own, that from the very first day of our setting out, till our return to Nagasaki, all the Japanese companions of our voyage, and particularly the Bugjo, or commander in chief, were extremely forward to communicate to me, what uncommon plants they met with, together with their true names, characters and uses, which they diligently enquired into among the natives. The Japanese are very reasonable and sensible People, and themselves great lovers of plants, look upon Botany as a study both useful and innocent, which pursuant to the very dictates of reason and the law of nature, ought to be encourag'd by every body. . . .

From this reasonable behaviour of the landlords, on our behalf, the reader may judge the civility of the whole nation in general, always excepting our own officers and servants, and the companions of our voyage. I must own, that in the visits we made or receiv'd in our journey, we found the same to be greater than could be possibly expected from the most civiliz'd nation. The behaviour of the Japanese, from the meanest countryman up to the greatest Prince or Lord, is such that the whole Empire might be called a school of Civility and good manners. They have so much sense and innate curiousity, that if they were not absolutely denied a free and open conversation and correspondence with foreigners, they would receive them with the utmost kindness and pleasure.[3]

The clandestine manner of obtaining knowledge of the West came to an end under the administration of the eighth shogun, Yoshimune, who, in 1720, lifted the ban on the importation of foreign books that had been in effect for nearly a hundred years. A new law stipulated that only works dealing directly with Christianity were forbidden. Yoshimune's interest in Western astronomy and mathematics and his desire to establish a more accurate calendar for Japan based on Chinese and Western sources seem to have been the chief motivating factors behind his relaxation of the restriction. For the first time, the study of Dutch language and scholarship received official government sanction and became a respectable scholarly pursuit.

The growing legitimacy of Western studies resulted in the gradual decline of Nagasaki as the cultural center for foreign learning. This was due also to the persisting strict surveillance exercised by government representatives there, under orders to enforce the prohibition against unofficial contacts between the Dutch and local inhabitants. Progressive currents shifted to the more metropolitan centers of Edo and Kyoto, where Dutch learning rapidly acquired increasing dignity and stature. Following the publication and circulation in 1774 of a translation of a Western book on anatomy, the former invidious appellation of *bangaku* (barbarian learning) gave way to the more respectable *rangaku* (Dutch studies), and scholars of Western learning became known as *rangakusha*.

Rangakusha did not, of course, represent the mainstream of Tokugawa thought. Theirs was a relatively small group—a few determined scholars quietly pursuing Western studies despite the severe handicaps imposed by a closed country restricting free association with Europeans. Yet these men formed a nucleus of intellectual life in the Tokugawa period. As scholars struggling against the insularity of their society, their objective was the acquisition of foreign knowledge, which they believed necessary for Japan to resist outside aggression, strengthen its government, and improve social and economic conditions. Their chief importance lies in the fact that they prepared a foundation on which their successors could build; their heirs provided much of the leadership for Japan's modernization when the country finally opened its ports to the world in the mid-nineteenth century.

If the *rangakusha* were not a predominant group in society, neither were the time-honored Buddhist intellectuals. Buddhism, with its emphasis on the necessity of obtaining release from the bonds of the illusory world, had proved a stabilizing influence and panacea for the miseries attending centuries of turmoil prior to the establishment of the Tokugawa regime. But the Buddhist clergy fell into disfavor during the era of peace and relative stability, partly as a result of malpractices and partly because of the shift in attention from the otherwordly to the world of here and now. New knowledge of geography and Western science further tended to discredit many Buddhist teachings concerning the nature of the physical world. Few secular scholars could find anything to praise in Buddhism; most were distinctly antagonistic. Shiba Kōkan, for one, detested both the Buddhist clergy and their doctrines and wrote vehemently against them.

The officially accepted moral doctrine of the Tokugawa period was neo-Confucianism—a code of ethical behavior appropriate to a hierarchical society with its emphasis on loyalties and obligations interacting through the whole structure of government. This doctrine was based on the teachings of a Chinese philosopher of the Sung dynasty, Chu Hsi, from whose system the Japanese had adopted those elements they thought best suited to the requirements and temper of their own country. Human loyalties and personal relationships were of utmost importance in maintaining order throughout the nation. Reason was the guiding principle of all learning and conduct; a ruler who used reason could be relied upon for effective government.

Reason, however, referred to moral principles, not to the methods employed by scholars who studied the Western empirical tradition, with its stress upon objective scientific inquiry into the operations of the natural world. Neo-Confucianists sought in nature sets of metaphysical symbols, as opposed to the *rangakusha,* who studied nature for its own sake. The neo-Confucianists condemned the examination of external forms as an irreverent quest that not only ignored the unanalyzable moral essence of the universe, but tended to deny harmony between man and nature by fracturing the unity of the laws governing both. To neo-Confucianists, nature was personal; Westerners, by assuming that the external world was governed by a mechanical order entirely removed from human will or morality, violated the harmony of Heaven and Earth. The *rangakusha,* committed to dissecting the nature that the neo-Confucianists held sacred, studied Western science precisely because the results of such exploration were useful and practical.

There was also a school of native learning, called *kokugaku,* which was originally devoted to the study of philology, ancient Japanese history and literature, and the indigenous Shinto religion. Unlike the neo-Confucianists, who by definition were committed to an admiration of Confucius and his successors in China, *kokugaku* scholars denied that China was in any way superior to Japan. Their anti-Chinese attitudes were seconded by the advocates of Western learning, who held that far more was to be learned from the countries of Europe than from decadent Chinese culture. The *rangakusha,* however, took exception to the *kokugakusha*'s often extreme xenophobia, which led them to assert that Hollanders were subhuman creatures with eyes like animals, born without heels, who lifted one leg like a dog when urinating; such notions were summarily discredited by the *rangaku* scholar Ōtsuki Gentaku. To a remark that Westerners were not better than animals, Kōkan replied: "If what you say is true, human beings are not as clever as beasts."[4]

Never intended to undermine government authority, the various intellectual currents of the eighteenth century had ultimately solidified into these distinct, conflicting schools of thought, whose divergent goals inadvertently created ever-widening breaches with orthodox policy. As new ideas gained credence, the Japanese became more responsive to change.

The two significant administrators in control of the government during Shiba Kōkan's lifetime were Tanuma Okitsugu and Matsudaira Sadanobu.[5] Neither held the top position of shogun, but wielded power by occupying key administrative posts. Okitsugu rose steadily to a position of authority under the administration of the tenth shogun, Ieharu, and in 1772 he became virtual ruler of the country by holding the two chief positions of Regular Senior Councilor in charge of public services and Grand Chamberlain in close attendance on the shogun. Like the eighth shogun, Yoshimune, Okitsugu looked upon Dutch learning as a partial solution to Japan's economic and social difficulties, encouraged land reclamation and the colonization of Hokkaido, and even went so far as to consider opening the country, especially the Hokkaido region, to foreign trade.

The general atmosphere of free spending and progressive spirit of inquiry prevailing during Okitsugu's rule changed when the reins of government were taken over by Sadanobu, regent for the eleventh shogun, Ienari, and the de facto ruler of Japan from 1786 to 1793. In an attempt to reassert government authority, Sadanobu promulgated reforms and sumptuary laws in 1790 designed to reduce expenditures, increase production, curb the rising tide of luxury, and re-establish orthodoxy in manners and morals. However well-intended these reforms were, they proved insufficient remedies for the ills of his society. Sadanobu failed to see that a policy of seclusion and a refusal to engage in foreign commerce were hindrances to the material and scientific progress of Japan. For this he was severely criticized by Kōkan, who maintained that foreign contacts through trade were essential to the national economy and well-being. Despite the restrictions placed upon society by the national policy of isolation, intellectual forces within the culture continued to expand and evolve. At the same time, pressure was exerted on Japan by Russia and other foreign nations to negotiate trade agreements. It became increasingly evident that more than mere exclusion edicts were necessary to ensure Japanese security.

Shiba Kōkan, neither a politician nor an economist, took no direct part in determining the policies of government. His writings, however, reflect his concern with contemporary problems, and he expressed his opinions unequivocally on such topics as the evils of Buddhism and neo-Confucianism and the need for foreign trade. He probably owed his escape from government censure and the unhappy fate of some unorthodox thinkers to his complete lack of political involvement. But though indirect, his influence on his age was no less pervasive: Kōkan was probably more responsible than any other man for the popularization of foreign knowledge and for awakening his countrymen to the world outside the confines of Japan. Were it not for him, the dissemination of European learning, techniques, and inventions would have progressed more slowly, remaining the property of a select few, passed down from teacher to disciple in the traditional Japanese manner. Kōkan's publications enabled men of all classes to discover the vastness of the world and the variety of peoples, arts, and sciences it contained.

Fifty years after his death, Japan was to enter a period of amazingly rapid modernization. Foreign observers were astonished by the suddenness of the change, but behind it were many years of often concealed activity by progressive thinkers, such as Shiba Kōkan. Kōkan holds a significant position as one of the early influences behind Japan's eventual emergence as a modern nation.

CHAPTER TWO

EARLY YEARS

SHIBA KŌKAN'S ANCESTORS migrated from Kishū (present-day Wakayama prefecture) to Japan's capital at Edo, where Kōkan was born in 1747.[1] His father was a townsman and probably belonged to the artisan class —the third-ranking level in the social structure.[2] During his lifetime Kōkan assumed such a bewildering variety of names we cannot be sure of his original family name, but Andō is generally accepted, because he was known during his youth as Andō Kichijirō.[3] He made no mention in his writings of brothers and sisters and may have been an only child.

From boyhood Kōkan was fond of drawing. He later wrote in his book of reminiscences, *Shumparō Hikki* (Notes by Shumparō):

> There must have been artists among my ancestors. My father's elder brother had a natural talent for painting, and perhaps I had some of his blood in my veins. At the age of five, seeing a design of sparrows on a bowl, I copied it on paper and showed it to my uncle. When I was nine, I used to make many paintings of Daruma to show him.[4]

His father may have been a swordmaker in Edo, for Kōkan's early ambition was to follow that trade:

> From my youth I was determined to become famous. I wanted to learn some art for which I would be so well known that my name would be remembered long after my death. My first idea was to design swords, for these are the prime part of a warrior's equipment, are handed down in the family, and the maker's name is remembered from generation to generation. The government had put down all opposition, however, and the country was at peace. Swords had become mere fashionable ornaments, and those worn by the military class were all antiques; there was no demand at all for new swords. Moreover, I did not like the idea

1. Killing Insects Inside the Mosquito Net. *Circa 1771–74. Woodblock print. Courtesy Hiraki Ukiyo-e Foundation, Tokyo.*

2. Summer Moon. *Circa 1775–81. Color on silk. Courtesy of the Freer Gallery of Art, Smithsonian Institution, Washington, D.C.*

3. Winter Moon. *Circa 1775–81. Color on silk. Courte Museum of Fine Arts, Boston.*

4. Ryōgoku Bridge, Edo. *1787. Copperplate etching. Courtesy of the Kobe City Museum of Namban Art.*

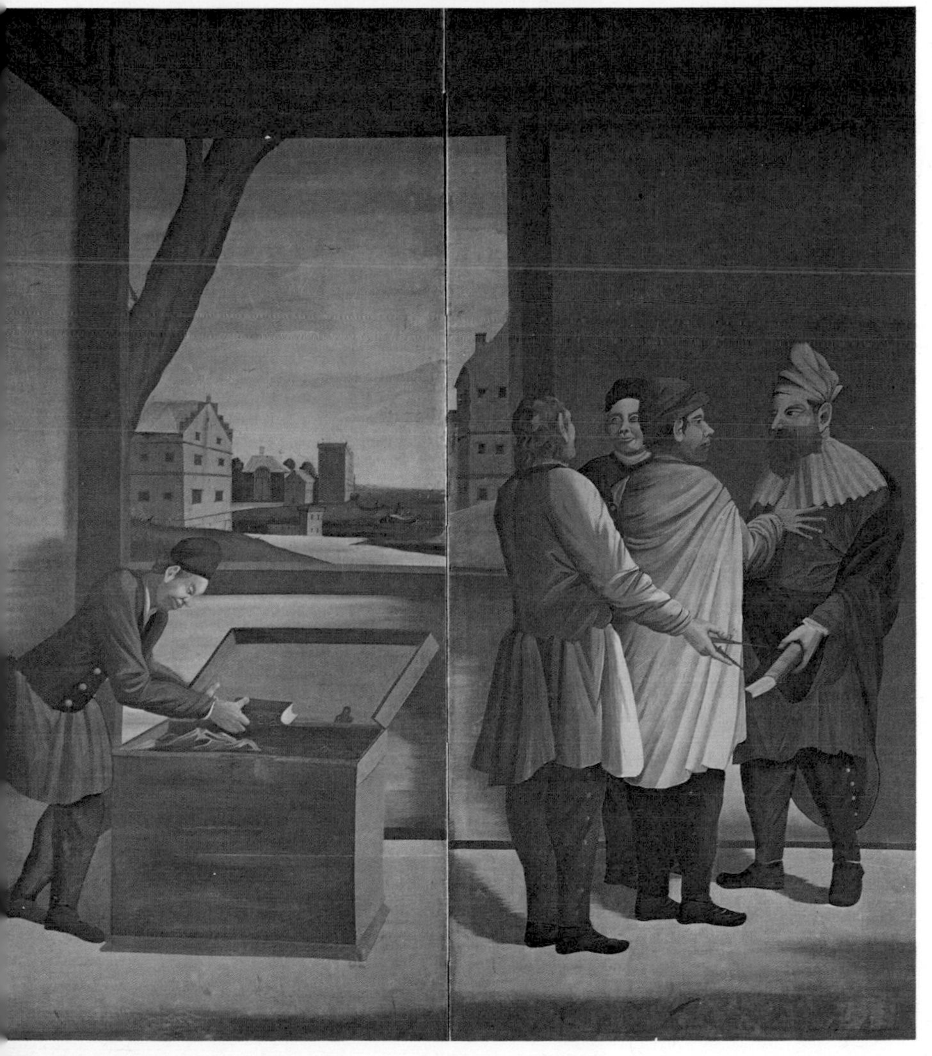

5. Scholars in Conference. *Circa 1789. Oil on paper. Courtesy of Yabumoto Sōshirō, Tokyo.*

6. The Shore at Shinagawa, Edo. *Oil on silk. Courtesy Museum of Fine Arts, Boston.*

7. Shichirigahama Beach, Kamakura. *1796. Oil on paper. Courtesy of the Kobe City Museum of Namban Art.*

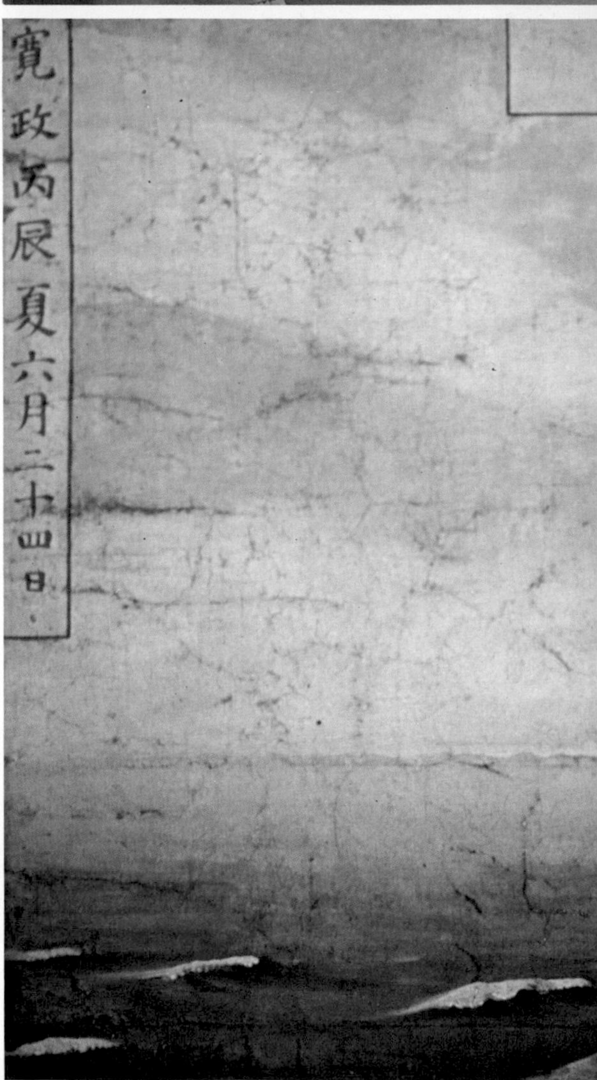

相州鎌倉七里濱

西洋畫士　東都

江漢司馬峻　描寫

A.o 1 8

9

8. The Shore of Kisarazu. *1800. Oil on silk. Courtesy of the Itsukushima Shrine, Miyajima.*

9. Tenkyū Zu *(Planisphere). 1796. Copperplate etching. Courtesy of the Kobe City Museum of Namban Art.*

10. Tenkyū Zu *(Planisphere). 1796. Copperplate etching. Courtesy of the Kobe City Museum of Namban Art.*

11. The Sun. *1796. Copperplate etching. Courtesy of the Kobe City Museum of Namban Art.*

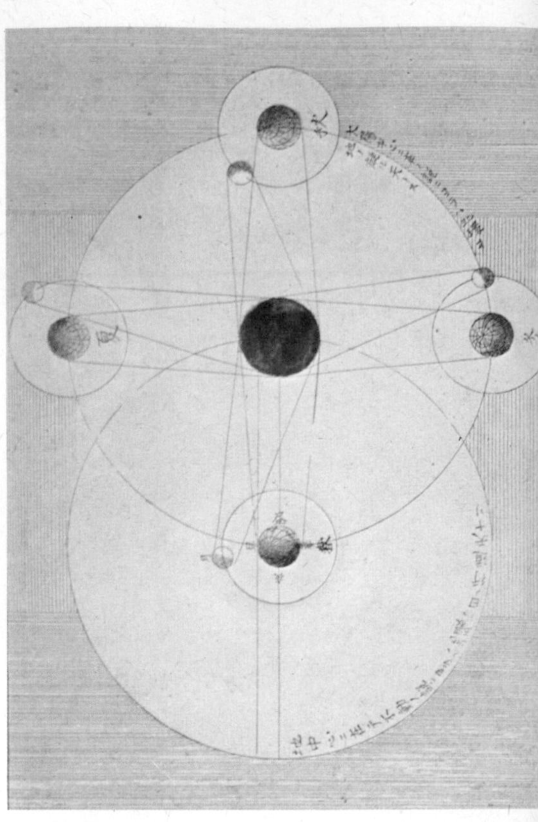

13. Heliocentric and Geocentric Universes *1796. Copperplate etching. Courtesy of the Kobe Cit Museum of Namban Art.*

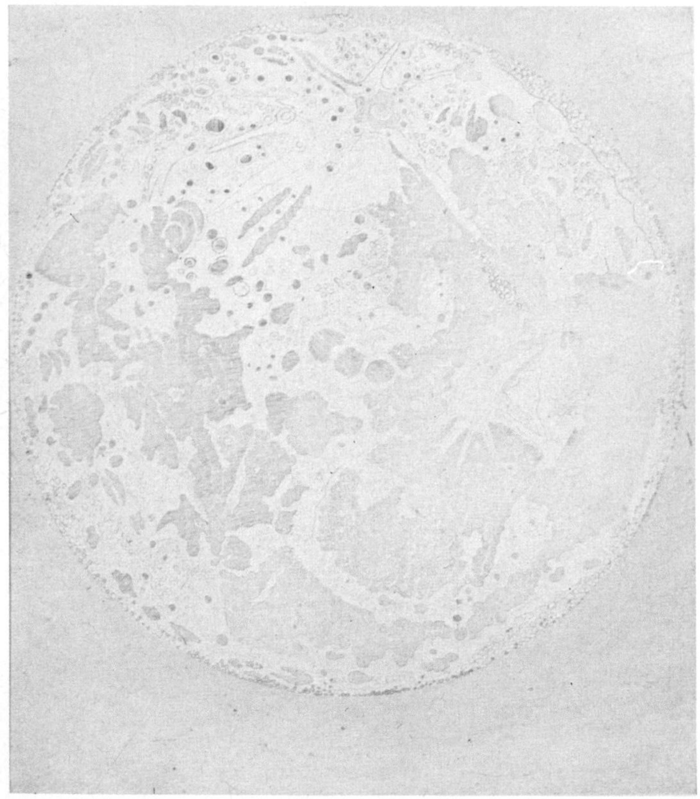

12. The Moon: Selenograph. *1796. Copperplate etching. Courtesy of the Kobe City Museum of Namban Art.*

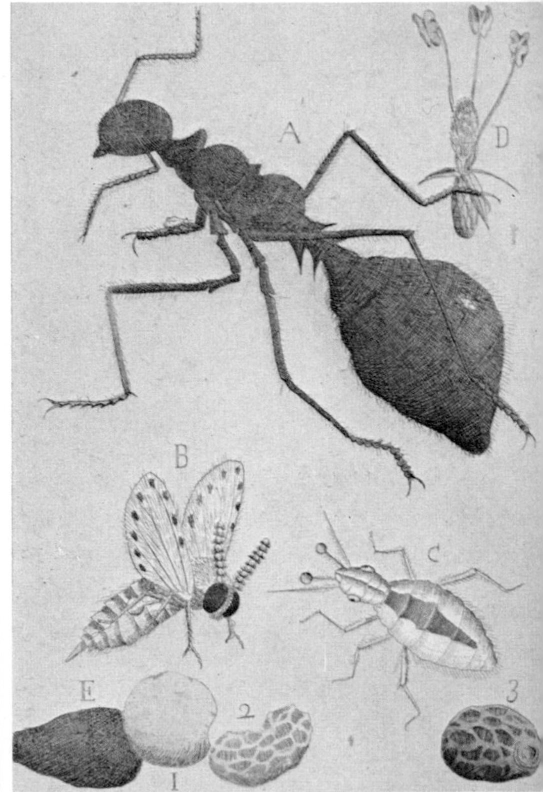

14. Insects and Seeds Viewed Through a Micro scope. *1796. Copperplate etching. Courtesy of the Kob City Museum of Namban Art.*

of making what, in intention, were instruments of carnage and slaughter, so I changed my mind and gave up that profession.[5]

Before dying in 1761,[6] his father enrolled the fourteen-year-old Kōkan under a teacher of the Kanō school. Established in the mid-fifteenth century, this school still represented in the eighteenth century the painting style officially recognized by the government. It was common practice for men seeking to learn painting to study first under a Kanō master, even though by Kōkan's time artists of this tradition were producing uninspired, mannered works. Kōkan wrote that he studied under Kanō Furunobu, but this is an error; Furunobu died before Kōkan was born. Furunobu, however, also used the name Eisen-in, the same name taken by his son, Michinobu Eisen-in; so possibly it was the son who became Kōkan's teacher.[7] In any event, Kōkan soon tired of academic Kanō training. In 1762, age fifteen, he switched allegiance and became the student of Sō Shiseki, master of the Chinese bird-and-flower style.

Besides his traditional training in Kanō art, Kōkan also received instruction in Chinese classics and poetry—an education ordinarily reserved for members of the samurai class. It was at this time that he chose the names Shiba, Kōkan, and Shun:

> Karahashi Sesai was a Confucian scholar who lived at Shitaya Takemachi. He often visited the house of my neighbor, a doctor named Sōgen, and read with him, sometimes giving dissertations on the texts. I used to join them, in order to learn what I could. Sesai would give out themes, and we had to write Chinese poems on them. It seemed to me that it would be more refined to have Chinese-sounding names to sign under my poems, so I chose Shun, Shiba, Kungaku, and Kōkan. My ancestors came from Kishū on the Kii Peninsula, where the great Hidaka and Kino rivers are located; I therefore chose the name Kōkan, meaning "broad river." Later Sesai told me that Kō and Kan are two different rivers in China[8] and was greatly amused that I had selected two rivers for my name. By that time, however, I was generally known as Kōkan and did not try to change it, even though I realized my mistake.[9]

Trained in both traditional Japanese painting and the Chinese bird-and-flower style, Kōkan had sufficient skill, talent, and popularity to afford a comfortable living. Throughout his life he made art his career, earned his livelihood by selling paintings, and never was obliged to enter the employ of another person. Shiba Shinsenza, the section where he lived, was the art center of Edo. Paintings of all types were sold both in shops and in numerous street stalls. Kōkan's art, of a higher quality than the pictures hawked to tourists at street corners, was exhibited at well-known halls, such as the Mampachirō Restaurant in Yanagibashi.[10] He also frequently performed painting demonstrations before wealthy and influential persons, receiving what he tactfully referred to as "monetary gifts" for his services, the amount depending upon the wealth and status of the person requesting the exhibition. Kōkan's description of one such performance, requested by the lord of Sendai in 1781, indicates his considerable fame and also offers insight into his personality; his candor, minor egotisms, and interest in his own activities are characteristic:

> Once Gotō Magobei, a retainer of the lord of Sendai, invited me to his lodging and requested me to paint a picture on the side of his desk. I drew with ink plum blossoms, explaining the method of handling the brush as I worked. . . . Everyone greatly admired my painting. Later, I was requested to visit the Edo residence of the lord of Sendai himself, together with Fukagawa Shinwa and his son. His Lordship's wife, the daughter of Mr. Kuga of the Kyoto aristocracy, was also present. She sat behind a bamboo screen to watch the proceedings. His Lordship sat facing me at some distance, and near him, his vassal Hiraga Kurando, who, at the

order from His Lordship, brought in silk and paper for painting. I then said: "I shall be honored to paint for you whatever you command." He told me to paint a Japanese beauty, so I took my brush and drew a quick sketch of a beautiful Japanese girl in a standing position. Then he requested a companion painting, and I drew a standing Japanese man. His Excellency was thoroughly delighted and took the two paintings himself to show his wife. I could hear the exclamations of astonishment from all her women in attendance. Then I executed many horizontal and vertical paintings on silk for His Lordship, and after that, at his command, made quick sketches of bamboo, plum, etc., for his retainers. The gathering lasted from 8 A.M. until 8 P.M., at which time Shinwa and I departed.... Shinwa said to me: "I had heard that you are a famous painter of the Chinese style, but did not realize until now that you also paint figures and landscapes in the Japanese manner and that you perform so admirably before such exalted personages! In twenty years you undoubtedly will be famous throughout the country." ... "My house is in Shinsenza, nearby," I told Shinwa, and he offered, jokingly: "Then I shall see you home." "No," I replied, "I have only a humble dwelling, with nothing to serve but tepid tea, so I could not permit that." "A most adept reply indeed!" said he, and continued: "When I next have a gathering at my home, you must be sure to come." Then we parted. I was twenty-nine years old at that time.[11]

Contrary to the contemporary custom of a man's ordinarily marrying at seventeen or eighteen, Kōkan remained single until after his mother's death in 1781,[12] when he was thirty-four years old. In his journal, he posited filial piety as the reason for his late marriage, but his referring to the poet Tantan's life style implies diverse motivations:

> By the time I reached manhood, I had only my mother, for my father had died when I was thirteen, and I had not married. My mother was by nature a woman of great moral integrity and fidelity, much like Mencius's mother,[13] and for her sake, even though I was over thirty, I remained celibate. I did not want ever to take a wife and thought that after my mother's death I would travel to various places in Japan, eventually settling somewhere near Kyoto. Years ago there was a poet named Tantan[14] who lived to be over eighty without ever having a wife or children. He kept round him a number of young girls about twelve years old, who took care of his needs. Specimens of his handwriting are extremely rare today because these children wrote everything down for him. I wanted very much to be like Tantan. When my mother died at the age of seventy-two, I made up my mind to leave home and go off by myself, wandering here and there, visiting all the famous mountains in Japan. But my relatives kept restraining me, showing me passages in the writings of ancient sages to the effect that man's duty is to marry and have descendants and that it is contrary to human nature to do otherwise. And so at last I acquiesced, though I know now it was a great mistake.[15]

Adopted into his wife's family, Kōkan assumed her surname, Tsuchida—a tradition still practiced in Japan when the woman's family possesses greater prestige or lacks male heirs. At the same time, he assumed two personal names: Magodayū and Katsusaburō.[16] Both Tsuchida and Magodayū were names used by the warrior class, suggesting that marriage advanced Kōkan in the social structure from artisan to samurai status. Unfortunately, his rise in social rank was unaccompanied by matrimonial bliss, and his wife shared nothing of his later travels or scholarly interests. According to a contemporary record, Kōkan divorced her:

> Shiba Kōkan, an artist famous for his oil paintings, lived opposite my house when he was an old man. . . . He used to live in Shiba Shinsenza and divorced his wife

for some reason. He had one daughter.[17]

His daughter seems to have been named Kino, the name signed at the end of the original manuscript of Kōkan's *Saiyū Nikki* (Diary of a Western Journey). Kōkan married her to a man named Sōemon, adopting him into his family. He asked his son to provide for him when he grew old, but Sōemon died before Kōkan, and Kino found another husband, whom Kōkan despised. Once, when asked about his daughter's choice, Kōkan replied: "I have never heard of such a man, not even in Holland."[18]

Apparently, Kino caused her father anxiety all his life; in his later years, he frequently wrote of the lack of filial piety among children:

> Persons who never have children lack a certain feeling of human tenderness. Through love of one's own children, one comes to love all young people, and no book or essay can describe the depth of this love. As children grow up, however, they begin to exert their own wills, which are bound to conflict with those of their parents; they fail to consider that their parents are responsible for giving them life. Very few children show any respect for the concept of filial piety; most assume a completely indifferent attitude toward their parents. But to the parents, the child is always a child, and their feelings toward him remain as deep as before, probably because they have borne him. I see now it is better never to have children.[19]

These musings reflect the thoughts and conclusions of an older man. Kōkan was sixty-four when he completed *Shumparō Hikki*—the text providing most of the information on his personal life. This manuscript and the numerous other writings of his mature years reveal the adult personality through discussions of his travels, art theories, and scientific interests. A quite complete picture of the man emerges after his retirement, when he entrusted to his journals his private thoughts and accounts of daily actions. His contemporaries, though offering few clues to his private life, reinforce the evidence of his accomplishments. To the sketchy biographical information, his extant paintings afford insight into his personality and abilities. All these combined sources, however, fail to bring into focus a total image of Kōkan's early years, and none of the facts known about his youth suggests the uncommon man he later was to become.

CHAPTER THREE

PAINTER IN THE CHINESE STYLE

THE STYLE OF PAINTING that Shiba Kōkan learned from Sō Shiseki derived ultimately from the colorful bird-and-flower compositions of the Shên Nan-p'in school of Nagasaki. Shên Nan-p'in arrived in Nagasaki in 1731. Two years later, when he returned to China, he left behind a well-established and eminently successful school of painting. His teaching placed extreme importance on detail, precise brushwork, and, frequently, illusionistic shading; vivid colors were integral to the decorative effect of bird, flower, or animal themes. Artists of the European manner, as well as painters of bird-and-flower subjects, inevitably fell under the spell of a meticulous rendition aimed at representing objects exactly as they appear in nature. Leading art centers from Edo to Kyoto to Akita all produced paintings reflective of Shên's influence.

Sō Shiseki went to Nagasaki around 1740 to study painting. Under the tutelage of Kumashiro Yūhi, a member of the Shên Nan-p'in school, Shiseki became an accomplished master of the realistic style. His admiration for the artist Sō Shigan (Chinese: Sung Tzŭ-yen), a later Chinese master of the Shên Nan-p'in school who taught painting in Nagasaki from 1758 to 1760, led him to assume the name by which he is generally known.[1]

The adoption of a name similar to one's teacher's or that of any person revered was not an uncommon practice. During his apprenticeship under Sō Shiseki, Kōkan, in his turn, assumed the name Kungaku in emulation of his master's pseudonym Kunkaku.

Among the few surviving paintings executed during his apprenticeship under Sō Shiseki, one, signed Kōkan Kungaku, depicts a grapevine with insects flying about clusters of fruit (Pl. 15).[2] A comparison with Sō Shiseki's *Grapevine* (Pl. 16) indicates the degree to which the pupil mishandled basic nuances of the naturalistic style. The master's painting is compositionally restrained: a single branch glimpsed as through a crack, but enlarged, brought close

15. Grapevine. *Circa 1769. Color on silk. Private collection, Japan.*

16. Sō Shiseki. Grapevine. *Color on silk. Courtesy of the Kobe City Museum of Namban Art.*

to the viewer. The curve of the branch frames leaves and fruit; self-contained in their enclosed pocket of space, they nevertheless suggest a larger world extending beyond the picture plane. An effective use of *tarashikomi*[3] in the leaves gives them a shimmering, spontaneous quality. Branches, fruit, and background space are modeled in barely perceptible gradations of ink wash, giving the impression of masses surrounded by atmosphere.

Kōkan's grapevine, on the other hand, exhibits the technical and compositional weaknesses of a young man who had not yet mastered the principles of his discipline. Rigid brushwork is evident in the heavy-handed application of ungraded ink tones; two nearly straight diagonal vines do not support but fan from leaves and fruit of similar dimension, with leaf veins appearing as lines scratched by the etcher's needle, grapes as circles bordered in black. Insects hang suspended on the surface in an airless void; leaves and grapes remain bound to the picture plane, expressing neither mass nor organic interrelationship. Rather than an integrated whole, the work is a patchwork of motifs. The absence of structural clarity and logic found in this youthful work never quite disappears from Kōkan's style; it lends a touch of labored awkwardness to even his most mature and accomplished efforts.

Two of Kōkan's later works in the Shên Nan-p'in/Sō Shiseki manner reveal a much improved technique (Pl. 17 and 18). The painting of a kingfisher perched on a withered limb beneath the overhanging branches of a willow tree bears the date "Winter, An'ei 4" (1775); the undated *Turtledove and Willow* was probably executed in the same year, as a companion painting to the former. Both display brushwork varying from a free, almost calligraphic use of ink to a meticulous rendering of detail. Strong, spontaneous strokes employed in the branches and in the lightly textured willow leaves have an affinity with *nanga* art.[4] In the kingfisher painting, the branch trailing in the water and the shrimp, fish, and clam shells beneath the surface are a sort of tour de force typical of Chinese bird-and-flower paintings of the Ming and Ch'ing dynasties —details one might expect would have had strong appeal to Kōkan, always interested in empirical observation.

Essentially, however, the paintings are rather uninspired works of Chinese derivation. Spatial relationships are implausible; the birds are perched on trunklike branches projecting awkwardly from the right, ending abruptly within the compositions, and seemingly affixed to no source beyond the picture planes. In the kingfisher painting, spatial zones are ambiguous, displaying a lack of coordination between the foreground plane of the branch and the background mountainscape meant to fall away below and behind it. This unclear extension from foreground to background is due to the absence of a well-defined middle ground; is it the plane of low-lying hills and willow or the massive rock from which the main branch projects? Even the identity of this branch—a withered peach tree among willows—is confusing, tending to destroy the thematic unity. The branch on which the portly turtledove squats is likewise a meaningless projection, its shape dictated by the need to fill a blank area of composition; negative space, too fragmentarily distributed, becomes vacuous. The ineluctable influence of Chinese bird-and-flower style is recognizable in the mannered quality of Kōkan's painting. His conception is clearly derived from a painting of a cormorant on a willow branch executed by Shên Nan-p'in, subsequently directly copied by Kumashirio Yūhi, and probably the source of a continuing tradition.[5]

The kingfisher painting is signed Kōkan Shun, followed by seals reading Shiba Shun and Kōkan. The turtledove painting is signed Kōkan Shiba Shun and bears the same two seals. Whatever weaknesses one might find in these works, the artist or his contemporary admirers would not have concurred with the criticism. At the lower

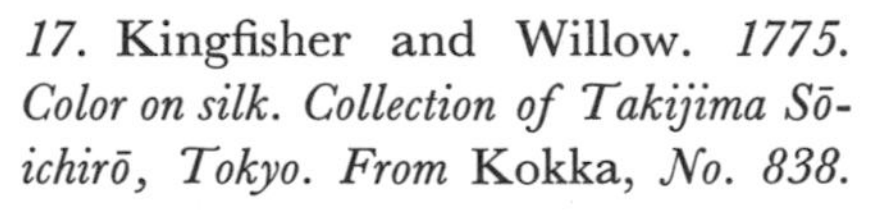

17. Kingfisher and Willow. *1775. Color on silk. Collection of Takijima Sōichirō, Tokyo. From* Kokka, *No. 838.*

18. Turtledove and Willow. *1775. Color on silk. Collection of Takijima Sōichirō, Tokyo. From* Kokka, *No. 838.*

19. Still Life with Rat. *Color on silk. Courtesy of Meredith Weatherby, Tokyo.*

left of the kingfisher painting, a seal reads *Fūryū daiichi nin* (Painted by a man of highly refined taste).

Still Life with Rat (Pl. 19), attributed to Shiba Kōkan, provides a final example of the Shên Nan-p'in naturalistic style filtered through Sō Shiseki. Fruit piled in a bowl, reminiscent of Dutch still lifes in the proliferation of forms, at first suggests a European model. But shapes and general handling are unlike anything found in Dutch painting. The immediate source of inspiration was more likely a work in the Chinese bird-and-flower manner, many of which had as subjects small animals or insects surrounding a central container of fruit or flowers. Kōkan's rodent is a close relative of the rats devouring a pumpkin depicted in a Yüan Dynasty painting attributed to Ch'ien Hsüan. The painting is part of a Chinese album that has been in the Japanese Hikkō-en collection since the sixteenth century; several leaves depict fruit-and-flower still lifes, any one of which could have served as prototype.[6] Originally, Kōkan's composition must have been somewhat larger, for the edges have evidently been trimmed, particularly at the left, where the rat has lost its tail.

Though the artist was attempting a naturalistic representation, his use of shadow is haphazard, unconditioned by a rational source of light and lacking the halftones necessary to the creation of believable textures and mass. Juxtaposed areas of shading and highlight thus resolve into flat shapes, a condition reinforced by precisely balanced colors. The black bowl, embellished with an intricate design of gold dragons, is a flat, unshaded strip. The precisely articulated rat nibbling on a pomegranate seed appears static and stylized, the artist's delineation of each hair of the coat resulting in a negation of furry texture and solidity of form. Due to the additive process of construction and excessive preoccupation with the particular, the painting lacks a sense of unity or rhythmic movement from one area to another. Whatever its technical shortcomings, however, the work displays a curiously appealing naiveté in its candid simplicity and directness.

In his writings Kōkan frequently referred to himself as a painter in the Chinese style.

20, 21. Left: Chinese Landscape. *Light color on paper. Above: detail. Courtesy Waseda University, Tokyo.*

His bird-and-flower art, derived ultimately from the Shên Nan-p'in school, qualifies as art in the Chinese manner. Further, he executed landscapes reflecting Chinese traditions, painted in the popular style of Japanese *nanga* or *bunjinga*.[7] *Bunjinga* artists created landscapes blending native Japanese traditions with Ming and Ch'ing formulas. Theorists as well as artists, *bunjin* were literary men, and often progressive and independent thinkers, some studying Western art and science as well as Confucian ideology. Although Kōkan did not identify himself with the *bunjin* group, he numbered among his acquaintances such literati as Tani Bunchō and Haruki Nanko, and undoubtedly he was familiar with current artistic developments in Edo, the center of *bunjin* activity. Kōkan's *Chinese Landscape* (Pl. 20) departs from several of the conventions normal to the *bunjin* manner of composition, as, for example, his establishment of a low horizon in lieu of the *bunjin* method of filling the picture with an aggregate of forms. Most aspects of his landscape, however—the idiosyncratic treatment of space, the loose dots and dashes employed to render foliage, and the quixotic contours of mountain peaks—are reminiscent of *bunjinga* aesthetics. The houses (shown in detail in Pl. 21), curiously constructed with high peaked roofs and raised on stilts, are derived more from the literati tradition of painting images according to the mind's eye than from a specific architectural prototype. Also in accord with literati practices, a poem is added at the top, composed by Hattori Genritsu, a descendant of the *bunjinga* artist Hattori Nankaku:

> The river widens, green cliffs rise;
> The boatman's shadow floats ahead.
> I see the beauties of the shifting landscape,
> Lacking words to describe its splendor.

CHAPTER FOUR

UKIYO-E ARTIST

The studio of Sō Shiseki was an appropriate setting for Kōkan's apprenticeship: there he encountered that concern with naturalism which provided a foundation for his later study of Western art. It seems all the more extraordinary, then, that just as he was becoming known as an artist of the Chinese style, he suddenly began devoting his main efforts to designing ukiyo-e woodblock prints in the established style of Harunobu.

His first prints were outright forgeries; since Harunobu would hardly have permitted them during his lifetime, they may be assumed to date from after his death in 1770. Kōkan confirms this assumption in his journal:

> While I was studying painting under Sō Shiseki, an artist of the ukiyo-e tradition named Suzuki Harunobu was illustrating the female modes and manners of his day. He died suddenly when he was a little over forty, and I began making imitations of his work, carving them on woodblocks. No one recognized my prints as forgeries, and to the world I became Harunobu. But I, of course, knew I was not Harunobu, and my self-respect made me adopt the name Harushige. I then employed the coloring techniques of such artists as Ch'iu Ying and Chou Ch'en in painting beautiful Japanese women. I painted *Summer Moon* [Pl. 2], depicting a girl dressed in thin robes through which one could see her body, and *Winter Moon* [Pl. 3], showing a thatched cottage in a bamboo grove and a stone lantern in the garden, all covered with snow. In painting the snow, I used thin ink washes in the Chinese manner. Side-lock ornaments used in dressing women's hair were coming into fashion at that time and were bringing about a great change in hair styling. I illustrated the new style, which consequently became exceedingly popular. But I feared that such work would damage my reputation, and I gave it up.[1]

When Harunobu died Kōkan was just twenty-three—young, talented, and cocky enough to dare to imitate a master artist. It seems surprising that Sō Shiseki should have permitted his pupil to forge Harunobu's signature, but Kōkan's restless and determined nature apparently gave Shiseki no choice.[2]

In his account Kokan offers no explanation for taking up the career of forger. He may simply have wished to satisfy his ego by deceiving the public with pictures no one could distinguish from those of a famous master. But a second inducement was no doubt financial: he could earn more money selling fake woodblock prints by the famous Harunobu than originals by Kōkan. A third possibility may have been a request for imitations by the company publishing Harunobu prints. A three-man team consisting of artist, block-maker, and color-printer was required for multicolor prints (called *nishiki-e:* brocade pictures), and in order to continue what must have been a lucrative business not only for the entrepreneur but for the block-makers and color-printers, a successor to Harunobu was needed. We shall probably never know whether the publisher requested Kōkan to execute forgeries or he asked permission, but some agreement between them undoubtedly existed.

Talented as Kōkan may have been, one is led to doubt that he could have produced perfect forgeries without having undergone some training in Harunobu's woodblock technique before the master died. The method of multicolor printing invented by Harunobu was known to few people at that time and required much skill and painstaking labor. Kōkan's own statement suggests no direct relationship between the two men; it does not, however, preclude the possibility. The book *Ameuri Dohei no Den* (Story of Dohei the Candy Vendor), written in 1769 by Ōta Nampo, contained illustrations by Suzuki Harunobu and a preface by Hiraga Gennai. Harunobu and Gennai lived in the same area of Edo, Shirakabe-cho. Gennai, a versatile scholar of Dutch learning, was a

22. Suzuki Harunobu. Kiyomizu Komachi. *Circa 1765–70. Woodblock print. Courtesy of The Art Institute of Chicago.*

23. Suzuki Harunobu. Kiyomizu Komachi. *Circa 1765–70. Woodblock print. Courtesy of the British Museum, London.*

major influence behind Kōkan's interest in Western art and science. It would seem quite plausible Kōkan and Harunobu were introduced by their mutual acquaintance. Though never formally listed as a disciple, Kōkan must have had an opportunity to observe Harunobu's technique.

For about a year Kōkan made no deviations from Harunobu's style, and indeed, there is no way to detect for certain the forger's work. The similarity between two unsigned prints, both depicting Kiyomizu Komachi and nearly identical in composition (Pl. 22 and 23), might suggest the hand of an imitator. Plate 22 is one of seven prints illustrating beautiful courtesans of Edo; the last print of the group is signed by Harunobu, and authorship of the series is undisputed.[3] The title—*Fūryū Nana Komachi: Kiyomizu* (Seven Elegant Komachi: Kiyomizu)— establishes the relationship between the courtesan and the Kiyomizu Komachi legend;[4] reinforcing the image, the Kiyomizu-dera temple appears within the cartouche at upper right. The accompanying poem expands the reference by parodying a poem from the *Kokinshū,* the tenth-century anthology of court poetry; Kōkan later included the same poem on his print *Girl on Temple Steps* (Pl. 27).

Although the figures of the courtesan and her attendant at first appear the same in both prints, slight changes indicate they were not printed from the same block: in Plate 22 they are set closer together to better fit the narrower format, and variations occur in the drapery folds, kimono patterns, and coloring. Background changes contribute to the creation of different moods: figures isolated against a plain mica ground appear divorced from nature, the cherry blossoms functioning only decoratively, while in the other print the branch is part of a symbolic setting established by a meandering stream dividing earth from sky. Although Plate 23 could have been executed by another artist, it is so undisputably in the Harunobu manner that such a supposition cannot be conclusively established. It could equally well be that a patron who admired

24. Lovers Enjoying the Evening. *Circa 1771–74. Woodblock print. Courtesy Homma Art Museum, Yamagata prefecture.*

25. Suzuki Harunobu. Courtesan Seated by a Window. *Circa 1765–70. Woodblock print. Courtesy of the Allen Memorial Art Museum, Oberlin College, Ohio.*

the first commissioned the artist to produce a second rendering—a not infrequent practice in ukiyo-e art.

After about a year of executing forgeries exactly in the manner of Harunobu, Kōkan began to experiment, adding his own personal touches. A comparison between *Lovers Enjoying the Evening* (Pl. 24), a forgery signed at left Harunobu, and Harunobu's *Courtesan Seated by a Window* (Pl. 25) reveals unmistakable differences in the handling of both figures and ground. Harunobu's courtesan, her legs tucked beneath her, leaning back with her elbow resting on the window ledge and wrapped about by long flowing sleeves, is the embodiment of youthful grace and flexibility, emphasized by the floral motifs of her kimono. In Kōkan's print, the position of the woman's lover derives from Harunobu's courtesan, though the verticality of his extended legs and straight left arm results in a nearly complete denial of curvilinear movement. The woman at right expresses a rigidity and angularity comparable to that of her lover, her stiffness emphasized by a kimono of plain vertical stripes. Sweet seriousness in the faces of all Harunobu's girls contributes to their aliveness and vulnerableness; Kōkan's faces reflect greater maturity and worldly experience. They have harder and less concisely defined features, having lost the delicacy that typifies Harunobu's conception.

Backgrounds are similarly conceived, with conjoining walls and an open area affording a view of landscape beyond. The concise statement of simple architectural planes in Harunobu's print suggests a light, airy atmosphere; in Kōkan's, the setting is described in greater detail, showing an attention to particulars reminiscent of Western genre scenes. Harunobu's use of traditional Japanese aerial perspective in the architectural setting contrasts with the low vantage point adopted by Kōkan. In both prints, architectural arrangements are consistent with the landscape, organized in Kōkan's print according to the principles of Western perspective, formed by the recession of riverbank and trees, and birds flying forward in echelon from the low horizon. Unity of setting, however, does not mitigate a dissonance in the total composition, for the two-dimensional figures are like cutouts set before a camera-obscura world.

As he wrote in *Shumparō Hikki,* self-respect caused Kōkan to adopt the name Harushige. Another reason was probably the confidence gained by making such perfect imitations that everyone was deceived; it must have given his ego a further boost to acknowledge as his own, prints accepted as Harunobu's. Interestingly, however, "Harushige" did not thereafter use his own name and seal consistently. Many works signed Harushige bear no seal, but some are stamped with the seal of Harunobu, while others bear Harunobu's signature and Harushige's seal. Possibly this was Kōkan's way of reiterating (not without a touch of insolence) his pride in having deceived the public.[5]

Even after he had assumed his new name, Kōkan continued to execute some of his prints in a style very close to that of Harunobu, as, for example, his portrayal of a children's celebration in autumn (Pl. 26), signed at left "Harushige." The season of festivals is established by traditional symbols of bush clover and chrysanthemums blooming near the garden fence and by the elaborate drum-patterned kimono and headdress of the performing girl, whose fan bears a design repeating the chrysanthemum motif. These details are enhanced by flat angular background planes, providing a foil for the dance to drum and flute. The interrelationship between costume and background details, contrasted with the

26. Children Playing. *Circa 1771. Woodblock print. Courtesy Tokyo National Museum.*

simple, enframing lines of veranda, shoji, and tatami, results in a well-integrated composition reminiscent of the best of Harunobu's works. Equally typical of his style is the quality of simplicity and directness evoked by the group's intense concentration appropriate to a child's world. A direct borrowing from Harunobu is the scallop-edged band of cloud at the top containing a poem, reflecting here the mood of the season:

Aki kaze no	Even when the autumn wind
Fukanu taema wa	Is still,
Yūtsuyu ni	They bend beneath the weight
Oki ni mo nabiku	Of evening dew,
Niwa no hagihara.	The clumps of bush clover.

Most of the prints signed Harushige, however, reveal marked differences from the manner of Harunobu. A typical example is Harushige's depiction of a girl on a flight of temple steps (Pl. 27), inspired by a Harunobu print of similar theme (Pl. 28). In the Harunobu woodblock, the girl is performing a ceremony known as *o-hyakudo,* a penance consisting of walking one hundred times up and down a flight of temple steps, each time dropping a counter in an offering box at the top. She carries as counters straw strings, twisted into knobs at the ends, used for stringing coins; the few remaining in her hand indicate she has nearly completed the ritual. Disheveled hair and wilting posture betray fatigue, an impression augmented by her frail form. A play of curves stressing downward motion contrasts with the upward direction of her course, reinforced by the raised branches of the tree and stairs stretching in an unbroken rhythm endlessly beyond the picture plane.

Inasmuch as Harushige's composition is derived from the Harunobu print, his girl too may be performing *o-hyakudo,* using twigs as counters. She carries them, however, in a bucket filled with water, suggesting that the scene is simply a depiction of a girl visiting a place of worship, the anise twigs and water intended as an offering at the grave of her ancestors. More rigid in posture than Harunobu's sinuous female, her stiffness is reinforced by the scrupulously balanced composition tightly framing her within a border of giant tree trunks and overhead branches. The stone steps of the background—employed in the Harunobu print to suggest depth and height by their slight curve into space, diminution in size, and shading—here, by their measured regularity, contribute to the general air of constraint. They are treated as flat bands, neither ascending nor descending, and afford no space-time dimension wherein the girl can move.

At the top right, the print is entitled: *Fūryū Nana Komachi: Kiyomizu* (Seven Elegant Komachi: Kiyomizu), indicating that it comprised one of a set depicting seven

27. Girl on Temple Steps. *Circa 1771. Woodblock print. Courtesy Tokyo National Museum.*

beautiful women of Edo.[6] The poem is the same as that of the Harunobu print of Plate 22—as noted, also one of a series:

<table>
<tr><td>Nani o shite</td><td>Why should my obi</td></tr>
<tr><td>Mi o itazura ni</td><td>To no point</td></tr>
<tr><td>Obi token.</td><td>Become undone?</td></tr>
<tr><td>Taki no keshiki wa</td><td>The waterfall</td></tr>
<tr><td>Kawaranu mono o.</td><td>Is just the same as
always.</td></tr>
</table>

If the girl unfastens her obi she will lose the purity symbolized by the waterfall of Kiyomizu. The girl's words could also be more prosaically interpreted: Why should I lose my virginity unless someone makes it worth my while? The contrast between people, who change, and nature, which does not, is frequent in Japanese poetry, as in the famous lines by Ariwara no Narihira compar-

8. *Suzuki Harunobu.* Girl on Temple Steps. *Circa 765–70. Woodblock print. Courtesy of The Art Institute f Chicago.*

ing his changed state with the unchanging spring and moon.[7] The parody, however, is based not on Narihira's *Tales of Ise,* but on a poem in the *Kokinshū* that treats the theme of transiency:

Nani o shite	Why is it
Mi no itazura ni	I have grown old,
Oinuran.	Accomplishing nothing?
Toshi no omowanu	Before we know it
Koto zo yasashiki.	The years so quickly vanish.

Analytical order is the forte of Harushige's style. A representative example of his ability to construct a composition using a complex juxtaposition of background and figures is the scene of a courtesan burning insects inside a mosquito net (Pl. 1). She holds a burning taper, catching the insects on a fan. Outside, her young attendant crouches on the floor asleep, while her lover appears at the curtained entrance. Strength of design results from erecting a geometric scaffold of architectural divisions as the foundation of the composition; floor, entranceway, and inner room comprise basic units enclosing three figures whose sizes and postures are accommodated to these areas. Attention is directed to the woman by strongly defined lines and simple patterns of an intimately conceived interior, by the inclined head of the figure at left, and by the arched body of the girl attendant, the directional flow continuing through the extended arms of the girl. The conjunction of wall column and lower triangle forces an outward movement counter to the inward-turned postures of the figures, resulting in a kaleidoscopic fusion of expanding and contracting segments, these countermovements interacting to create an intricate play between figures and setting.

In a Harunobu print, the figures usually contain within their own forms a complete expression, the background serving only as a pleasant and not obtrusive adjunct; in this work by Harushige, the appeal lies in the organization of the whole, the background contributing details indispensible to the enhancement of the subject. Within the scalloped cloud above, the poem expands the scene of woman and lover to the theme of an unexpected liaison:

Ikuyo ka wa	How many nights
Omoi komeshi	Wanting you, yearning,
Neya no to o	I stare at the empty doorway
Sashi mo hatasade	Our love still unfilled,
Matsu wa kurushiki.	The anguish of waiting.

Kōkan's works exploiting the stylistic possibilities of flat patterning are better integrated than prints utilizing a background organized by rules of linear perspective. This is seen, for example, in *The Archery*

29. The Archery Gallery. *Circa 1771–74. Woodblock print. Courtesy of the Kobe City Museum of Namban Art.*

Gallery (Pl. 29). The figures of the young man seated in the foreground and the girl offering him an arrow present an odd contrast to the lines of architecture focusing on the target at the far end, the illusion of depth being augmented by a distant landscape glimpsed through open windows. On the sign above is inscribed the name of the woman and the establishment: "Fumi-e of the Keimon," as well as the fee for shooting: "Ten arrows for two *mon*." Though the arrangement of figures in contrast to their setting is unlike any composition by Harunobu, the perspective employed has prototypes in works by other ukiyo-e artists.

Pictures of this type drawn by rules of Western mathematical perspective were known as *uki-e*. The first *uki-e*, executed in Japan around 1734,[8] were generally small in size, hand-drawn with a fine brush or printed with woodblocks, and distinguished by the use of exaggerated one-point linear perspective to create the illusion of depth. At the outset, Japanese *uki-e* were copies of illustrations imported from Holland or of woodblock prints from China; gradually, Japanese subjects replaced exotic views.

The earliest known *uki-e* artist was Okumura Masanobu, whose familiar perspective scenes of theater interiors first appeared about 1740. While Masanobu's work in this genre evoked startled admiration, *uki-e* did not acquire general popularity until 1759, when executed by Maruyama Ōkyo. Ōkyo produced quantities of *uki-e* at the request of his employer Nakajima Kambei, proprietor of a toy shop in Kyoto, who found the demand greater than the supply he could import from China. Though his first efforts were hand-drawn, Ōkyo soon switched to woodblock *uki-e*, which he continued to create until 1761. His works brought about a shift in taste in the Kyoto area from interior scenes to landscapes. One of his most ardent imitators was Utagawa Toyoharu, whose prints fostered a craze for perspective pictures. Kōkan's depiction of the archery gallery appears especially reminiscent of Masanobu's theater views; the success of Ōkyo's and Toyoharu's *uki-e* suggests that Kōkan's composition was a concession to continuing popular demand.

Kōkan's prints cannot be dated precisely, but all were produced between 1770 and 1774, a period determined from his statement in *Shumparō Hikki* and from the hair style worn by the women in his ukiyo-e paintings after 1774. This fashion was distinguished by the use of *binzashi:* objects made of bone or metal that held the hair out flat on either side of the face. Not yet in vogue during Harunobu's lifetime, the hair style is depicted in none of his works, nor in any of Kōkan's woodblocks. It became popular around 1775, as evidenced by its appearance in prints executed at that time by Koryūsai, Shigemasa, Toyoharu, Shunshō, Kiyonaga, and Utamaro. Kōkan, then, must have abandoned woodblock prints about 1774, before *binzashi* came into fashion, and turned to paintings of ukiyo-e women about 1775, using the signature Harushige or Shōtei Harushige.

In his ukiyo-e paintings, Kōkan wrote, he used the coloring techniques of Ch'iu Ying and Chou Ch'en, but this does not actually distinguish his style, for Harunobu and other ukiyo-e artists were also influenced by those Ming-dynasty painters, especially Ch'iu Ying, whose delicate and colorful studies of beautiful women had achieved great popularity in China. Imitations of Ch'iu's paintings, executed in woodblock prints and imported into Japan, received wide acclaim in the ukiyo-e art world. The characteristics of Kōkan's paintings are the same as those distinguishing his prints: taller figures, longer, more angular faces, and more elaborate backgrounds showing traces of experimentation with Western techniques.

The two paintings Kōkan cited in his journal as representative of his style at this time are *Summer Moon* and *Winter Moon,* both signed Shōtei Harushige and stamped with the seal of Harunobu. *Summer Moon* (Pl. 2), depicting a girl on a veranda examining a cage of fireflies, is especially noteworthy for the fine color harmonies and the masterful craftsmanship displayed in illusionistic techniques. Using a method known to both Chinese and Japanese artists, Kōkan painted on the back of the silk; the white lattice of the shoji screen, painted on the underside, convincingly describes the texture of paper covering a wooden frame. Blue and green washes over the girl's arm and leg evoke the impression of a sheer outer kimono. Concern with naturalistic effects is further evident in the hair highlighted with grey, the cloth textured as if of watered silk, the roof painted in dry-brush giving the impression of thatch, and the base of the shoji simulating wood grain; a blue-washed sky perhaps indicates the influence of Western painting. Harushige has thus departed from the traditional ukiyo-e aesthetic of attention to detail employed solely to produce an effective surface pattern and concentrated instead on manipulating detail and color to illustrate tangible forms from the visible world. Clear notes of the girl's costume contrast with muted tones of the moonlit landscape of rocks, tree, and stream. The somber background is enlivened, however, by touches of blue-green over the leaves and brightly colored flowers echoing the tones of the kimono; interaction of hues provides a unifying element between the carefully described foreground and the loosely defined landscape.

Similar in conception and composition, *Winter Moon* (Pl. 3) reveals the same preoccupation with illusionism and the same striking contrasts between bright hues of the girl's costume and muted tones of surrounding landscape. The girl, standing on a veranda enjoying the snow-covered garden while inserting a *kanzashi* in her hair, is dressed in winter robes of lavender-grey decorated with an unusual mixture of motifs: a blue wave pattern, butterflies, and bamboo; her underrobe of deep scarlet seems to vibrate against the soft tonalities of a pinkish-grey veranda and pale green room interior. Freely brushed washes of grey in the area of sky establish the mood of a winter evening. The boneless method of application, leaving areas of unpainted silk to represent piled-up masses of snow, is remi-

30. A Courtesan Blowing Soap Bubbles. *Circa 1775–81. Color on silk. Courtesy of Kimiko and John Powers, New York.*

31. Enjoying the Cool of the Evening. *Circa 1775–81. Color on silk. Courtesy of the Kobe City Museum of Namban Art.*

niscent of the *bunjinga* painting tradition.

A third example of Kōkan's ukiyo-e style is a similarly conceived painting called *A Courtesan Blowing Soap Bubbles* (Pl. 30). Here the familiar device of using background elements to focus on the figures is again evident: the triangle of woman and child is set within the angles of the veranda and a larger triangle composed of the water basin at lower left, garden screen at right, and *sudare* at upper left. As in *Summer Moon,* the girl is dressed in diaphanous material, her arms and heel revealed beneath summer attire. This touch of naturalism is echoed at upper left where the tree is glimpsed behind the *sudare* window blind. Harushige's meticulous observation and the same color harmonies found in *Summer Moon* are revealed in the garden flowers, and subtle adjustment of tones distinguishing the kimono: cloth of a muted blue-green decorated with patterns of brighter blue and green is transformed into pink, rose, and blue as it falls over underrobes and flesh. Completing the impression of light-heartedness imparted by the girl's simple pastime, the frolicking boy tugs at the woman's robe blown partly open by the summer breeze, staring at her with the unabashed curiosity of a child. A poem inscribed above and signed Tankyū, reinforces the theme, combining a suggestion of eroticism with a mood of gentle melancholy:

Shōfu risshin nite takezutsu o fuku
Dandan to tobisari kumpū ni matataku
Jidō hirugaeru suso no uchi o yubi de ukagau
Enken ganshū gyokū kyō no beni.

A young girl blows bubbles through a bamboo pipe;
Gently they rise skyward and vanish in the summer breeze.
A child, slightly parting her wind-stirred kimono, peeks beneath;
Like pretty jewels the girl's cheeks flush.

Another example of Kōkan's ukiyo-e painting style is the often reproduced *Enjoying the Cool of the Evening* (Pl. 31). The foreground organization is reminiscent of

32. A Japanese Man. *Ink and color on paper. Collection of Andō Kyūbei, Fukushima prefecture. Reproduced with permission from* Kokka, *No. 726.*

Harunobu's manner, and the woman herself, with the exception of her legs pendent rather than tucked beneath her, is seated in a position nearly identical to the Harunobu of Plate 25. This painting too reveals Kōkan's empirical concern with naturalistic renderings of textures and genre motifs; the result is a forced composition—a vehicle for the artist's far-ranging observation of bits and pieces of the material world.

Less complex pictures constitute some of Kōkan's finest work. Among them are impromptu sketches—known as *sekiga*—such as those referred to in the account of his performance before the lord of Sendai. Executed usually in the presence of an audience, drawn with brush and ink, sometimes with color added in quick washes, these creations were spontaneous, requiring the artist to have complete control of his brush at all times. *Sekiga* was therefore an important type of painting by which to judge technical proficiency. Kōkan's picture of a male figure (Pl. 32) shows clearly his masterful command of the techniques. Conceived with illustrative strokes that capture a characteristic posture and natural drapery folds, the drawing is a direct, expressive statement. It is given life by swift brush strokes and bold ink tones appropriate to the alert pose, and displays a sureness and lightness of touch rarely found in his more formal efforts. Frequent references to this type of art in the diary Kōkan kept during his journey to Nagasaki in 1788 indicate that the sale of *sekiga* provided a major source of income during his year of travel.

Though he continued to execute *sekiga* as a means of livelihood, Kōkan wrote that he gave up ukiyo-e painting for the sake of his reputation. There was probably an additional reason. In his search for variety and new mediums to bring him fame, he discovered during this period the existence of European art techniques unlike anything known in his own country. Paintings were executed with oil, and illustrations were printed, not from wooden blocks, but from copperplates. When, around 1780, he finally obtained a book explaining Western methods of painting, he set about the study in earnest. Copperplates attracted him equally, and he readily turned from woodblocks to the study of etching, a technique permitting greater accuracy of detail. Ukiyo-e art ceased to interest him; about 1781 he gave it up entirely, both for his reputation and because the "new art" filled his thoughts. At the same time he abandoned the name Harushige; from then until late in his life he signed most of his paintings Kōkan Shiba Shun.

CHAPTER FIVE

GRAPHIC ARTIST

KŌKAN'S EARLIEST ACCOMPLISHMENT in Western art research was not only his rediscovery of the method of copperplate engraving but his discovery of the more complex art of etching. European graphic techniques of engraving on a copperplate had been known in Japan as early as the sixteenth century, when Portuguese Jesuits, as an aid to their proselytizing activity, brought to Japan engravings of religious subjects. They also produced religious engravings in Nagasaki and taught the art to Japanese converts.[1] With the subsequent expulsion of all missionaries, however, knowledge of the technique was lost.

So far as Kōkan was aware, no Japanese had ever executed or even evinced interest in copperplates; he described what he presumed their first importation:

> When I was a young man, Hiraga Gennai told me that many years ago a Hollander arrived in Japan bringing with him several hundred Dutch copperplate pictures. He offered them for sale, but the Japanese, too frivolous and superficial to realize what a rare and wonderful opportunity this was, declined his offer! They knew nothing of the technique involved, and this, in fact, was their first indication of the existence of copper engravings.[2]

This and other information from Hiraga Gennai spurred Kōkan to his enthusiasm for Western knowledge and techniques. Gennai, one of the most accomplished of the Edo *rangakusha,* was a sort of Renaissance man. His chief interest was botany, particularly the study of medicinal herbs; he was also a talented metallurgist and zoologist. Further, he mastered the art of pottery making, and incidentally was a popular novelist and playwright. Among his collection of foreign texts, Gennai possessed a highly prized zoology book. According to Kōkan,

> To pay for it, Gennai was obliged to sell everything in his house, down to his very

33. View of Mimeguri, Edo. *1783. Copperplate etching. Courtesy of the Kobe City Museum of Namban Art.*

bedclothes and washing things. This book gives pictures, drawn from nature, of all the live things in the world, including creatures, such as lions and dragons, that one cannot see in Japan. Nowadays there are several people who have the book; but at that time it was quite unknown.[3]

The text was written by John Johnston, and illustrated with 296 etchings by the Swiss artist Matthieu Mérian.[4] Both Kōkan and Sō Shiseki had opportunity to study the pictures, and both attempted detailed copies.[5] Their drawings, curious mixtures of naturalism and decorative flourishes, were hardly comparable in precision and clarity to the Western models.

Kōkan then determined to research graphic methods for himself. He recorded his enthusiasm for the foreign illustrations, indicating also where he found an explanation of the etching technique and how he mastered it:

Starting from the Dutch zoological encyclopedia by Johnston, the technique of making copperplates improved markedly, so that more recent publications reaching us from abroad all contain carefully detailed engravings, so realistic the pictures almost come alive. Even though we often cannot read the descriptions written in the Dutch language, we still can get a thorough understanding of many of the things described merely by studying the pictures carefully. This fact alone proves the brilliance and superiority of Western art. . . .

No one in Japan knew the proper method of making a copperplate. I therefore turned to the formula given in a book by a Hollander named Boisu. I consulted with Ōtsuki Gentaku, who assisted me in

> translating the text so that I could manufacture copperplate pictures in Japan. In 1783, I produced the first engraving.[6]

In a later essay Kōkan wrote that he discovered the engraving method "in a Dutch book called 'Boisu.' "[7] The foreign text referred to was almost certainly *Huishoudelijk Woordenboek,* a Dutch translation of a dictionary of the arts and sciences written by the French priest Noël Chomel.[8] Japanese scholars of Dutch learning considered the book one of the great treasures acquired from abroad. Ōtsuki Gentaku, who translated the section on etching for Kōkan, was perhaps more skilled in the Dutch language than any contemporary Edo *rangakusha.*[9] He continued to assist Kōkan in later endeavors, providing information for his studies of geography and map making.

Kōkan's first copperplate, executed in September, 1783, when he was thirty-six, was a landscape of the Sumida River viewed from the bank near the shrine at Mimeguri, Edo (Pl. 33). For a first attempt, it is a noteworthy effort. His success in deciphering a complicated technical process from a foreign text; in employing parallel lines and crosshatching to create impressions of depth, three-dimensional form, highlight, and shadow; and in applying the new method to an original conception rather than copying a foreign composition warranted his pride. One senses the artist's thorough scrutiny of each component of the scene, from the foreground ferry boats and people to the cluster of houses on the far distant river shore, and even to the smoke on the horizon rising from the kilns at Imado, where roof tiles were manufactured.

Though not directly copying, Kōkan presumably adhered closely to Western models representing a secular landscape tradition well-established in the Netherlands by the seventeenth century. As he himself acknowledged in his essay on Western art, however, his picture is less skillfully executed than a European engraving, for the lines are shallow and imprecise. These technical inadequacies are partly obscured by the addition of hand coloring, an innovation Kōkan did not derive from his Western prototypes, but probably employed in order not to have to rely upon graphic techniques alone for tonal gradations. Aside from the problems raised by the medium, the scene exhibits immature coordination of perspective, which results in spatial distortions and inconsistencies: the river bulges in the middle until it becomes almost a lake, the horizon is raised so that it appears one is viewing the scene from a great height, and the path breaking through the center does not extend from a well-established foreground plane. The mood is one of almost maplike detachment; figures do nothing to evoke special interest but are set up like tenpins on a broad promenade.

34. Camera obscura made by Kōkan. 1784. Wood. Courtesy of the Kobe City Museum of Namban Art.

The following year Kōkan devoted all his energies to etching. For viewing his copperplate landscapes he constructed a device immensely popular in Japan, the camera obscura (Pl. 34).[10] This invention had been introduced from the West into China during the seventeenth and eighteenth centuries, and many were manufactured around the area of Soochow. From China it was imported to Nagasaki in 1718 but attracted little attention until brought to Kyoto and Edo, where camera obscuras and accompanying woodblock prints created a furor of popular demand. Maruyama Ōkyo constructed his own in 1739, for viewing woodblock pictures drawn by rules of mathematical perspective (*uki-e*). Kōkan's camera obscura, though hardly new to Japan by 1784, still proved a novelty, and he delighted in the resounding praise received from those who used it to examine his graphics. The heightened illusion of three-dimensionality achieved, he felt, the maximum in Western realism. On the bottom he drew diagrams explaining the correct placement of the pictures, and included the statement:

> Shiba Kōkan, living in Shiba, Shinsenza, Edo, is an artist of the Chinese style. In his spare time he studied Dutch scholarship and learned the Dutch method of copperplate engraving. This method was unknown in China or Japan, for Oriental peoples do not understand the principles of Western art and are unable to make such pictures. It took him a great many years to study and master the technique, but finally, in September, 1783, he succeeded in making a copperplate picture. The technique is a Western one, and his engravings are the very first ever made in Japan. Artists in the future who plan to make copperplates, do not forget that Shiba Kōkan made the first one.
>
> Shiba Kōkan has made the first copperplate picture in Japan. Five of the engravings contained herein depict Japanese landscapes; one is a copy of a Western work. May, 1784.[11]

One of the more accomplished of the five Japanese landscapes referred to is *Shinobazu* (Pl. 35), a lake in Edo, still extant in the present-day Ueno Park area of Tokyo. In contrast to the Sumida River landscape, the artist was able to utilize effectively a rudimentary knowledge of perspective to create the illusion of a vast expanse of sky and water. The tall grass along the lower edge of the composition establishes a foreground plane, although it functions as a screen rather than as a shelf extended into depth. Paths along the water's edge and the diminishing perspective of trees carry the eye back into space. Tiny figures stroll on both sides of the lake and across the sandbar and bridge leading to the Bentendō Shrine, which occupies the middle ground at the center of the lake. The horizon set below eye level, as well as distant trees in marked contrast to repoussoir grasses and the large tree at right, contributes to the sense of spaciousness.

A painting of Shinobazu Lake by Odano Naotake, now in the Akita Prefecture Museum, may have provided inspiration for Kōkan's composition. Fundamentally, however, Naotake's work is more reminiscent of the Shên Nan-p'in manner than of Western composition, for its focus is a carefully studied urn and peonies in the immediate foreground rather than the lake and shrine beyond. Another small painting of Shinobazu attributed to Naotake (Pl. 36) is closer in arrangement and focus to Kōkan's version.[12] Kōkan's original contribution was, of course, the use of a copperplate.

Curiously, although all three works clearly are intended to depict accurately the same scene, the two paintings by Naotake, as well as another by Ōta Nampo, include at the entrance to Bentendō a cluster of buildings, replaced in Kōkan's version by a promenade and woods, with buildings in smaller scale on the opposite shore. Since the works by Naotake and Nampo depict the buildings at the bridge entrance, it seems probable they were located there; Kōkan's decision to omit them would then indicate the extent to which he relied on his own artistic intuition rather than faithfully reproducing actual appearances. At any rate, the substitution resulted in a more open composition, imparting an effective impression of panorama. Of the four depictions, Kōkan's work gives evidence of a closer adherence to the Dutch landscape tradition: there is greater stress on sky filling more than half the composition, and hori-

35. Shinobazu Lake, Ueno, Edo. *1784. Copperplate etching. Courtesy of the Kobe City Museum of Namban Art.*

36. Naotake, attributed. Shinobazu Lake, Ueno, Edo. *Color on paper. Courtesy Yabumoto Sōshirō, Tokyo.*

37. The Serpentine, Hyde Park, London. *Circa 1784. Copperplate etching. Courtesy of the Kobe City Museum of Namban Art.*

zontal lines used to suggest clouds convey the impression of light-filled atmosphere rather than mere blank space.

The "copy of a Western picture" completing the set of six etchings for his camera obscura may have been the depiction of either the Serpentine in Hyde Park (Pl. 37) or the European hospital (Pl. 38). Illustrations of these exotic locales—described in glowing terms in Kōkan's later geography texts—no doubt held special appeal to Japanese curious about the Western world. Both scenes were certainly based on European models, but in Kōkan's versions, the severity of one-point perspective and the rigidity of shapes and tonal gradations create a strained artificiality. In *The Serpentine,* though the arrangement of trees is borrowed from a Western composition, Kōkan has distorted the image: one dominant tree thrusts up dizzily above all the others in echelon along the shore, bending forward with branches reaching down in echo of the foreground man feeding swans. Nevertheless, there is great charm in the depiction of this manicured British landscape so filled with anecdotal detail. It is, in effect, a composite of the wonders and pleasures he fancied must comprise a park in so beautiful a city as London.

The quality of verdant lushness in *The Serpentine* is totally lacking in the *European Hospital,* creating a very different mood. Kōkan's chief interest was in delineating details of European life unknown to Japanese: the odd shape and impressive height of the stone tower entrance, the multistoried hospital constructed of masonry with glass windows, and the strange costumes of the foreigners; by comparison, the flat landscape is uninspired. The picture exemplifies the artist's intense concentration on the new technique and manner of expression; Western concepts of composition are realized in the firmly established, unbroken horizon, in the clearly lined perspective, and in the

38. A European Hospital. *Circa 1784. Copperplate etching. Courtesy of the Kobe City Museum of Namban Art.*

exaggeratedly dark shadows that result in a design of almost geometric precision and abruptness. The conjunction of deliberate lines and black and grey shapes set up according to a gridwork of intersecting horizontal and vertical planes creates an air of twilight stillness.

For the next several years after 1784, Kōkan apparently turned his attention to Western oil painting. The only extant dated etching of 1785 is a picture of a European leather tanner printed on a fan. From the following year too there remains only one etching: a small picture of Toranomon in Edo, differing both in size and style from his other works, and more closely resembling the small woodblock prints made at the time by Toyoharu and Shigemasa.

By 1787, however, Kōkan resumed his work in graphics, perhaps in preparation for his Nagasaki journey, when he took with him copperplate pictures and camera obscura. Compared to those of 1784, the later etchings display marked technical improvement, the lines deeper, more varied, and precise. All have titles written in large roman letters on banners inside the top borders rather than relegated to the margins.

One of the most successful is the view of Ryōgoku Bridge (Pl. 4), a famous site in the Asakusa area of Edo. The foreground presents an interesting contrast between blocky shapes of roofs and shoji and fine details of human interest in the busy street. People of various social classes—priest, warrior, and townsman—mingle in the area before the row of street stalls; the huge shrimp emblazoned on the restaurant screen proclaims the speciality of the house. Recession into space is more skillfully handled than in his earlier engravings: the bridge thronged with people forms a central dividing line between contrasting wedges of buildings and merchant stalls and the broad river extending beyond. In the distance to the right, the roof of the Asakusa Shrine appears hazy in

39. View of Mimeguri, Edo. *1787. Copperplate etching. Courtesy of the Kobe City Museum of Namban Art.*

the autumn sky. The feeling of openness typical of Kōkan's pictures probably indicates, in addition to the influence of Dutch compositions, a reaction to the two-dimensionality of Kanō form and the tiered planes of Chinese landscapes.

Spaciousness, achieved through multiple vanishing points, is stressed by the establishment of a low, curved horizon. The earth is not a flat plane measured according to the vantage point of man, but a globe suspended in space. This more cosmic notion of the relationship between earth and universe was first exploited in Western art in the sixteenth century, in response to Copernicus's discoveries. Perhaps Kōkan employed it to illustrate and emphasize his awareness of the earth's roundness. The curved horizon was used at least as early in Chinese paintings, however, and utilized also by Kōkan's contemporaries—not only by those painting in the Western tradition, but by others motivated by an essentially Chinese orientation, such as the *bunjinga* master Ikeno Taiga. While it is therefore possible that Kōkan attempted to reproduce a European idea of spatial extension, it is not necessarily true that the composition was so inspired, especially considering the absence of any Western counterpart to Kōkan's handling of foreground buildings. Kōkan has combined a European system of mathematical perspective with the traditional Japanese solution of diagonally oriented architectural planes to define spatial boundaries. He also displayed a touch of bourgeois snobbery when he inscribed the picture with a title in Dutch: "Tweelandbruk," a translation of *Ryōgokubashi* (bridge connecting two provinces).

The following month Kōkan again executed *Mimeguri* (Pl. 39), the same scene as his first etching of September, 1783. The decision to execute a second version demon-

40. Mount Fuji Viewed from Suruga Province. *Sketch for an etching. Location unknown.*

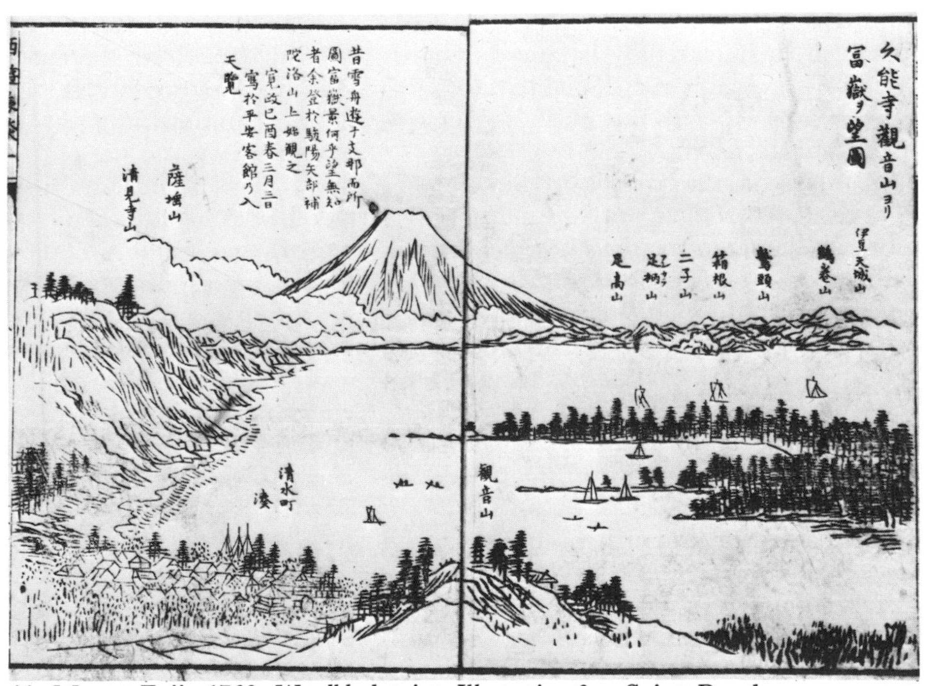

41. Mount Fuji. *1789. Woodblock print. Illustration from* Saiyū Ryodan.

42. Mount Fuji. *Circa 1789. Color on silk. Courtesy Center of Asian Art and Culture, The Avery Brundage Collection, San Francisco.*

strates his recognition of his improved skill in handling Western techniques and formulas. Immediately apparent is the lowered horizon corresponding to eye level, describing a more convincing projection into depth. Despite its greater sophistication, however, the work is more inhibited and contrived in its carefully balanced details placed at regular intervals, heightening one's awareness of Kōkan's essentially schematic approach.

The date on the picture in the upper-right corner corresponds to November, 1787. Chinese characters reading "Mimeguri no Kei" are in mirror image because the picture was to be seen through Kōkan's camera obscura. If the image is reversed, the Dutch letters will appear backwards; their order, however, was of little importance to the Japanese audience, who could be expected to admire their decorative rather than didactic purpose.

During his travels en route to Nagasaki, the etchings Kōkan carried with him proved greatly valuable in impressing his various hosts. Especially proud of his accomplishment in this medium, he gratuitously showed his works to everyone. After his return to Edo in 1789, he continued to execute copperplate pictures, though chiefly of a scientific nature. From this period, one of his few extant sketches for an etching is a view of Suruga province (present-day Shizuoka prefecture) with Mount Fuji in the background (Pl. 40), a simplified composition that discloses the extent to which Kōkan had matured in technique. His earlier, more ambitious attempts to delineate human activity and the multiplicity of nature have here been restrained. Minute trees, patchwork fields, and darkly massed mountain ranges leading to the cone of Mount Fuji establish a mood of cool, detached tranquillity not only appropriate to the theme, but believable as an expression compatible with Kōkan's basically objective temperament.

The engraving was derived from a diary sketch (Pl. 41), on which he wrote:

> A view of Mount Fuji from Kunaji-Kannon. Long ago when Sesshū visited China, he drew a picture of Mount Fuji. No one could guess the spot from which he had viewed the mountain, but I discovered it when I climbed Mount Daraku

in Yabe, Suruga. Sketched on March 29, 1789, at the Heian Inn. One of my pictures of this scene was presented for imperial inspection.

Kōkan depicted this landscape many times: again, during his journey to Nagasaki, for an innkeeper in Kyushu, and as noted on his sketch, for the emperor, Kōkaku. Which picture was set before imperial eyes is impossible to say because several works illustrating this theme are extant. In one of these (Pl. 42), the viewer is led easily into the composition by the tree-covered sandbar curving back from fore to middle ground. A broken horizon lends added depth and interest, and tonal values establish lively contrasts, capturing a mood and atmospheric effect rarely seen in Kōkan's paintings. Whether or not this is the work shown to Emperor Kōkaku, it is certainly a painting worthy of imperial inspection.

Taken as a whole, Kōkan's etchings suffer from his attempt to superimpose Western techniques on basically Oriental compositions. His efforts to combine entirely different and often conflicting aesthetics led frequently to disharmony and confusion. The conviction shown by earlier Oriental artists in their scheme of patterning gives way in Kōkan's works to an insecure decorativeness, the result of wavering between two traditions. His creations find echoes among the works of many artists from various nations who, caught between the conflicting ideals of East and West, have sought to bring the two together by efforts on a material or stylistic level. In aesthetic terms, such efforts are doomed to fall short of masterpiece, but as cultural-historical documents, they provide the links necessary to understanding the development or modification of national styles and are valuable clues in tracing the history of ideas.

Rather than stress the inevitably discovered faults of design and execution in Kōkan's etchings, the historian might more profitably marvel at the level of sophistication and often strikingly appealing moments he was able to achieve. Remembering that he was self-taught, and not only working in an unfamiliar medium, but with an exotic body of artistic theory learned through books or inferior models, one cannot fail to admire the range and adventurousness of Kōkan's vision. His eye and spirit were by nature fundamentally scientific rather than poetic; if his creations fall short of great art, they must be respected as uncommonly fine evidence of a man's pioneer energy and determination to extend the boundaries of his mind, as well as the minds of his countrymen.

Kōkan did not transmit the art of etching to any disciple. He was, in fact, unjustly criticized for this by Matsudaira Sadanobu, who wrote that Kōkan made copperplates but kept his method a strict secret.[13] Matsudaira was a patron of Kōkan's rival, Aōdō Denzen, which accounts at least in part for his antipathy.[14] Both Matsudaira and Denzen were from the northern province of Ōshū, and perhaps Kōkan had them in mind when he wrote:

People in Ōshū are stubborn and opinionated, never changing their minds. For the past twenty-five years now I have been executing oil paintings of Mount Fuji and other famous Japanese landscapes by the Dutch method. I have contributed them to shrines and temples throughout the country, as well as to rulers of provinces and other noble lords, and everyone has admired and praised them. A great many persons request paintings from me, but all of them are from the Kyoto area or west of there. Even now people from Ōshū have not learned to appreciate my art. How very stupid they are![15]

Kōkan fully intended to make public his copperplate method along with his other discoveries in a never completed book entitled *Shumparō Gafu* (Illustrations by Shumparō), announced at the end of his essay on Western art.[16] Certainly he had no intention of concealing the technique; on the contrary, his objective always was to enlighten his countrymen. He was eager to let the whole world know it was he who first made copperplates in Japan.

Kōkan, who advertised his achievements so insistently, seems to have been unduly proud of his accomplishments as a graphic artist. He was indeed the first Japanese to discover the etching process, but many other men, following closely on his heels, attained superior proficiency.[17] It was due to his initiative, however, that the process came to be adopted in Japan. His accomplishment prepared the way for all future graphic arts, whether purely pictorial or accurate technical illustration. His own scientific etchings are in themselves impressive, but of even greater importance was the progress in scientific research they initiated.

CHAPTER SIX

TRAVELER

IF ONE COULD ASK KŌKAN what he considered the most interesting experience of his life, he probably would choose his journey to Nagasaki in 1788. He was already forty-one when he decided to fulfill his lifelong desire to travel, which had been frustrated in his younger days by family ties. His youthful ambition had been to explore the area around Kyoto and Osaka, but developing interests in Western art and scholarship expanded his goal, and he determined to make his destination the port of Nagasaki on the western coast of Kyushu, some 830 miles from Edo. Along the way he planned to visit as many famous places as possible, and in order to have sufficient time for study and sightseeing, he decided to devote three years to the journey. As it turned out, he was away a little less than a year, but managed nevertheless to see much of Japan. He returned to Edo with fresh vigor and a far broader outlook on life. Moreover, his travels greatly spurred his interest in foreign studies and determined the future course of his career.

Throughout his journey Kōkan sketched everything that struck his fancy, from mountain landscapes to the fish he received as presents. He also kept a diary. In 1794, five years after his return to Edo, he published a travelogue called *Saiyū Ryodan* (Account of a Western Journey) describing and illustrating his experiences. The book apparently proved a popular success, for a second edition was printed in 1803. The first edition contained an illustration of Shogun Ieyasu's grave at Kunōzan in Shizuoka, an indiscretion offensive to the Tokugawa government; Kōkan was obliged to omit the sketch from his second edition, and he also changed the title of the book to *Gazu Saiyūdan* (Illustrated Account of a Western Journey). In 1815, after he had retired and enjoyed greater leisure, he rewrote the book entirely; the revisions are mentioned in a letter written April 29, 1815, to Yamane Kazuma, a scholar and magistrate who served the Nabeshima clan in Arita:

> Many years ago I published a book called *Saiyū Ryodan,* which I am now rewriting and enlarging to three or four hundred manuscript sheets. I am giving the new work, which is illustrated, the title *Saiyū Nikki* [Diary of a Western Journey]. So far the manuscript is only two-thirds complete, not yet ready for publication. I am describing everything in detail, to the last cup of tea or sakè I drank. I am eager to show it to you.[1]

Although both *Saiyū Ryodan* and *Saiyū Nikki* describe the journey of 1788–89, their contents vary considerably. The first is basically a narration of facts; the second, an all-inclusive journal recounting in detail Kōkan's thoughts and impressions, as well as his activities; it is therefore the more valuable source for insight into his character and personality. *Saiyū Nikki,* moreover, illustrates particularly well Kōkan's keen artistic perception: his eye for detail, color, and humor make it more interesting than the usual travel book. The intimate tone gives the reader the feeling of participating in the journey. Kōkan was interested not only in persons of wealth and power, but in the lower classes as well. His scholarly interests did not preclude many hours of theater-going and other pleasures. He was fond of sakè and women: he frequently mentions his hangovers and describes in detail the songs and dances performed by prostitutes, as well as conditions and prices at the various brothels he visited. He records local dialects, dress, and superstitions. As if to demonstrate his own freedom from convention and contempt for religious injunctions, he frequently mentions the delicious pork, venison, rabbit, raw beef, chicken, and duck he enjoyed, though Japan was a Buddhist country and the faithful were enjoined not to eat meat. Once he shocked even his companions by cutting off the ear of a freshly killed deer and sucking the warm blood—a highly efficacious medicine, he claims. Trivia are usually treated with a quiet, unassuming humor:

> There were signs in the area saying that people gathered mushrooms there, so I went mushroom hunting. Apparently, everyone else had been gathering before me, for there were none left to be picked. I found just one solitary mushroom—which someone else had dropped.[2]

The diary reveals a self-confident, fastidious, and gregarious man of astonishingly varied interests.

Kōkan left Edo on May 28, 1788. It was his first venture out of his native city, and to embark on a journey to the other end of the country was no easy undertaking. Most of the way would be on foot, and the dangers to be encountered required courage and energy. Rivers were often flooded and the traveler had to wait days or weeks before crossing. In mountains and remote areas there was always the threat of attack by bears, wolves, or bandits. Furthermore, government restrictions made travel within Japan difficult; it was generally forbidden to cross from one province to another except on official business. To enforce these restrictions, originally intended to prevent farmers from deserting their lands, barriers had been established at the provincial borders, where travel permits were examined. Kōkan had no official status, but surmounted legal restrictions through letters of introduction received from local governors. Nearly everywhere he went he was, in fact, warmly and enthusiastically received, treated with great respect, given free lodging and free meals. Except for the preparations and subterfuge necessary before he could enter the Dutch compound at Deshima in Nagasaki, he makes no mention of trouble with the authorities during the journey.

At the outset, Kōkan was accompanied by a young man of twenty who had lived as an apprentice in his house in Edo. They did not go far together, however; one month after their departure, the youth "did something outrageous" and Kōkan dismissed him. He found another youth the following month—the sixteen-year-old son of Konishi Shōbei, at whose home Kōkan stayed from July 24 to 29. The boy, called Benki, proved a more suitable companion, and the two traveled together the rest of the way to Nagasaki and back to Edo. At the end of his diary Kōkan writes:

> My servant Benki comes from Fujieda, Suruga province. Last year, at the age of sixteen, he accompanied me to Nagasaki, Hirado, Ikitsuki-shima (where we stayed thirty days to watch the whaling), Kyoto, Osaka, and Edo, thereby seeing many thriving cities. He might be likened to a fly on the rump of a fine horse.[3]

With the exception of those who accompanied him for short distances, Kōkan had no other traveling companions. To handle baggage, he hired local guides and carriers along the way. When possible he took boats and occasionally rented a palanquin, but generally he walked.

Ostensibly, the purpose of his journey was to improve his painting techniques in Nagasaki; this was probably why he so readily obtained his travel permits. He writes of his visit in Iwakuni:

> October 19. A low-ranking clerk of the town magistrate arrived and told me to submit a report of my business. I wrote that I was paying a courtesy call, that I was on my way to Nagasaki in order to polish my painting techniques, and that I would take great pleasure in presenting him with a painting on silk. From then on my stay was financed by the clan, and three luxurious meals including soup and sakè were provided each day.[4]

Kōkan's hearty welcome everywhere was undoubtedly due to the unique information he possessed and the many curiosities he could show his hosts. He delivered highly successful lectures on Holland, foreign inventions, and world geography. Among other unusual objects, he brought with him magnifying glasses, copperplate etchings, and a camera obscura, and demonstrated them with alacrity to people of all classes, including peasants and prostitutes:

> August 1. . . . My guides asked me to tell them what Edo looked like, so I showed them my pictures of Ryōgoku and Edo bridges through the camera obscura that I personally manufactured. They were all utterly dumbfounded and could scarcely believe their eyes! Jokingly, I told them that they would have to pay me thirty-two *mon* apiece for the privilege of viewing the pictures. They took me seriously and pulled out their money. People in the mountain districts are all terribly naive.[5]

> September 4. . . . To my embarrassment, at least twelve or thirteen women waited on me at the brothel. According to the custom of that district, neither sakè nor food was served immediately, and I felt extremely awkward just sitting there doing nothing. Finally, food and drink were brought in and we began chatting. The women were completely dumbfounded when I showed them my pictures *Ryōgoku Bridge* and *Enjoying the Evening Cool by the River* through the camera obscura that I brought with me. In this way the ice was broken, and from then on we chatted freely. When I left the brothel, the women begged me to return the next day to talk with them again.[6]

The aristocracy, too, admired Kōkan's etchings; the eight views of Edo, he writes, were shown to Prince Kan'in of the Kyoto nobility.[7]

Besides the finished works that Kōkan carried with him, he had a good supply of materials, enabling him to execute pictures for his hosts upon demand. Mostly *sekiga* sketches were requested, but he also mentions commissions for more formal works, including landscapes and various screen paintings depicting plum blossoms, puppies, tigers, lions, fish, and birds and flowers, as well as many flower paintings on silk and on fans. His paintings and performances were

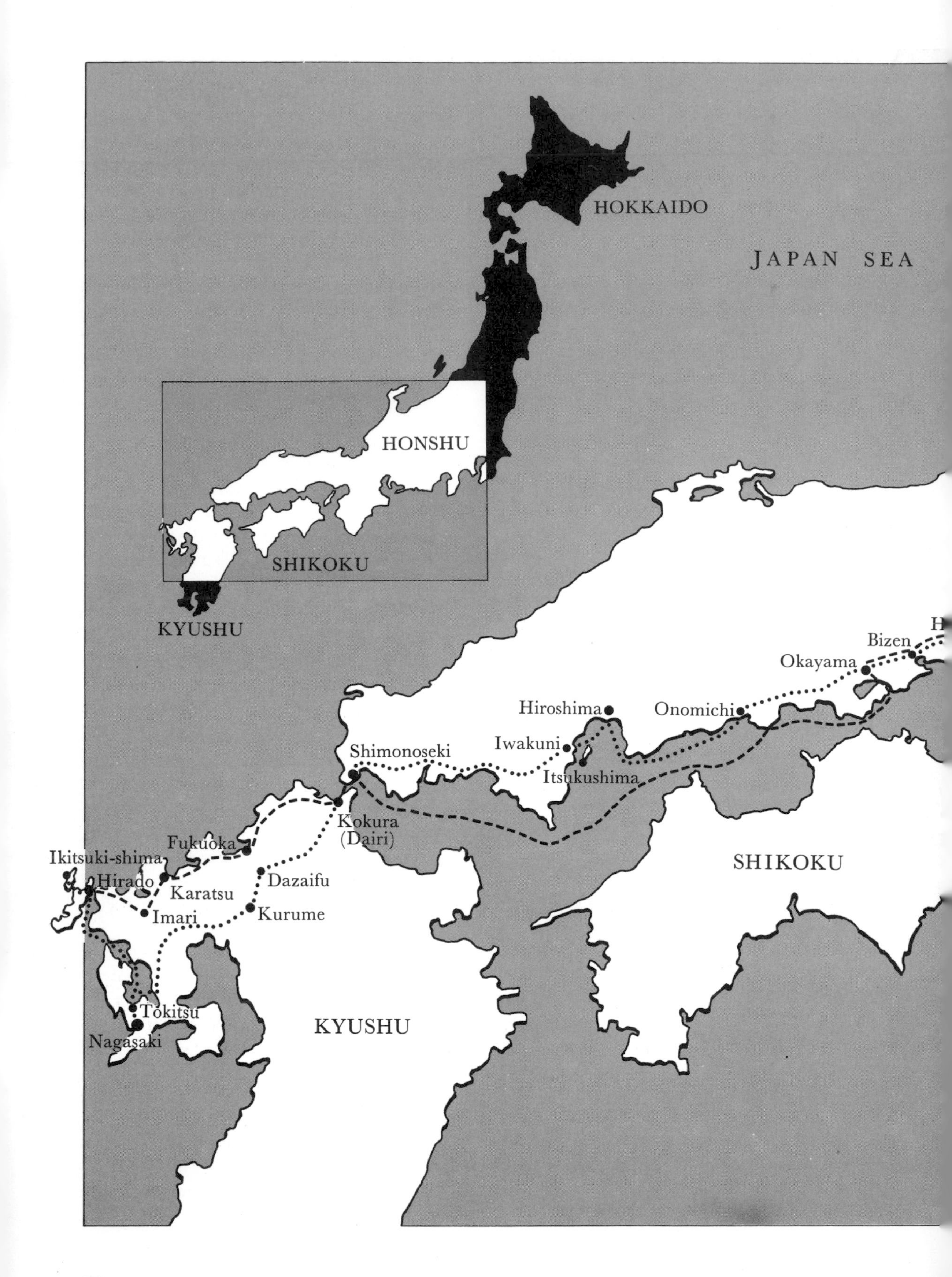
HOKKAIDO
JAPAN SEA
HONSHU
SHIKOKU
KYUSHU
Bizen
Okayama
Hiroshima
Onomichi
Iwakuni
Shimonoseki
Itsukushima
Kokura
(Dairi)
Fukuoka
Ikitsuki-shima
Hirado
Karatsu
Dazaifu
Imari
Kurume
SHIKOKU
Tokitsu
Nagasaki
KYUSHU

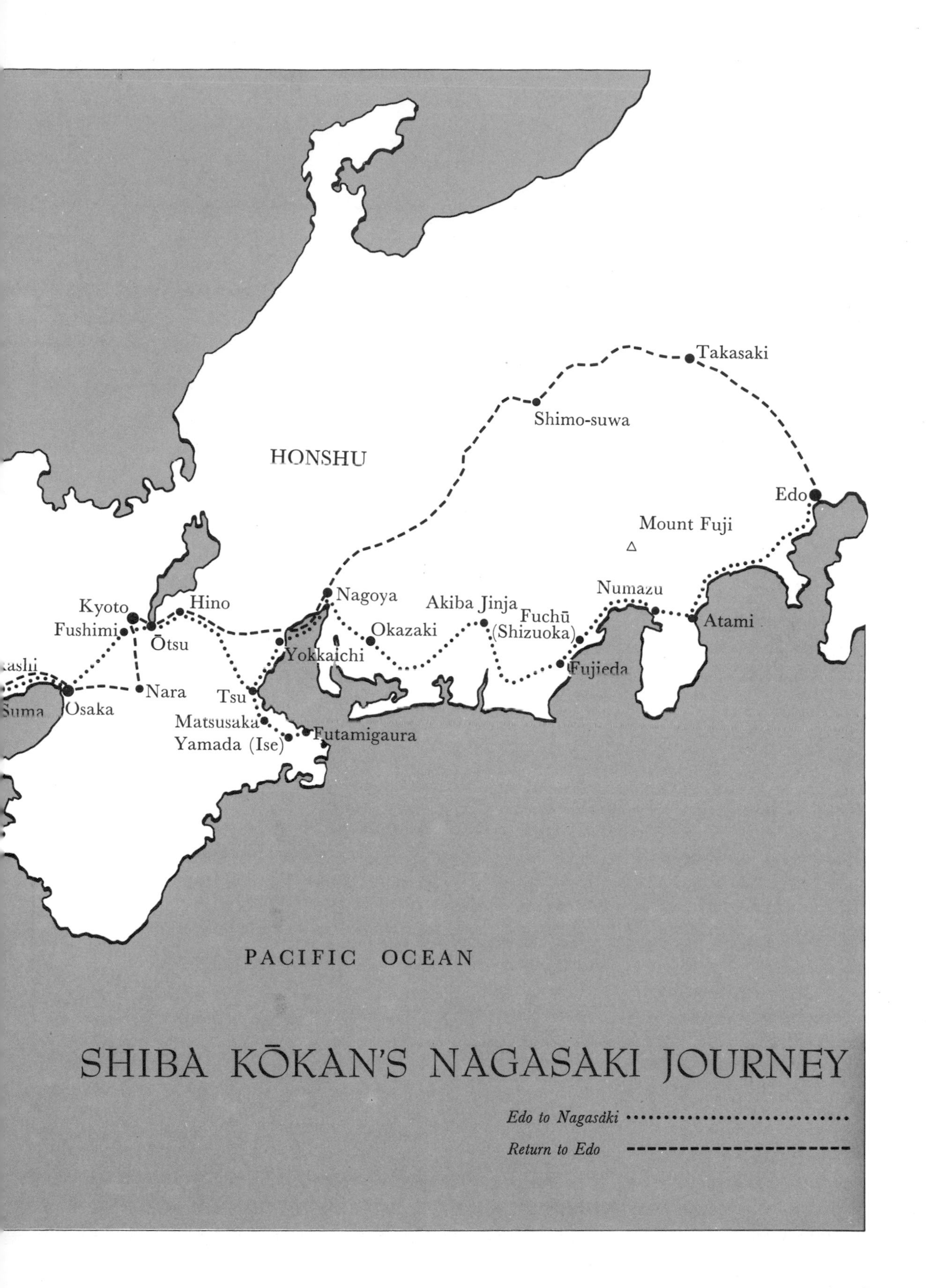

HONSHU
Takasaki
Shimo-suwa
Edo
Mount Fuji
Numazu
Atami
Fuchū
(Shizuoka)
Fujieda
Akiba Jinja
Nagoya
Okazaki
Yokkaichi
Kyoto
Fushimi
Hino
Ōtsu
Nara
Osaka
Tsu
Matsusaka
Yamada (Ise)
Futamigaura
PACIFIC OCEAN
SHIBA KŌKAN'S NAGASAKI JOURNEY
Edo to Nagasaki
Return to Edo

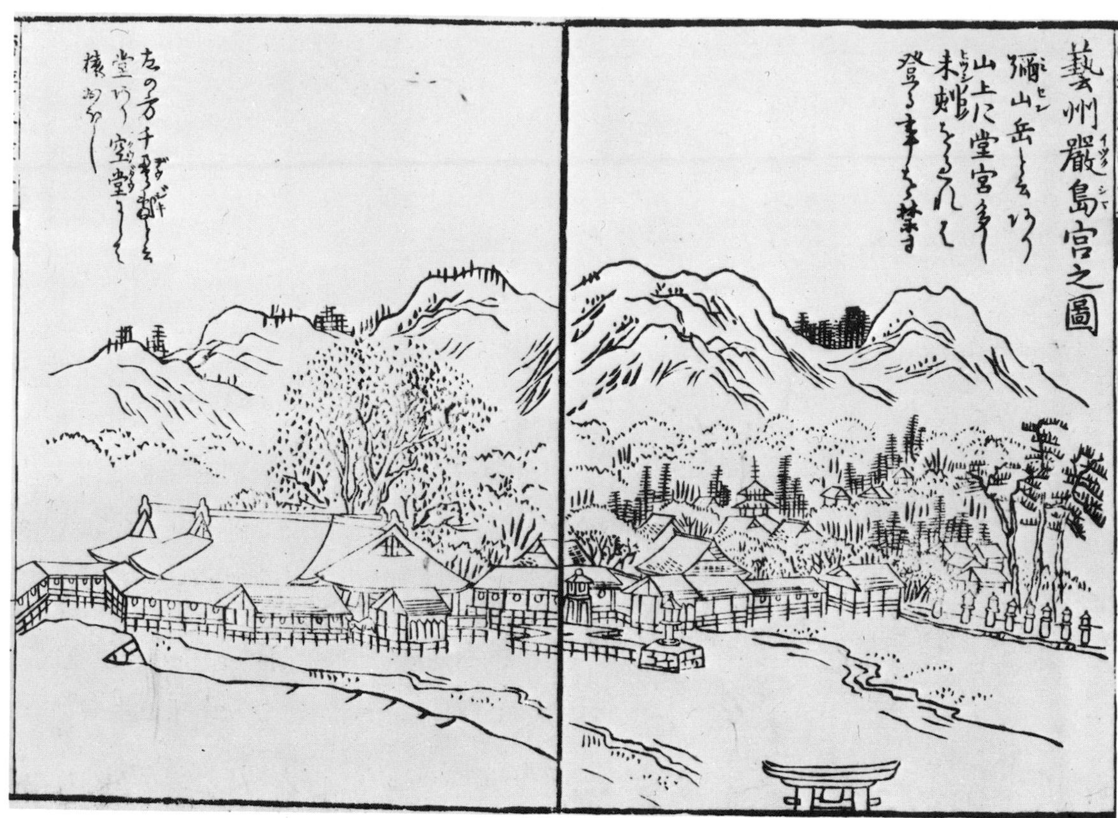

43. Itsukushima Shrine. *1788. Woodblock print. Illustration from* Saiyū Ryodan.

so well received that invariably he was rewarded with "monetary gifts" after each interview, a regular source of financial support for his journey. When he left one place, he often was presented with gifts of food; these he usually offered to his next host.

Several of the scenes Kōkan sketched during his travels and included in his diary he later redrew, apparently as preliminary designs for copperplate etchings. These include views of Itsukushima, Kintai Bridge in Iwakuni, and Nagasaki harbor (Pl. 43–48). The wash drawings are competently handled, the view of Kintai Bridge being especially effective in the mature treatment of spatial recession and compositional balance. But they also express a certain mannered quality, suggesting the artist's habitual attempt to follow rules and consciously imitate Western conventions of drawing. The corresponding sketches hold the greater charm. Lacking studied insistence on perspective and precise shading, they possess spontaneity, a more appropriate filling of spatial areas, a clarity, vitality, and precision of line, and therefore are more arresting compositions.

The famous shrine of Itsukushima in the Inland Sea has changed little since Kōkan depicted it in 1788 (Pl. 43 and 44). He diverted his route from Hiroshima in order to visit the island, traveling, he writes, in company with Haruki Nanko, a fellow artist from Edo who was on his way to Nagasaki by order of his feudal lord Masuyama.[8] At Itsukushima they parted, but met once more the following month at their destination. The diary reports:

> I walked three and a half miles to Kusazu and soon reached Inokuchi, where I boarded a small boat and traveled the seven and a half miles to Miyajima. It was raining. First I went to the shrine to

44. Itsukushima Shrine. *Circa 1790. Drawing designed for an etching. Location unknown.*

pay homage. Corridors are formed so as to let in the tide beneath them. The shrine reportedly was built by Heisokoku [Taira] Kiyomori. It is an old and fine structure, with lanterns along the corridors reflected in the water. The island is seventeen and a half miles in circumference and has more than one thousand houses, but no fields and farms. The place abounds with monkeys and deer. At that time a theatrical group was performing and teahouses were thriving.

I stayed there the next day and parted with Haruki, who wrote for me: "A poem for Mr. Shiba, with whom I traveled to Itsukushima in the late autumn:

> "For a short while we traveled together
> Amid splendid scenery of mountains and river.
> We shared a lodging in Itsukushima in the autumn
> And parted at the Hyaku-hachi Corridor,
> Sacred lanterns shedding light over a lone boat."[9]

The inscription on the sketch explains:

> A picture of Itsukushima Shrine, Geishū province. On the hill called Misen-dake are many halls belonging to the shrine. Climbing is prohibited after two o'clock in the afternoon. The building at the left is called the Hall of a Thousand Mats and is empty. There are a great many monkeys in this area.

Kōkan's next stop after Istukushima was the famous Kintai Bridge in Iwakuni (Pl. 45 and 46). He spent the first night in an inn at the foot of the bridge, staying several days in the vicinity in order to study its construction. On the sketch he notes:

> Picture of the Kintai Bridge, Iwakuni. I

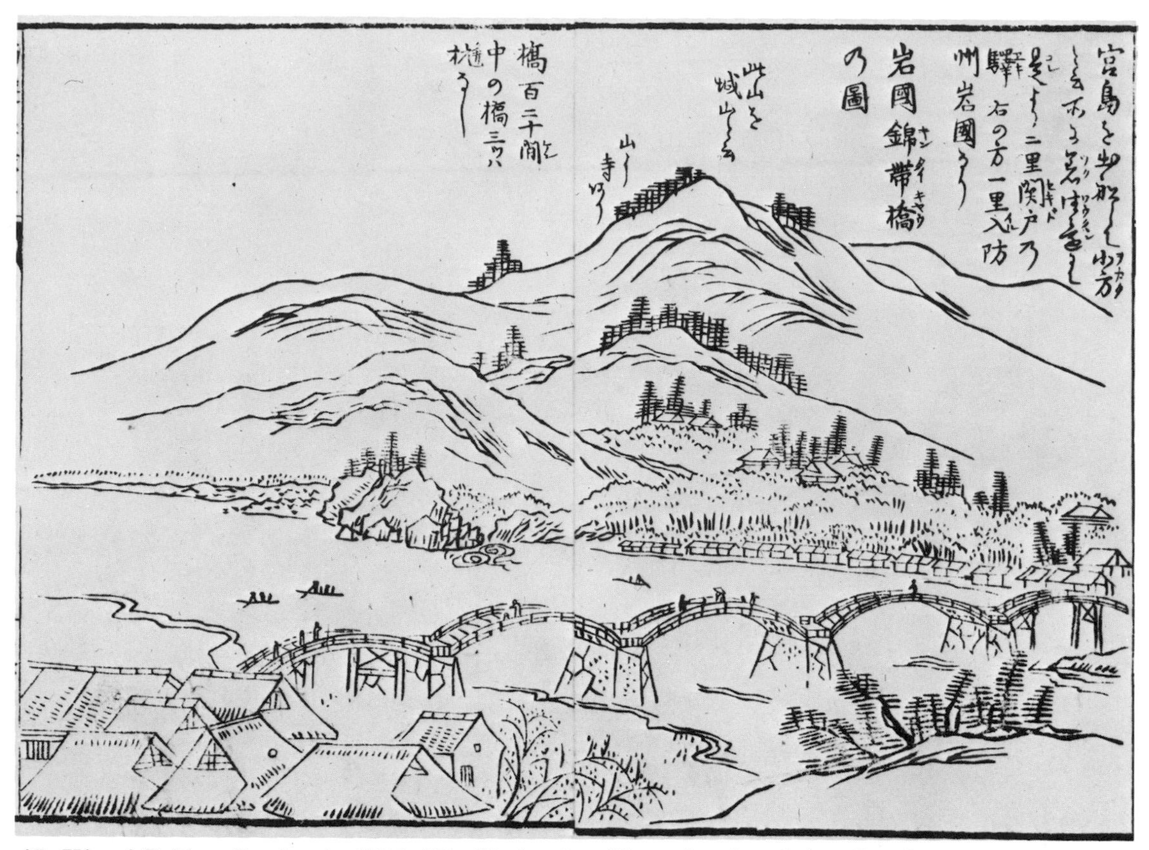

45. Kintai Bridge, Iwakuni. *1788. Woodblock print. Illustration from* Saiyū Ryodan.

left Miyajima by boat for Okata, walked five miles along the highway to Sekido Station, and another two and a half miles to the right from there to reach Iwakuni in Bōshū province. The mountain with a temple on it is named Shiro-yama. Kintai Bridge is 250 yards long, and the three spans in the middle have no supporting posts beneath them.

Several years later, in 1809, Kōkan executed an oil painting of this same scene, which he offered to the Asakusa Shrine in Edo.

To reach Nagasaki, Kōkan had to cross from Honshu to Kyushu by boat, a treacherous journey vividly described in his journal:

October 31. Fine and windy. Shimonoseki is the embarking port for Kyushu, seven miles from Kokura and three and a half miles from Dairi. About 10 A.M. I boarded the small ferryboat,[10] but the boat's departure was delayed by the strong wind. To kill time, I took out a flask given me by Uchisaka of Iwakuni to buy sakè. What I couldn't drink myself I passed around to the other passengers. Everyone was eager to get started, and finally we set sail, but the west wind grew stronger and stronger and huge waves sloshed into the boat. Kokura is a little southwest of Dairi. The wind blew violently, filling the sail and blowing it out almost horizontally. The boat heeled sharply, and those sitting in the gunwales were so drenched by the sea they appeared to have just come out of a bath. People were vomiting all over the place and acted as though they were dying. One man about fifty who seemed to be a courier sat opposite me on the gunwales. Waves were breaking right over our

46. Kintai Bridge, Iwakuni. *Circa 1790. Drawing designed for an etching. Courtesy of the Tenri Library, Nara prefecture.*

heads, so I threw an oilcloth over myself in order to get a good view of the waves and sketched them. The sakè helped a great deal. I didn't even get seasick! Sakè makes us very brave, I realized.

The boat barely managed to stay afloat for the three and a half miles; it took an hour to reach Dairi. Only the three crew members did any work during the crossing. The other people were all screaming and shouting to pull down the sail, but the sail was full blown and wouldn't come down. The three crewmen did all the bailing as water poured into the boat, while all the passengers looked like corpses. It was indeed a horrible experience, and everyone was enormously relieved when we finally docked at Dairi.[11]

Arriving safely in Kyushu, he approached his destination—the window to the Western world. From a nearby hill he sketched the harbor (Pl. 47), a view he redrew on several occasions. The notation on the drawing is typical of Kōkan's discursive, alert mind:

> A view of Nagasaki from Nishizaka. The spot where the flag is flying is the Dutch sector, called Deshima. Chinese ships are seen in the waters nearby. Dutch ships leave Kosaki, two and a half miles from Nagasaki, in September. The Chinese residences, located in the lowland named Jūzenji, are not shown in this picture. Surrounding mountains have cultivated fields.

In Osaka on his way home he depicted the harbor (Pl. 48) for Kimura Kenkadō, a wealthy sakè merchant and scholar of Dutch learning.[12] This drawing and a later one executed after his return to Edo are nearly

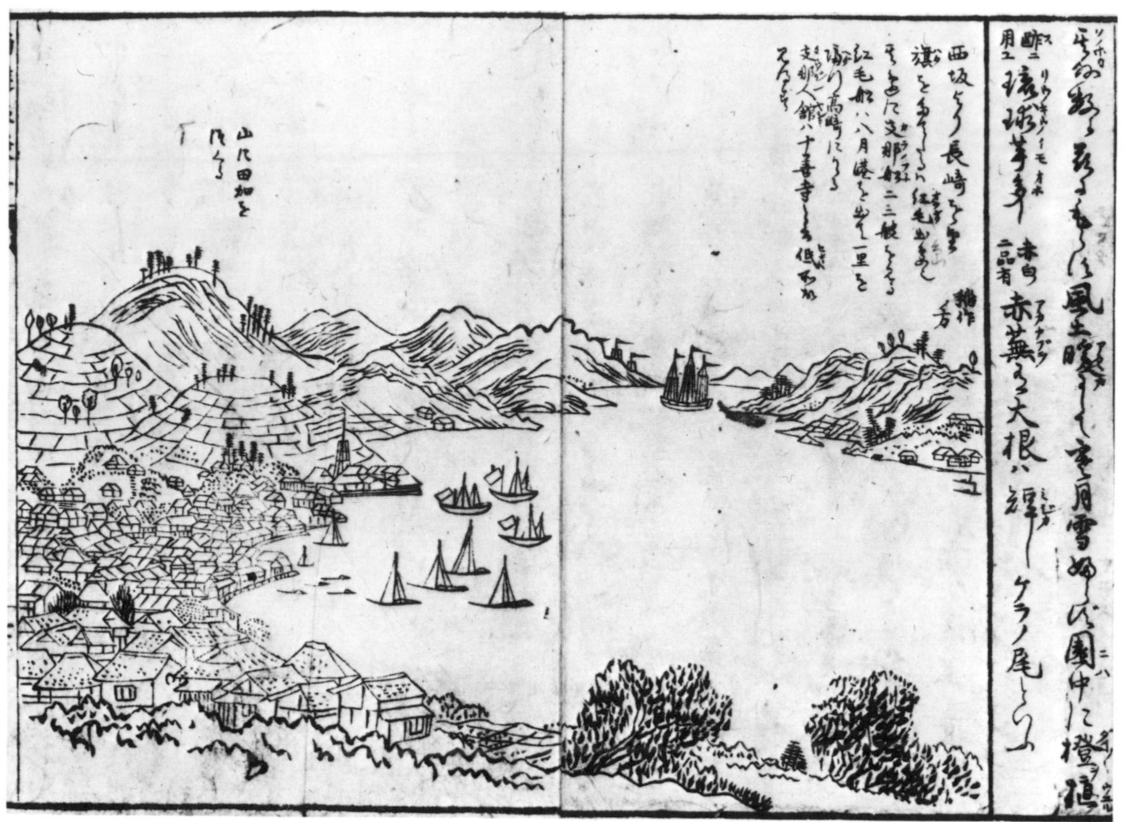

47. Nagasaki Harbor. *1788. Woodblock print. Illustration from* Saiyū Ryodan.

identical in composition, but the Osaka work has a particular distinction: it is drawn on Western paper with pen and ink, materials Kōkan may either have brought from Nagasaki or obtained from Kenkadō. The finished drawings are in reverse of the diary sketch, perhaps because Kōkan intended them for viewing through a camera obscura.

Kōkan stayed in Nagasaki a little over a month, from November 7 until December 11.[13] His hope of finding a teacher to instruct him in the methods of Western painting was destined to be frustrated, for no one seemed capable. He visited Araki Gen'yū, a respected artist and Foreign Art Inspector for the Japanese government,[14] but Kōkan was unimpressed:

> I called on Araki Tamenoshin at Kajimachi. As the official connoisseur of pictures he is somewhat capable of drawing but is not a good artist.[15]

Undoubtedly his period of study would have extended to three years as originally planned had he discovered a suitable teacher; his pursuit of other interests, however, apparently compensated for this disappointment.

Most of his time was spent visiting acquaintances and exploring the town; the event of greatest significance was his admittance to the secluded Dutch compound on the manmade island of Deshima in Nagasaki harbor. In order to gain access, he was obliged to disguise himself as a merchant engaged in official business with Dutch residents. With the assistance of his friend Katsuki Rihei, a minor government official, Kōkan applied for an entry pass on November 21 and visited Deshima the following

48. Nagasaki Harbor. *Circa 1789. Pen and ink drawing with color added. Courtesy Nagasaki Municipal Museum.*

day. He recorded his impressions as follows:

November 22. After receiving my pass from the government office, Katsuki Rihei and two other Nagasaki men accompanied me to the Dutch compound. At the gate we were examined to make sure we were not carrying anything in our bosoms or sleeves, for nothing can be taken inside. Just inside the gate we met Stutzer, a Dutch surgeon, whom I had met the year before at the Nagasaki-ya, an inn for Hollanders at Ishi-machi in Edo. I had promised him that I would visit Nagasaki, and as soon as he saw me, he showed me to a deserted cowshed. As we walked he talked to me, but I could not make out what he was saying. All I understood was "tekenen," which meant that he wanted me to draw pictures for him of Marunouchi and other areas in Edo. Then he said, "Mijnheer kom kamer," which I understood perfectly well. "Mijnheer" means "you," "kom" is "come," and "kamer" is "room." I followed him to his room upstairs.

We sat in chairs placed on the dirty matted floor, leaving our footgear on. Cups of liquor were served on a table that resembled a low Japanese dining table. Lamps and other decorations were all made of glass and silver. A white bird something like a parrot and as large as a dove was kept uncaged in the room, and the Dutchman petted the bird, which perched on his hand, pressed it against his cheek, and put its head in his mouth. I have never seen that type of bird since, but apparently it was a kind of parakeet. The liquor looked like unrefined sakè and tasted sour, so I said "sushi sushi" [sour]. The Dutchman, pointing to an egg, re-

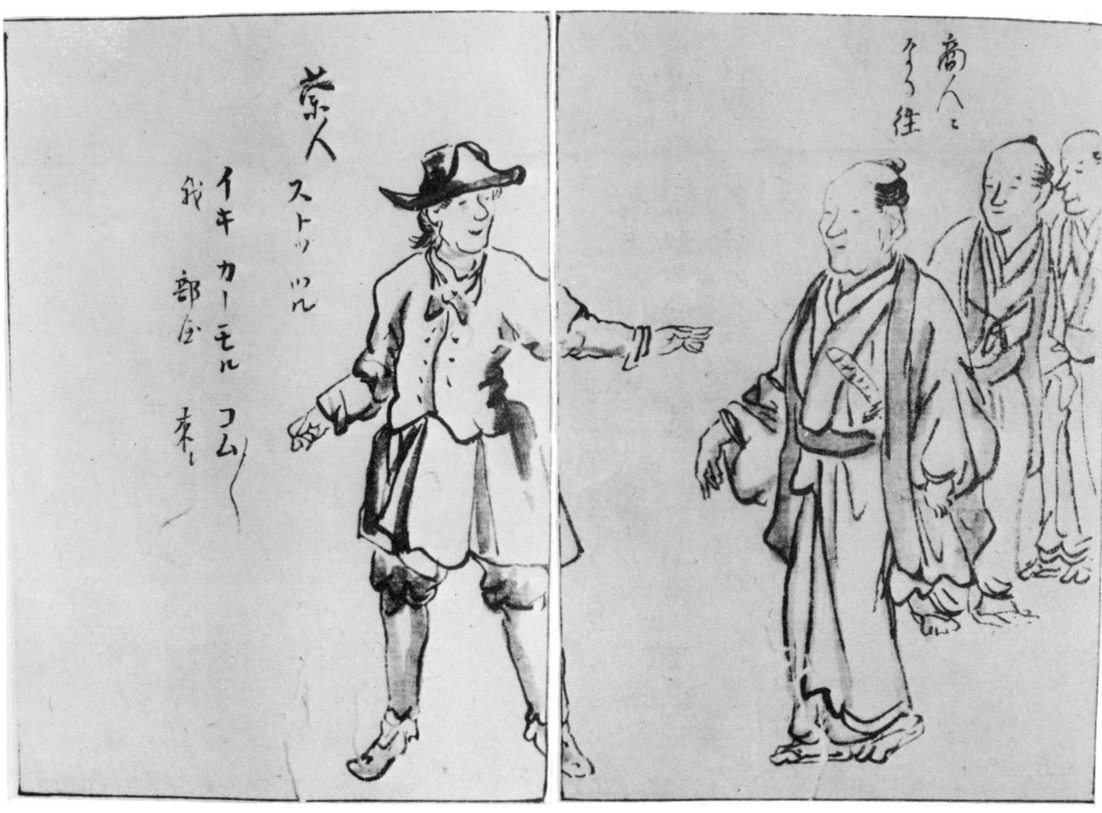

49. Kōkan and Dr. Stutzer. *1788. Woodblock print. Illustration from* Saiyū Nikki.

plied in Japanese, "kusuri" [medicine].

We then proceeded to the interpreter's room to meet the official interpreter, Kōsaku.[16] At his orders, two lesser officials, Tokutarō and Matsujūrō, escorted me to the captain's room, reached by ladders from three directions. Matsujūrō guided me through the corridor upstairs, and again we kept our footgear on. A black-skinned man walked by, and Matsujūrō asked me to make a good sketch of him. Black-skinned men are not Dutchmen, but are born in tropical countries, such as India, Dutch-controlled Java, or the African continent. They have dark complexions, frizzly hair, and features strikingly different from ours. In summer they wear something like a Japanese priest's surplice, but in winter, when I saw them, they had on narrow-sleeved coats given them by the Dutchmen, breeches, and leather-soled sandals. They carry tobacco pouches made of Japanese leather at their sides, and they cover their heads with red-striped cotton cloth. They have no hair around their mouths, and they speak an Indian language that Dutchmen cannot understand. They are dirty indeed.

The captain's room was twenty mats in width, and the walls had transoms on all sides. Beneath the transoms were hung framed pictures painted on glass. There was a row of chairs, beside each of which stood a silver spittoon about two feet high, looking like a flower vase. On the floor matting was a rug with a flowered pattern; a glass chandelier hung from the ceiling. Behind a red curtain there was what appeared to be a small den. All the windows were made of glass.

Soon the captain appeared, holding a long pipe in his hand, and greeted us. According to Matsujūrō's translation, he boasted that his room was most splendid,

50. The Dutch Factory Director's Room, Deshima. *1788. Woodblock print. Illustration from* Saiyū Ryodan.

probably because he felt that we Japanese don't decorate our rooms and have only simple, primitive tastes. I therefore replied: "I am dazzled." Two black-skinned servants appeared with gold-colored glasses and a flask on a silver tray and stood by our side. From the glasses we drank anise wine, which is made from fennel. It was so strong that I gave mine to my companions. The captain, Hendrik Casper Romberg, had visited Edo five times, and therefore we were already acquainted. There was another captain too, but he did not live upstairs in the building.

We then went out and along a path bordered with flowers, crossed a bridge with a resting place over a small pond, and were ushered into what appeared to be a guest room. There was a table for pocket billiards—a game that Dutchmen play just as Japanese play dice games. The table is about four by seven feet, and the top is covered with a woolen cloth. Balls placed on the table are hit with a stick like a riding whip, and the object is to drop the balls into holes at the four corners of the table. I was not on intimate terms with the other captain, for he had just made his first visit to Japan that year. We then left Deshima.

My three companions, though natives of Nagasaki, had never seen Dutchmen before; access to the Dutch residences on Deshima is strictly prohibited. My companions were truly astonished to see me talking with Hollanders on familiar terms, all the more so because I was acquainted with the captain! Nagasaki citizens see Chinese but never have an opportunity to see Hollanders because when Dutchmen visit temples in the city they always travel by palanquin. Nagasaki citizens still marvel at the fact that I was

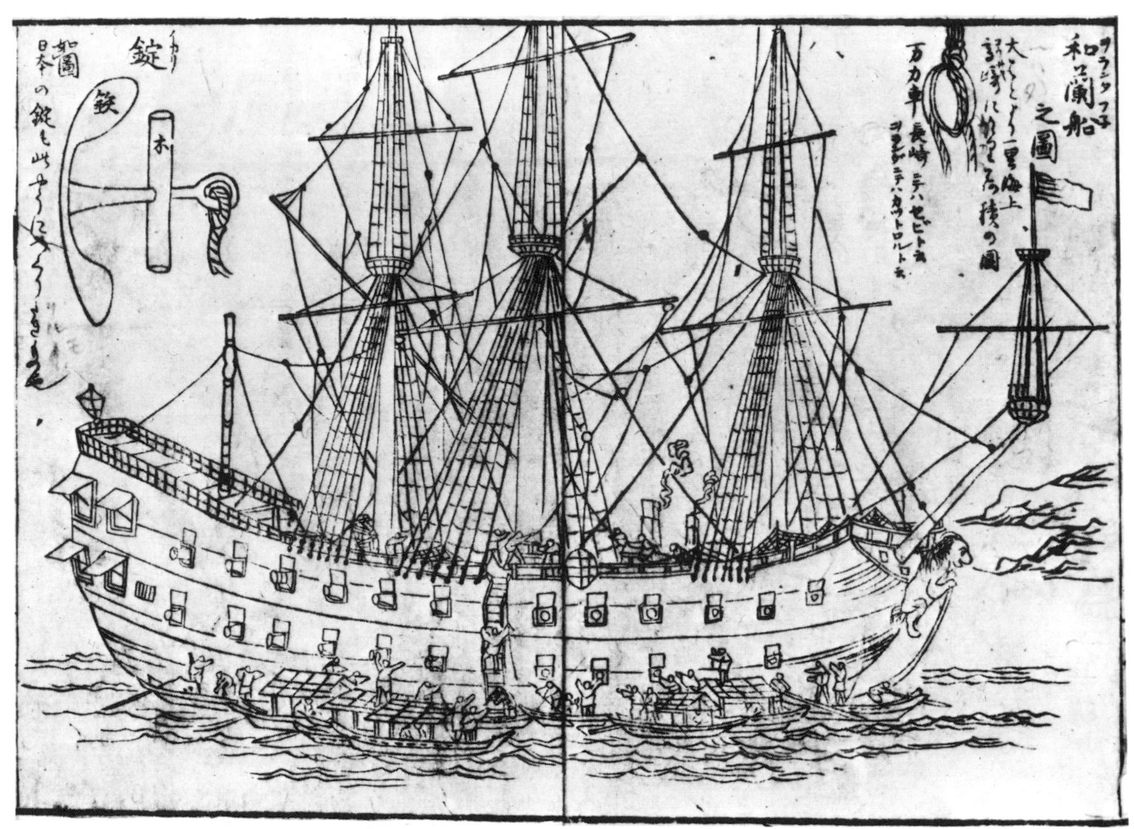

51. A Dutch Ship. *1788. Woodblock print. Illustration from* Saiyū Ryodan.

able to mingle freely with the Hollanders. Even feudal lords in western Japan near Nagasaki visit Deshima only once during their entire reign.[17]

Several incidents of the visit are illustrated in the diary, among them Kōkan's reception by Doctor Stutzer (Pl. 49) and a picture of Captain Romberg's room in all its European splendor (Pl. 50). The sketches are informal examples of lively draftsmanship and unreserved expression directly capturing a mood; through them one senses the artist's enthusiasm for his subject and something of the excitement of his travels.

Kōkan's only other contact with Hollanders in Nagasaki was a visit on November 24 to a Dutch ship anchored in Nagasaki Bay. The diary sketch (Pl. 51) and accompanying description reveal his powers of observation, and, in the mention of the firing of the cannon, his rejection of popular superstition:

> November 24. Frequent showers. About 8 A.M. I went with Sadanosuke (Yoshio's son, who is an interpreter) to a Dutch ship anchored at Kosaki about a mile off shore. Sadanosuke went to supervise the ship's loading, and I accompanied him as his letter carrier. We took a small boat out to the ship, which was about twenty feet high. It was a difficult climb up the rope ladder, and when I reached the deck, I felt that I was looking down from a rooftop. The huge size of the ship defies description. It was painted black with pitch except for the railing, which was yellow. On one side there were twenty-five cannons, and in all there were sixty. At the stern was a roofed room with glass windows through which one could look

out on the sea. There were three masts with so many ropes they looked like cobwebs. . . . The style of shipbuilding differs every year, and the ship I saw had an image of a lion painted yellow on the bow. The sailors, known as "matroos," are all Dutchmen and dress like Dutchmen except that they go barefooted even in winter, so that they can easily climb the masts to rig the sails. They do not go on land at all, but remain on the ship at all times. Their jumping from one sail rope to another is an acrobatic feat, and they are also excellent swimmers. The black-skinned servants can perform no such feats. The cannon is fired once every morning, and two or three times on festival days. It is merely a custom, rather like our custom of using fire for purification, and the conjecture of Nagasaki citizens that the guns are fired to move the ship is sheer nonsense. Ships arrive in the harbor in June and stay until August; then they remain at anchor off Kosaki until the new and former captains settle their accounts and conclude their trading. In November, the sailors wait for an easterly wind and set sail under the direction of the captain.[18]

In Nagasaki Kōkan also visited a foreign cemetery. On his sketch of a Dutch tombstone he explained:

> This is the grave of a Dutch captain named Duurkoop at the Goshin-ji temple.[19] It is a Dutch custom to bury the corpse in a lying position. The stone is engraved with gold-colored letters, and above the epitaph is carved an hourglass, which symbolizes that the time of a man's life must run out. Dutchmen frequently use proverbs as teachings, and pictures are often metaphorical, portraying winged persons and other figures intended purely as symbols. There are no winged persons on earth.[20]

Although Kōkan's active scientific career began after his journey to Nagasaki, his interest was stimulated by two interpreters and scholars of Dutch learning he met there, Yoshio Kōsaku and Motoki Ryōei. After his first few weeks in the city, he told his host, Inabe Hanzō, that he was leaving for Hirado; under that pretext he moved into Yoshio Kōsaku's house on December 1. Undoubtedly during the ten days with Kōsaku he gleaned various bits of information on Western science. He also had an opportunity to meet there other men acquainted with Hollanders or with Dutch learning. Not without a touch of pride he notes that they all treated him with respect; he describes his surroundings with great precision, as if to impress his readers by his familiarity with the world of scholars of the exotic. Characteristically, these descriptions are filled with such incidentals as the fact that Kōsaku's house, in the Western manner, had two stories:

> December 9. I drew a portrait in ink of Kōsaku in a sitting position, wearing Japanese *haori* and *hakama* and holding a Dutch book. Above him I drew angels in a cloud, one blowing a trumpet. This portrait I gave to Hakku, a physician from Kurashiki, Bitchū province. I also drew a portrait of Chang Chung-kuei and gave it to Yamayoshi Taihaku, a physician from Sanshu who lives in Nagasaki. In the evening Reibun, a physician in the employ of Lord Matsudaira Suho, from Iwami, came to receive lessons from Kōsaku. His nose was deformed. The four met on the second floor of the house. All the visitors learned my name.[21]

Many diary references allude to portraits Kōkan executed during his travels; always in demand, they provided an income contributing considerably to his support. The extant portrait of Kōsaku (Pl. 52) is drawn with unvarnished realism, his features outlined carefully with a fine brush and slightly modeled. Clothing, drawn in rapid, sure brush strokes in the manner of Kōkan's *sekiga* art, is shaded with ink washes to produce the illusion of three-dimensional form. The attempt is unsuccessful, however, resulting only in an overworked pattern of indiscriminate lines and tones. The painting does not contain the transitional range of values necessary to indicate volume, and thereby fails to create the illusion of naturalism and corporeality basic to Western portraiture. Equally, it is without the simplicity and precision of design achieved through flat patterned areas and unmodeled color found in Japanese portraiture. By superimposing a veneer of Western technical methods on a traditionally Far Eastern style, Kōkan produced a portrait lacking the essential values of either aesthetic.

Kōsaku's name appears at the top in roman letters, placed above two incredible cavorting angels, one indeed blowing a trumpet. The motif undoubtedly was employed to stress the painter's acquaintance with Western symbolism, for as Kōkan the empiricist asserted, "there are no winged persons on earth."

52. Portrait of Yoshio Kōsaku. *1788. Private collection.*

In the diary, Kōkan also mentions painting on glass. Glass painting, called *biidoro-e* from the Portuguese word for glass, *vidro,* consisted of meticulously executed miniatures painted on one side of the glass and viewed through the other. Kōkan wrote simply that he "painted on glass," without naming the technique, but it seems certain his pictures were in fact *biidoro-e* (or *garasu-e,* as they are called today). Glass was a rare and hence extremely expensive commodity in Tokugawa times, and very little was produced in Edo; it was hardly likely an artist there would use it as a substitute for silk or other materials.

Biidoro-e were particularly popular in Nagasaki, where Ishizaki Yushi and Araki Jogen were well-known practitioners of the craft. It seems probable that Kōkan learned the art in Nagasaki. His interest, however, had been aroused even before his visit, for in Osaka, en route, he visited a plate-glass maker. Both in Nagasaki and in Kyoto on his return journey he stopped in glass shops, where, he writes, he "gave instructions on sheet glass." Considering Kōkan's propensity for exaggeration, one may conjecture he received rather than gave instructions. The statements are vague and could, of course, refer to either the making or painting of glass, for probably he knew both processes. Scientific curiosity may have led him to investigate the method of producing the glass itself; his artistic interests, in any case, very likely included glass painting. Among the announcements of future publications written at the end of his book *Chikyū Zenzu Ryakusetsu* (Explanation of the Complete Map of the World) is this listing:

> *Oranda Kikō*. The book includes a method of making copperplate engravings, the technique of mixing oil paints, and the art of plate glass.

But the scarcity of glass in Edo seems to have caused him to give up such painting after his return from Nagasaki. He makes no later mention of the art, and none of his *biidoro-e* is extant.

Kōkan sent back by ship from Nagasaki to Edo some personal belongings, including souvenirs acquired in his travels. On December 11 he departed for the former Dutch trading port of Hirado, where he was enthusiastically welcomed by the local ruler, Lord Matsu-ura:

> When I arrived at the gate of His Lordship's mansion, he received me immediately. He had with him seven retainers and four lesser servants. After he had shown me a number of foreign books, I painted *sekiga* for him, and he then entertained me with sakè, food, cakes, and ceremonial tea, which he personally prepared for me in the tea room. When I returned to the inn that evening, I found the whole town in an uproar. I described the events of the day, how I had been entertained with ceremonial tea prepared personally by His Lordship, and how he had presented me with fine cakes. The innkeeper was utterly astonished, and said this was completely without precedent. "Anyone received by His Lordship in his own mansion is certainly an extremely important person," he said. "Your visit to my humble inn is therefore as great an honor as it would be if His Excellency himself were to stop here." I gave him the cake I had received from His Lordship, and the innkeeper wept over it in awe and trepidation. He insisted that the cake was far too valuable to eat; he would keep it always as a good-luck charm.[22]

From Hirado, Kōkan proceeded to the small island of Ikitsuki-shima off the coast of Kyushu. This was the westernmost point reached during his journey, and in many ways the most extraordinary place he visited. He spent a month on the island[23] and had ample opportunity to study the local whaling industry; the high point of his sojourn was a whale hunt, vividly described and illustrated in his diary. After he returned to Edo, he used the illustrations as models for a horizontal scroll painting, executed probably around 1793–94. Each section contains a written explanation adding pertinent information to the visual description. Nearly thirteen feet in length, the scroll is painted in monochrome with light washes of color added. Its general effect is that of an Oriental painting, but the use of mathematical perspective, shading, and realistic detail mark it as a typical example of Kōkan's eclectic style.

The scroll opens with a view of Usukaura harbor, Hirado, where Kōkan departed on a cold winter morning for Ikitsuki-shima, in a boat manned by five oarsmen. Weather conditions interrupted the crossing, illustrated in Section 2:

> At 10 A.M., December 30, 1788, we left from Usukaura for Ikitsuki-shima but were obliged by high winds and rough seas to make port at Sukusa, a wild, rocky place with only a tuna storehouse. There were more than fifty tuna boats, and we changed boats and set out again for Ikitsuki-shima. My clothes were soaking wet from the high waves. Finally, at dusk, we reached the island.

Section 3 (Pl. 53) presents a carefully detailed image of Ikitsuki-shima, pinpointing

53. Ikitsuki-shima. *Circa 1793–94. Light color and ink on paper. Section 3 of* Picture Scroll of Whaling. *Courtesy Tokyo National Museum.*

fishing villages, lookout towers, boats, and floats of fishing nets on the sea. Perspective augments the naturalistic effect, but along with Western techniques there is an equally strong Oriental vision. The mountains, though given mass through modeling, have the rapidly executed quality of *bunjinga* painting, and the rocky crags are typically Chinese in shape and conception, their power conveyed through proportional relationship and broken contour lines. Here Kōkan has attempted to assimilate the best of two artistic worlds by extracting desirable elements from each. He was torn between an interest in realistic depiction and an inclination to portray mountains in the traditional Chinese manner. Though mountainous, Ikitsuki-shima has not the precipitous silhouette Kōkan drew. His desire to depict reality gave way to a more artistic urge to impart dramatic effect to the landscape. This, of course, was no different from the approach of Western artists, but Western art, as Kōkan conceived it, consisted of a near literal transcription of surface appearances.

The corresponding diary sketch (Pl. 54), freer in its sweeping linear movement and entirely unconstrained by attempts at Western modeling, appears the more dynamic representation; by comparison, the formal painting conveys the spirit of a Brobdingnagian island. Kōkan labeled in greater detail the various places of interest: the watchtower, tuna net, islands ostensibly Chinese, the mountains Yayako-ga-dake (left) and Biwade (right), the area at right where whales were brought in and dismembered, as well

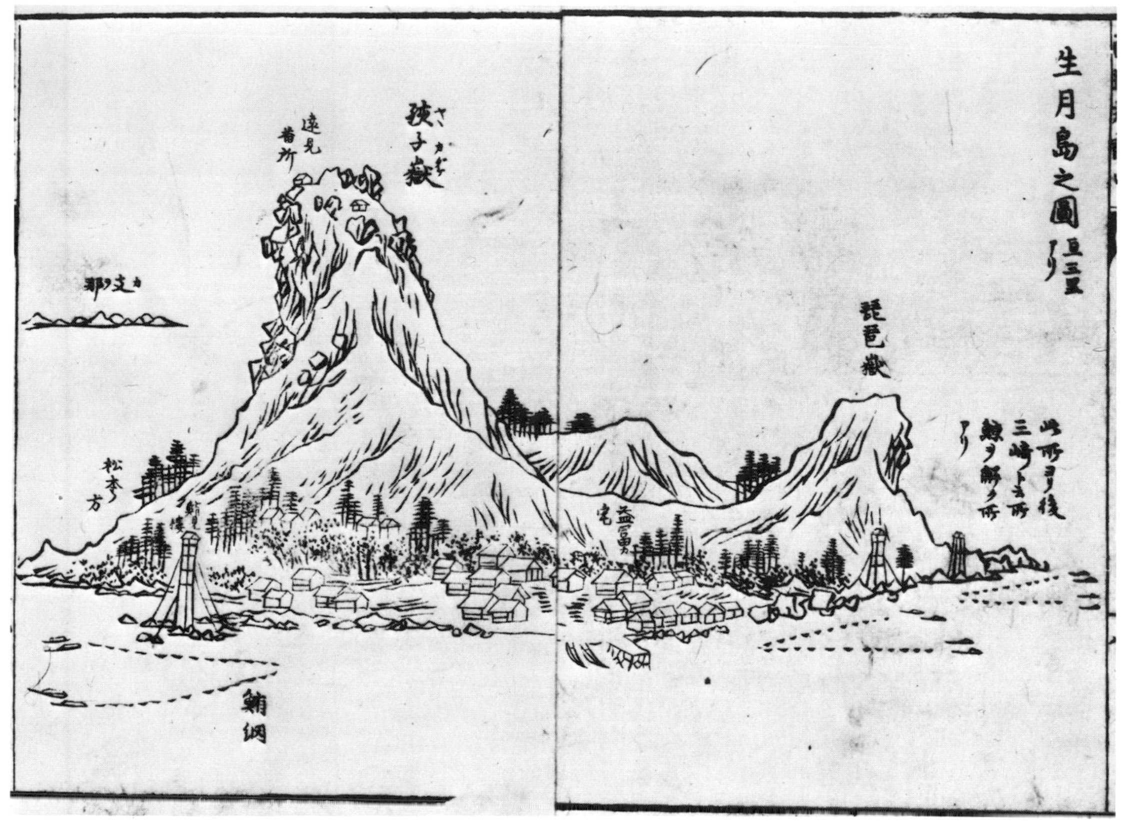

54. Ikitsuki-shima. *1788. Woodblock print. Illustration from* Saiyū Ryodan.

as the house of Masutomi Matazaemon, proprietor of the whaling industry. The inscription on the painting reads:

> The mountain of Ikitsuki-shima is called Yayako-ga-dake. I climbed it, reaching the top just at sunset. Far to the west, the land that appears to be islands in the evening glow is actually China.[24]

Kōkan's account of his climb presents more than a simple description of the event. His observations capture the tempo of life on that remote island, the naiveté and provincialism of its inhabitants, the customs, attitudes, and atmosphere so alien to a man from the metropolis of Edo:

> December 31. Fine calm weather. At 10 A.M. we began the climb up Yayako-ga-dake, the highest mountain on the island, taking with us tea, cakes, and sakè. There were four in our party: Matanosuke,[25] Shinshirō, my attendant, and I, plus a child who carried a mat. While passing through the village we met an old man who fell prostrate on the ground before us. Matanosuke shouted at him to move on. In a place like this, Matanosuke is indeed nobility! We reached a house made of stone, which was the home of Matanosuke's old nurse, and stopped to visit. The old woman was having her lunch, and while listening to our conversation, she suddenly burst out laughing, blowing the rice in her mouth all over the table. I had no idea what the outburst was all about until Matanosuke explained that the peculiar language used by the stranger

from Edo had struck her as terribly funny.

The slope up to the top of the hill was grassy with no trees, and six or seven hundred yards from the top it became steeper. Altogether, the hike was about a mile and a half. The watchman in the tower at the top told me that in the evening light distant mountains in the west can be seen three times a year. These are Chinese mountains and not a part of Japanese territory. Possibly they are Chinese islands near Japan.

We spread out the mat on a rock at the top of the mountain and drank sakè, looking at the blue sea below. I felt as though I were in a foreign country. The watchman, a man of about sixty, said he had lived in Edo for ten years. He described the city as twenty miles square, with rows and rows of houses. On the outskirts of the city, he said, are farms where radishes ten inches wide are grown. We all laughed at his description.

After a while we descended the mountain, and again dropped in at the old woman's house, where we had a meal of steamed Ryukyu potatoes. We then returned to Masutomi's house.[26]

The fourth section of the scroll illustrates the harpoons and cutlery used in whaling. Typical of his concern for detail, Kōkan drew harpoons and a sword in his diary, giving the length of each weapon and an explanation of its use.

Section 5 depicts the actual whale hunt (Pl. 55), the high point of Kōkan's visit to Ikitsuki-shima. The diary account brings the event vividly to life:

A whaling net is constructed of ropes like a large screen and attached to floats in the water. It is from 1,400 to 1,600 yards long, joined together in sections of about 20 to 30 yards, and extends to the ocean floor. Whales are driven toward the net, and when one strikes it, the sections separate, the part struck wrapping about the head of the whale and impeding its flight. Then the boats take up the chase. The men do not throw harpoons until the boat is nearly on top of the prey. A rope is attached to each harpoon, so that when one is lodged in the whale, one boat is pulled, when two harpoons are thrown, two boats are pulled, etc. The more boats pulled, the slower the whale's flight. The boats encircle the whale and are pulled about wherever it flees. When the beast throws its head above the water and blows, a fisherman hurls a sword at it repeatedly. Greatly weakened, the whale is

55. The Whale Hunt. *Circa 1793–94. Light color and ink on paper. Section 5 of* Picture Scroll of Whaling. *Courtesy Tokyo National Museum.*

unable to blow and can only inhale the air. At this moment a young man dives into the sea, sits astride its back, and slashes a hole in it, running a large rope through the hole. The whale sounds again, thrashing and beating the waves, and the man hangs on, disappearing beneath the surface with the whale. In a moment they reappear, and another man dives into the water and runs a heavy rope beneath the whale's belly. Two poles are run between two boats, and the ropes tied to them. These boats serve as tugging boats, pulling the whale near the shore. The animal is not yet dead and still moves its fins as the boats approach the port. If it should die before reaching the shore, it would sink immediately, making it extremely difficult for the boats to bring it in to port. The manipulation of the swords, therefore, must be done with precision so that the whale will not die

56. The Captured Whale. *Circa 1793–94. Light color and ink on paper. Section 6 of* Picture Scroll of Whaling. *Courtesy Tokyo National Museum.*

before reaching land. I personally witnessed the entire operation. The fishermen who capture the whale perform like soldiers on a battlefield, and the sea turns scarlet from the blood of the leviathan. The sea off the island of Ōshima is the whaling ground belonging to the Hirado clan, stretching as far as the islands of Iki, Tsushima, and far-off Korea.[27]

Kōkan's remarkable facility with words and ability to select pertinent facts in his verbal description conjure such sharp imagery that the painting inevitably disappoints, for it fails to capture the same degree of drama and excitement. The body of the whale, however huge in proportion to the attackers, appears motionless; only agitated, foaming waves carry the dramatic content. Contributing to the absence of tension are the light washes of color, which convey a quality of delicacy quite out of keeping with the violence of the theme. The harpooner is almost lost, off-center, not emphasized in any way. Orderly fishermen wait in boats miraculously suspended above the water.[28]

Section 6 portrays the captured whale (Pl. 56), with an inscription at right:

> Misaki, the place where the whales are dismembered, is about two and a half miles from Masutomi's house. I was there at night when it was low tide and the moon was full, so I was able to see the entire whale. The man standing on the whale is Masutomi, and the one sitting on its back is myself.

The sketch (Pl. 57), through the placement of the whale close to the foreground, suc-

57. The Captured Whale. *1788. Woodblock print. Illustration from* Saiyū Ryodan.

ceeds better in representing the limpness of the dead mammal. The focal point of the composition is the two men on the back of the great whale; the liveliness of both conception and draftsmanship evokes an impression of immediateness less apparent in the more polished work. In general, Kōkan was most effective when he restricted himself to the principles of his native artistic idiom: form realized through line, ranged in parallel spatial zones on the picture plane. Like his *sekiga,* his diary sketches are free of the intellectual self-consciousness so often evident in his paintings.

No detail was too insignificant for Kōkan's attention; in the seventh section he illustrates crustacea parasitic to whales, which are described more precisely and illustrated more fully in the diary.

Section 8, the longest of the scroll, depicts a scene of great activity, with swarms of fishermen flensing the whale (Pl. 58). Men are cutting the blubber, which is being peeled by a giant winch turned by two dozen workers. One man is beating a small drum to set a rhythmic pace for the operation. Part of the tail has been severed and is about to be hauled away, while pairs of workmen carry pieces of blubber suspended from poles slung over their shoulders. Kōkan has taken great pains to illustrate the scene as it actually appeared, and his didactic approach minimizes the potential emotional impact of the activity. Units of space are organized according to the Japanese scroll-painting method of enclosing areas of action within diagonals; the row of buildings and stone pier at left fuse the scroll tradition with Western linear perspective. The major scene of activity is set

within a square block of space established by the pier at left and waves at right; extended lines of the winches continue a directional movement from this area to the enclosing buildings. Interestingly, the corresponding sketch reveals a rounded pier, evidence that Kōkan manipulated nature for a more controlled composition.

The final section, illustrating a humpback whale, bears the inscription and signature:

> *Picture Scroll of Whaling.* The pictures to the right concern the whaling activities I witnessed at Ikitsuki-shima, Hishū. Shiba Kōkan of Edo.

Though five types of whales are illustrated in the diary sketch,[29] Kōkan noted that he himself saw only two: the humpback and right whale. He did not explain where he found his information and illustrations for the others, but an anonymous illustrated book on whaling entitled *Isana Tori Ekotoba* (Picture Book of Whaling), owned by a descendant of Masutomi Matazaemon with whom Kōkan stayed while on the island, bears an attached inscription giving the publication date as 1786. If this date is correct, Kōkan, who visited Ikitsuki-shima in 1788, could have had access to it.[30]

The unusual theme of the whaling scroll and its use of both Oriental and Western techniques make it an outstanding example of Kōkan's art; the wealth of detail provides an informative historical document of whaling practices in eighteenth-century Japan. Kōkan fulfilled his purpose admirably in informing the public about a little-known industry in a concise, direct, and rational manner. Clearly, the painting was highly regarded during his lifetime, for the inscription on the box indicates it was owned and treasured by the *rangaku* scholar Takami Senseki, perhaps known best to art historians as the subject of many portraits by Watanabe Kazan.

58. Dismembering the Whale. *Circa 1793–94. Light color and ink on paper. Section 8 of* Picture Scroll of Whaling. *Courtesy Tokyo National Museum.*

After a month on the island, Kōkan departed Ikitsuki-shima on January 29, 1789. On the return journey to Edo he again stopped in Osaka, and also in Nara and Kyoto, but these visits were brief, for he was eager to return home. He reached Shinsenza, Shiba, on May 7, 1789.

The journey to Nagasaki can be considered the turning point in Shiba Kōkan's career. It confirmed his confidence in the superiority of European technical and artistic accomplishments, and in the value of Western learning to his own nation. European science, he discovered, was an exact discipline concerned with the investigation of natural laws; through scientific inquiry men had determined the earth to be round, not flat as Asian philosophers contended. Westerners had learned to plot the geography of the entire world, to build ships and navigate them across seas, steering their course by the stars, and so to engage in trade with all countries, enriching themselves and the nations of Europe. European art, Kōkan felt, contributed much to the extraordinarily high level of achievement in the West. Rather than stressing the "spirit" of brush strokes and subjective interpretation important to the mainstream of Oriental art, Western artists emphasized precise descriptions of visual reality readily understood by all. This was the proper aim of art, he concluded; the Oriental approach to painting, by comparison, seemed totally useless.[31] Having seen for himself the foreigners and their trading vessels in Nagasaki, Kōkan had found his purpose: he devoted his main energies from that time on to the study of European science and to the creation of art in the Western manner. Like many of his contemporaries who studied European culture, Kōkan envisioned an ideal world of humane and industrious citizens and scholars working together for the betterment of mankind; enthusiasm precluded doubts or criticisms of his Utopia.

CHAPTER SEVEN

PAINTER IN THE WESTERN MANNER

It would be absurd to suggest that Japanese oil paintings of the eighteenth century compare favorably with the European examples the artists were attempting to emulate. Obvious weaknesses cannot be wholly attributed, however, to inept or inexperienced painters. Materials available to would-be practitioners of the European manner equally conditioned the inferior quality of Japanese oils, for the homemade paint was not of a consistency to permit the precise delineation or lustrous finish characteristic of Western prototypes. Each artist was obliged to mix his paint from materials at hand, generally Japanese vegetable or mineral pigments, chalk (ground from clam shells), glue, alum, pine resin, egg yolks, and soybean oil. The ingredients were boiled, stirred, strained, and blended in different proportions according to the color and texture desired. A few pigments, such as Prussian blue, were imported from Holland, but for most colors, artists had to be content with indigenous materials. Western canvas was almost unheard of and paintings were executed mainly on silk, hemp cloth, wood, or paper.

Tokugawa-period paintings in European style are generally referred to today as *doro-e* (mud pictures), so called because of the opaqueness of the pigments and their dullness of color.[1] Usually small in size, *doro-e* were produced mainly for tourists who visited Edo, Kyoto, or Nagasaki. A typical subject might illustrate a beach in the foreground and a broad expanse of blue sky and sea, with gleaming white buildings for contrast on a distant shore. Other favorite themes were the whitewashed houses of wealthy noblemen set against blue sky, white sails on a sea, views of Edo, well-known national landmarks, and foreign landscapes. Because they were sold cheaply and in quantity, they were made of the least expensive materials available—low-grade paper and chalk paint with a water base.

Strictly speaking of course, a *doro-e* made of chalk and pigments with size as the binding medium cannot be designated an "oil painting." Since the term is not fully adequate, a distinction is sometimes made between water-based paint bound with egg white or glue and paint having oil mixed with the pigment; the latter is then raised above the category of ordinary *doro-e* and often referred to as *rōyuga* (wax-oil painting). It is impossible, however, to differentiate clearly between the two in all instances. Shiba Kōkan's paintings might be called *doro-e* because he used chalk as a base, resulting in the somewhat murky appearance of his colors; his medium did not permit the underpainting, glazing, and scumbling techniques that gave translucency to European paintings, nor did it contain the chemical mixture necessary to high gloss. His are, nonetheless, oil paintings, if only because he mixed oil with the chalk. Further, they belong to a higher category than common *doro-e,* being more carefully executed, larger in size, and often painted on silk.

Before his journey to Nagasaki, Kōkan had already become aware of Western painting techniques—as he had learned of copperplate engraving—through his acquaintance with Hiraga Gennai. During his visit to Nagasaki in 1770, Gennai had been greatly impressed by the foreign art-forms he observed, and particularly by the naturalistic chiaroscuro effects achieved in European painting. Although not an artist himself,[2] he seems to have taken a dilettante's interest in European art insofar as it comprised part of Western studies. He described the new technique to Kōkan, as well as to Akita artists,[3] especially Odano Naotake:

> It is said that while Gennai was on his way to the Ani copper mine, he happened to see at his lodging in Kakudate a folding screen painted by Naotake. When Naotake called on Gennai at his invitation, Gennai asked him to draw a round mirror-shaped rice cake as seen from directly above. Naotake mused for a while, then drew it. Gennai, glancing at the picture, offered the criticism that the rice cake could in no way be differentiated from a tray or a circle; after this he taught Naotake the Western technique of shading. Naotake, just twenty-four at that time, had considerable confidence in his ability and must have been extremely embarrassed to find he was unable to represent a spherical form. Gennai pointed out the great defect in Oriental painting that represented a ring, disk, and spherical form all in exactly the same manner with no differentiation. This lesson in how to depict relief by means of shading awakened Naotake to the exactness of Western art.[4]

This incident took place in the summer of 1773. In December, when Gennai returned to Edo, Naotake joined him, taking up residence with Gennai for five years.[5] It was an active household, filled with the comings and goings of artists and scholars. Though he had been sent to Edo by the feudal lord of Akita, Satake Shozan, ostensibly to learn metallurgy, Naotake devoted most of his time to the study of painting. In 1774, he was chosen to illustrate Ōtsuki Gentaku's book on Dutch studies, *Rangaku Koto Hajime.* Shozan was apparently little disturbed by his retainer's predilection, for he too was a painter and developed a great enthusiasm for Western art practices.

Interestingly, Naotake's early art education was similar to Kōkan's. Trained in Kanō tradition at age eleven, he worked in the ukiyo-e style of Suzuki Harunobu when he was eighteen, studied the Shên Nan-p'in bird-and-flower method in his early twenties, and began his career as painter in the Western manner at twenty-four, after his meeting with Gennai. His death at the age of thirty-one cut short a promising career. The Akita style of painting developed by Naotake and Shozan was a mixture of several influences, never as faithful to European art as the works of Shiba Kōkan. Basically, Akita painting was a naturalistic bird-and-flower style incorporating Western techniques of shading and perspective. Interest was focused on foreground objects drawn in large scale, with a background landscape set low in the picture plane. Sō Shiseki was more instrumental in the formation of Akita style than was Hiraga Gennai, and more significant yet was the influence of the Shên Nan-p'in school of Nagasaki.

When Naotake began his study of Western painting in 1773, Kōkan was still engaged in the creation of ukiyo-e prints. Undoubtedly the two men had occasion to meet in Edo, and it would seem likely that Naotake explained to Kōkan some of the principles of Western painting—a supposition supported by extant Akita documents.[6] Gennai, after all, did not have the practical painting experience that Naotake possessed, and the latter would therefore have been of greater assistance to Kōkan. Kōkan's rudimentary attempts to incorporate chiaroscuro into some of his ukiyo-e paintings and to experiment with linear perspective in his prints might reflect Naotake's instruction. As noted, two of his copperplate engravings of 1784 are reminiscent of works by Naotake executed at least four years earlier. The painting *Willow and Waterfowl in Winter* (Pl. 74) also reflects the Akita manner of composition. Kōkan's failure to credit Naotake with instructing him appears typical of his egocentric nature; Naotake, who died in 1780, could hardly protest.

For his inspiration and the themes of most of his early oil paintings, however, Kōkan turned directly to a study of the illustrations available to him in European books. One text in particular, from which he learned the fundamentals of Western painting, he claims was presented to him in Nagasaki by the director of the Dutch factory of Deshima, Isaac Titsingh:

> When I visited Nagasaki some years ago, a Hollander named Isaac Titsingh gave me a book on art entitled *Konst Schilderboek*. Perusing this work carried me into an intoxicating world. After a careful study of it, I finally attained a perfect command of its principles, and can now draw whatever I wish with complete ease—landscapes, birds, flowers, men, or beasts.[7]

The content of this statement is reiterated in a later essay:

> I went to Nagasaki and looked for a Western-style painter to instruct me, but could find no one. I managed, however, to obtain a Dutch book on the technique of Western painting. It was presented to me by a Hollander named Titsingh. I have devoted much time to studying this book, and have finally attained a perfect command of its principles. Now I am able to paint whatever I wish.[8]

The work was the *Groot Schilderboek* (Great Painter's Book), compiled by Gerard de Lairesse and first published in 1707 at Amsterdam.[9] De Lairesse described and illustrated in detail methods of sketching, composition, coloring, shading, perspective, landscape painting, portraiture, architectural drawing, ceiling painting, still life, flower painting, and book illustration. Though unable to read the text, Kōkan was able to study techniques by closely examining the seventy plates providing clear visual explanation.

Kōkan's assertion that he obtained *Groot Schilderboek* in Nagasaki is highly questionable and may have been intended to add importance to that journey. If he received the text from Isaac Titsingh, it must have been before he went to Nagasaki, when Titsingh visited Edo in 1780 or 1782. When Kōkan traveled to Nagasaki in 1788, Titsingh was not in Japan.[10] Kōkan's interviews at the Dutch factory at Deshima were with Captain Hendrik Casper Romberg and the surgeon J. A. Stutzer. Nowhere in his travel account did he mention receiving a European book of any kind, and surely such an important event would not have gone unnoted.

Unlike the average Hollander in Japan, Isaac Titsingh was a scholar interested in Japanese culture.[11] The *rangakusha* in Edo were, of course, eager to obtain whatever information he could provide, and Titsingh readily made friends with them. In 1780, Kōkan was on good terms with the group; there can be little doubt he met Titsingh at that time. Foreigners were forbidden by law to purchase any material describing the customs, manners, or scenery of the country. Titsingh could therefore obtain pictures and other scholarly evidence only in the form of gifts from Japanese friends. Kōkan, a much better artist than any of the *rangakusha,* was best equipped to provide the captain with local scenes, much as he later drew pictures of Edo for Dr. Stutzer in Nagasaki. It would seem logical, therefore, that Titsingh would cultivate Kōkan's friendship. He might have presented Kōkan with the European art book in gratitude for illustrations.

It is further possible, of course, that Isaac Titsingh had no more to do with Kōkan's obtaining *Groot Schilderboek* than did the Nagasaki journey. An Akita sketchbook dated 1778 contains a picture illustrating a method of drawing the human figure that quite clearly was copied from the de Lairesse book. Information in the sketchbook on art materials and color preparations is taken from a previous text by Hiraga Gennai.[12] If the 1778 date is correct, *Groot Schilderboek* was known in Edo before Titsingh arrived. Kōkan may have obtained it from Gennai, an avid collector of foreign texts, and claimed Titsingh as donor merely to assert his friendship with the Dutch captain.

Morishima Chūryō, in *Kōmō Zatsuwa* (Miscellany of Dutch Studies), also referred to *Groot Schilderboek.* His insistence on the need to study nude models must have raised not a few eyebrows in a country where no tradition of drawing the nude figure existed outside the realm of pornography:

> Hollanders are extremely proficient in painting. Anyone wishing to study this art must first master the anatomy of men and women, have a clear understanding of human bones and joints, and learn to draw nude figures. After that he can draw figures fully clothed. The method is explained in the *Schilderboek,* illustrations from which are given here. They are offered for study to anyone interested.[13]

Western texts were a rare and highly prized commodity in Tokugawa Japan, and those who possessed them nearly always passed them among comrades in a cooperative effort to gather as much information as possible on foreign scholarship. Kōkan and Chūryō are known to have been acquainted; Kōkan's illustrations of Adam's Peak in Ceylon and pictures of insects seen through a microscope are included in *Kōmō Zatsuwa.* If, as seems likely, Kōkan lent the book to Chūryō, he certainly had *Groot Schilderboek* before 1787, when *Kōmō Zatsuwa* was published.

In his travel diary, Kōkan repeatedly mentions painting in oils—further indication that he had knowledge of the technique before going to Nagasaki. Had his painting in the European style not progressed beyond a rudimentary stage, he would hardly have volunteered so freely to display his ability in that domain, nor would he in his diary have criticized so severely the Nagasaki artist Araki Gen'yū, well respected as a painter in the European manner.

As an aid in evaluating Shiba Kōkan's paintings, literary sources provide invaluable clues to the artist's intent. Two published essays specifically devoted to art remain, one entitled *Seiyōga Dan* (Discussion of Western Painting) and the other *Seiyōga Hō* (Principles of Western Painting). *Seiyōga Dan* was a slim volume published separately in 1799; *Seiyōga Hō* appeared in 1805 as part of a longer work entitled *Oranda Tsūhaku* (Dutch Navigation), a miscellany of information on foreign manners, customs, art, and science. Unfortunately, both essays are couched in extremely ambiguous language. Kōkan alludes only vaguely to his own art, giving no dates to assist in establishing a chronology of his paintings. Moreover, *Seiyōga Hō* is little more than a reiteration of

Seiyōga Dan, adding nothing to the theories presented in the earlier text. Both works are redundant, and employ numerous examples to define the qualities Kōkan believed basic to true art. In outline, these can be restated as follows:[14]

1) Art must be a true representation of reality
   a) Only Western art techniques can capture reality
   b) Japanese painting is mere child's play
   c) The living quality must be apparent in the thing represented, not merely in the brushwork
2) Reality in a painting is achieved through shading and color
   a) Shading expresses depth, shallowness, and three-dimensional shapes
   b) Color helps create an accurate image of the object portrayed
3) The primary function of art is utilitarian
   a) A painting must represent an object or scene in a manner that informs the observer of its exact appearance
   b) Paintings are an aid to understanding facts and fulfill the same function as words

Kōkan's contention that paintings should be practical, and therefore accurate, tends to reduce the motives of the artist to the most simplistic level. Though he asserted in his essay that Western art must not be considered artisan's work, he judged the merit of painting according to functional values more legitimately applied to the craftsman. It is doubtful whether his views, born of deep respect for Western culture and the naturalistic aesthetic of the works he knew, ever went deeper. In opposition to Oscar Wilde's "All art is quite useless," one surmises that Kōkan would have posited: "All art must be useful."

Kōkan's view was typical of the concept of European art held by most Western-style artists of his era. Admiration of European style was focused on its capacity to represent the external appearance of objects, that is, on photographic accuracy. Japanese had, in fact, little other basis on which to admire it. Although notations in various sources indicate a smattering of Dutch paintings were imported throughout the seventeenth and eighteenth centuries,[15] their number was exceedingly few, mainly because the government held them in little esteem. More numerous than oil paintings were book illustrations and engravings, which were, for the most part, artisan efforts. It was on the basis of these works that the would-be practitioners of the Western manner formed their theories.

When occasionally a painting of significant stature was imported, it caused tremendous excitement, as, for example, the floral still life brought to Japan in 1726, painted a year earlier by Willem Frederik van Royen.[16] Praise of the work inevitably was directed to its outstanding feature—meticulous realism:

> No painting in all the world can excel Dutch works in live delineation, and it is said there is no finer painting even in Holland than the picture of birds and flowers at Rakan-ji temple in Honjo, Edo. The paint is softened with oil, painted not on paper but on silk cloth, and therefore referred to in foreign lands as an "oil-silk painting."[17]

The artist Ishikawa Tairō and his brother Taketaka made a copy of the painting in 1796; subsequently it was copied by Tani Bunchō.[18] Kōkan, an associate of Bunchō, must also have been familiar with the Dutch work, though in his writings he makes no mention of it.

A painting by Kōkan depicting flowers in a bowl (Pl. 59), however, may well have been inspired by the van Royen oil. Unlike the copies by Tairō and Bunchō, Kōkan's painting is an original creation incorporating notions peculiar to the Far East. Though based on the Dutch still-life tradition of massing together a variety of flowers to exploit the richness of textures and colors, Kō-

59. Still Life of Flowers and Grasses. *Circa 1797. Ink on paper. Courtesy Yamato Bunkakan, Nara.*

kan restricted his choice of flowers to those indigenous to Japan and, surprisingly, he painted his still life entirely in monochrome ink. The use of monochrome sets off the textures and shapes of grasses and blossoms to striking effect.

Though this painting recalls Kōkan's earlier studies in the Shên Nan-p'in tradition, such as his *Still Life with Rat* (Pl. 19), it avoids the flatness of that style. It is more reminiscent of an earlier Northern tradition in the West of carefully executed nature studies, as exemplified by some of the water colors of Albrecht Dürer. The signature on the vase is unusual not only in the horizontal arrangement of Chinese characters above the roman letters, but in the manner of writing the character for *kan*. This same character seems to have been used in Kōkan's signature on only one other painting: a now lost depiction of the landscape of Kanazawa in snow.[19] In technical perfection, both these paintings may be ranked among Kōkan's finest works, executed during his mature years, perhaps around 1797.

Whether or not Kōkan's art was directly influenced by Odano Naotake and Satake Shozan, his views expressed in *Seiyōga Dan* are strikingly similar to those in the text attributed to the lord of Akita, reflecting in turn the thoughts of Hiraga Gennai:

> A picture is of value when it accurately represents the thing portrayed. Pictures of celestial and terrestrial objects, humans, flowers, or birds are valuable when all details are faithfully depicted. If a picture of a tiger looks more like a stone than an animal, people will laugh at it. An illustration of a monarch cultivating fields is intended to encourage agriculture; that of a great general in the heat of battle glorifies military strategy. If such pictures are not realistically illustrated, how can they possibly serve their intended purposes? There is a theory that claims the spirit of a painting is more important than realistic representation; this concept, however, loses sight of the real aim of painting. In the final analysis, how

> can one possibly distinguish such things as plants, trees, birds, animals, fish, shells, insects, gold, precious stones, and soil unless their true forms are accurately portrayed?[20]

Affirmation of these ideas is found throughout Kōkan's essay. For example:

> Fundamentally, a brush is a tool for drawing pictures. If one attempts to draw an ox without expressing the actual appearance of the ox, if one is concerned mainly with the impression given by the brush technique, then a mere spot of ink could just as well be called a picture of an ox.[21]

Similar views, in fact, were held by most leading scholars of Dutch learning. In his book *Seiiki Monogatari* (Tales of the West), Honda Toshiaki expresses beliefs probably inspired by Kōkan's *Seiyōga Dan:*

> "Why is it that European painting differs from Japanese and Chinese painting?" someone asked. I replied: "European paintings are executed in great detail, and it is attempted to make them resemble exactly the objects portrayed, so that they may be of some use. There are rules of painting to achieve this effect. They observe the division of sunlight into light and shade, and also what are called the rules of perspective. For example, if one wishes to depict a person's nose from the front, there is no way in Japanese painting to represent the central line of the nose. In the European style of painting, shading is used on the sides of the nose, and one may thereby realize the height of the nose. Again, if one wishes to draw a sphere, there is no way to make the centre appear to stand out in Japanese painting, but the Europeans shade the edges to permit one to see the height of the centre. In Japan this is called *uki-e*. Since it is the custom in Europe to consider above all whether something is of use to the nation, there is an academy which examines all books before they are printed so that no books of a frivolous or indecent nature will be published."[22]

However unsophisticated these notions may appear, they were in advance of the ideas held by many contemporary artists of the European manner. Their progressive nature becomes evident when contrasted with the naive and simplistic explanation of the function of Western art offered by a Nagasaki author writing as late as 1826:

> Nagasaki artists have become proficient in Western-style art, many rivaling European artists. Westerners in Japan often commission pictures to take back to Holland.
>
> Western women have very long noses and white complexions. Though extremely beautiful, they neither talk nor smile. They move people by inner emotions, which they are careful never to reveal outwardly. For this reason, artists can draw only their countenances but are unable to reach their inner feelings.
>
> Hollanders often have pictures painted of their Japanese concubines to take back home as remembrances.
>
> The captains in Nagasaki always carry pictures of their wives with them.
>
> When Dutchmen return to Holland, they send pictures of themselves to their concubines in Japan to inform them of their safe arrival.
>
> The Dutch-language interpreter Yoshio Kōsaku has hung two glass pictures of Hollanders on the wall of his house in order to remember the men.[23]

A few of Kōkan's contemporaries in Nagasaki achieved equal proficiency in Western art techniques, but their paintings were rarely more than carefully executed copies of foreign designs.[24] Moreover, Nagasaki residents, more provincial than Japanese in the larger cities, seem not to have been motivated by the idealistic desire to assimilate new knowledge into their culture. Unlike Shiba Kōkan, leading Nagasaki men painting in the European manner never thought of themselves as freethinkers attempting to break with tradition by defying public opinion and government censorship for the sake of their beliefs. Kōkan, on the other hand, considered himself the chief prophet of Western art in Japan, and his works a crucial tool in the struggle to modernize his country. This proselytizing image drove him to a stronger stand than he might normally have taken had he been painting merely for his own profit and pleasure.

In his two essays, Kōkan's descriptions of Western techniques are surprisingly brief. His sole explanation consists of three basic rules of shading for depicting an object in direct sunlight, light shade, and deep shadow. At the end of *Seiyōga Dan* he promises that a later book would examine the techniques of Western art in greater detail, and announces his intention of publishing a thorough explanation of the method of copperplate engraving; neither promise ever materialized. His essay further proclaims in the advertisement section the future publication of a book entitled *Shumparō Gafu* (Illustrations by Shumparō) in three parts; from the description it is clear that Kōkan intended to present in the first two parts a discussion of Western painting and engraving techniques respectively.[25] Although advertised in 1799, fourteen years later *Shumparō Gafu* still had not been published. Kōkan again mentions the anticipated appearance of the book in two letters he wrote to Yamane Kazuma in 1813;[26] according to these sources the manuscript was completed, but for some reason it remained unpublished. So highly technical a study could not have been expected to pay for itself, and possibly Kōkan was unable at the last moment to finance the publication due to lack of funds.[27]

To what extent was Kōkan able to incorporate into his work the European techniques so strongly advocated in his writings? Examining his paintings, one cannot but recognize a gap between what he preached and practiced. Not only Kōkan, but every Japanese artist of the period displayed influences of Oriental brushwork, coloring, and composition in his "Western paintings." There simply was not sufficient knowledge of European techniques to enable an artist to discard his native tradition. Painting in the European manner amounted to experimentation with Western style, technique, and subject matter. Japanese traditions were always just beneath the surface and often obtruded into the effect artists sought to achieve. In Japan, Western painting ultimately remained derivative, with all the qualities of misapprehension that attend any derivative style.

The earliest examples of Kōkan's painting in the Western manner, executed around 1780, are studies of Daruma, the legendary founder of Zen Buddhism, a favorite theme of Japanese artists since the introduction of Zen to Japan in the early thirteenth century. Both Chinese and Japanese models were available to him, and the theme was still considered relevant, as evidenced by such compelling portrayals as those by Ekaku Hakuin. Traditionally, the subject was made the more difficult by the necessity of catching beneath the grizzled human visage the penetrating spark of Zen enlightenment. Though as a boy Kōkan had shown talent in portraying Daruma, in light of his anti-Buddhist sentiments the theme might appear curious at this juncture of his life, especially as an introduction to the European style. His choice, however, was inspired not by traditional renderings in monochrome ink but by portraits of Daruma executed between 1596 and 1614 by the Namban artist Nobukata and similar works by Nobukata's contemporaries, all of whom employed chiaroscuro to effect solid form in the manner of Western portraiture. Kōkan, working nearly two hundred years later, was still indebted to this tradition.

The Daruma portrait illustrated (Pl. 60) typifies Kōkan's many versions of this subject.[28] Chiaroscuro is employed in painting the highly exaggerated bone structure of the head, the large, deep-socketed eyes, broad nose sharply accentuated with outline, and the great gold ring dangling from an elongated earlobe. Though the basic concept is the same as Nobukata's, the latter's Daruma (Pl. 61) appears the more expressive and naturalistic. Nobukata achieves greater direct-

60. Daruma. *Circa 1780. Wax oil on paper. Courtesy of the Kobe City Museum of Namban Art.*

ness by enlarging the area of the head and bringing it closer to the viewer who, while not confronted with a direct gaze, is held by the alert expression that seems to communicate an intense acumen. Although Kōkan has darkened the same planes of the face, he has not succeeded in producing an equally naturalistic effect; compare, for example, the curved lines of the brow, bridge of the nose, and ear with Nobukata's faithful rendition of shadow. Kōkan's shading is more a hardened and conventional device and consequently is less illustrative of solid form.

Paintings by Christians of priests and other Western figures provided models for other portraits by Nobukata and his followers. Apparently, Kōkan himself had in his possession one of the early Christian-influenced works, modeled after a Portuguese portrayal of Saint Paul. When he traveled to Nagasaki in 1788, he took the painting with him, and in his diary recorded the enthusiasm it aroused among all who saw it:

When I explained that the oil paint used in coloring Dutch paintings gives them

61. Nobukata. Daruma. *Oil on paper. Collection of Kuga Ichio, Osaka.*

a glossy, lifelike quality, I was urged to show an example. . . . The oil painting I possessed was a half-length portrait of a foreigner named Paul, whose frizzly whiskers were extremely realistic. Upon seeing the picture, my listeners were astonished.[29]

In the morning I departed, crossed the Miyagawa river, and arrived at Yamada [Ise], a bustling town with rows of tile-roofed houses. People from all over the country visit this place, and it is therefore very prosperous. First I paid my respects at the Outer Shrine, then stopped at the Jakushō-ji temple in Nakano Jizō, where I called on the priest Gessen, who was known for his paintings.

Gessen appeared, looked at me, and inquired: "Who are you?"

"I am Shiba Kōkan from Edo. Haven't you heard of me?"

"Indeed I have not," he replied.

Thereupon I took out the various paintings I had and showed them to him. Among them was the portrait painted in the Dutch manner of a man with frizzled whiskers who looked so lifelike. Seeing this, the priest immediately changed his attitude, and said:

"After you have visited the Ise Inner Shrine, won't you please come back and stay at my house this evening?"

So I went to the shrine and then returned to his lodging, where the priest, now a model of hospitality, entertained me lavishly with food and drink. I was supposed to have spent the night there, but when he asked me to execute a Western painting, I replied that European pictures were painted with oils and could not be produced in an instant like the ordinary, clumsy pictures he drew. After that remark, I fled to the brothel across the street.[30]

Kōkan's own painting of a priest (Pl. 62), like his portrayals of Daruma, closely reflects the style of Nobukata.[31] Again, most evident in this painting is the artist's preoccupation and experimentation with European chiaroscuro effects. This was the aspect of Western art he most consistently stressed, and it forms a unifying link in all his oils. In order to avoid possible censure for a work displaying Christian overtones, Kōkan depicted a shrimp in the hand of the priest, thereby identifying him as the Zen master Kensu, who achieved enlightenment while catching and eating shrimp and other shellfish.[32] Written on the painting are roman letters that seem to spell "Sint Paap" (i.e., holy priest).[33]

62. Priest Kensu. *Early 1780s. Oil on paper. Courtesy of the Kobe City Museum of Namban Art.*

Japanese paintings executed in the Western style were sufficient models for Kōkan's paintings of Daruma and the priest. For his more ambitious compositions, depicting large, full-length portraits of Europeans against foreign backgrounds, Western models were essential, and for them he turned to illustrations in the European books available to him. One book in particular provided prototypes for several of his works (Pl. 63, 68, 69, 71) and motifs for a great many more. Written in 1699 by Father Abraham van St. Clara and reprinted several times in Europe, *Iets Voor Allen* (Something for Everyone) was a collection of moral

63. Hollander on a Pier. *Mid-1780s. Wax oil on silk. Courtesy of the Kobe City Museum of Namban Art.*

64. Abraham van St. Clara. Sailor on a Pier. *1759. Copperplate etching. Illustration from Abraham,* Iets Voor Allen.

precepts applied to various occupations of Europeans.[34] Each brief section describing a profession was preceded by an etching. These illustrations were ideally suited to provide Kōkan opportunity to display not only his virtuosity with artistic techniques and technology, but also his familiarity with Western themes.

His first painting based on a European illustration depicts a Hollander on a pier (Pl. 63). Though working from a Western model (Pl. 64), he did not directly copy. From the small black and white etching he borrowed the major forms, but added his own motifs to complete the vertical composition, simplified background elements, and added color. Unfortunately, his attempt to create a large painting from a small illustration resulted in inconsistencies in both human proportions and spatial relationships. Individual figures are anatomically absurd. The main figure, his head too small for his body and his Dutch hat, is curiously drawn: hunchbacked, round-shouldered, with protruding stomach, and a face distinctively Oriental. The influence of Harunobu persists in Kōkan's rendering of the hands, incongruously delicate and feminine. Further, the figures lack all sense of scale relative to each other: were the man bent over the basket to straighten up, for example, he would be only half the height of the other adult beside him. Due to illogical proportional relationships, the treatment of space is also ambiguous. Recession is established by the men on the foreground pier, the warehouse, oarsmen in a boat in the middle ground, and figures in a second boat near the horizon; the two silhouettes in the most distant rowboat, however, appear as giants in relation to the Dutch trading vessel anchored in the harbor.

When one compares Kōkan's painting with the illustration, many of the reasons for his misrepresentation become clear. Figures in both painting and etching, though they manage to suggest volume, reveal an equivalent rigidity. The central figure of the illustration, standing on flat pointed feet extended in opposite directions, gestures at nothing, while the man beside him consists solely of a small hat and squared bulk of clothing suggesting a posture somewhere between a standing and kneeling position. This engraving and all the others Kōkan used as models were created solely for the purpose of illustration. They were easily reduced to formulas of simple volumes, and could not serve to enlighten Kōkan in his comprehension of human anatomy and foreshortening.

The bent tree at left in Kokan's painting is a motif he used repeatedly. Its roots are somewhere beyond the picture plane, the trunk projects into the composition, twists back, is cut off again higher up, and the upper branches reappear at the top. Use of this S-shaped tree as a compositional element has, of course, a long tradition in Oriental painting. It is also found in various forms illustrated in both *Iets Voor Allen* and *Groot Schilderboek,* justifying its appearance in an ostensibly Western context.

In the companion painting (Pl. 65), a European woman—presumably Dutch, although like the Hollander, her face is unmistakably Oriental—is portrayed with one arm extended, seated on a chair. Behind her stands a barefoot child echoing her gesture, the two reminiscent of the classical theme of a muse accompanied by a genie. The woman's position is an echo of many figures found in European illustrations. In *Groot Schilderboek,* for example, a woman of similar type is represented before a mirror, and in Egbert Buys's *Encyclopedia* a woman is portrayed seated beneath a tree with two naked children at her feet; either composition could have inspired Kōkan's rendering. Unlike the prototypes, however, the outstretched arm and widely spread fingers of Kōkan's woman, by reaching for or grasping nothing, fail to function purposively, a disorientation of gesture suggesting a pastiche. Kōkan appears to have gathered here into one scene a set of quotations borrowed from several sources. The hand, in fact, seems a disembodied segment copied from another figure in the de Lairesse illustration.

Unmodulated hues of the woman's robes are keyed up through the application of white highlights, particularly in the upper portions of the quasi-Roman tunic. This type of shading, perhaps motivated by the desire to impart dimension to the clothing, results in a series of nearly parallel folds that neither generate interest in themselves nor accentuate the body beneath. The landscape reveals a growing sensitivity to European conventions of painting nature as a setting for the human form. The broad diagonal path and curving tree echo the movement of the figures, reinforcing them, while the background falls away in intersecting diagonal planes to the archaically severe blocks of what appear to be a Romanesque church and campanile.

In the upper corners of both paintings the artist's signature appears in black Chinese characters, Kōkan Shiba Shun, and beneath, in place of a red seal commonly used on Far Eastern paintings, are roman letters written with red paint. The portrayal of the Dutch woman bears the signature Siba Sun, and on the companion scroll, an in-

65. Dutch Woman Beneath a Tree. *Mid-1780s. Wax oil on silk. Courtesy of the Kobe City Museum of Namban Art.*

scription in quasi-Dutch frequently used by Kōkan on later works: "Eerste Zonders in Japan. Ko" (First sinners in Japan. Kōkan).[35] It has no apparent relation to this or any of his later pictures; Kōkan seems simply to have wanted to impress others with his knowledge of Dutch letters.

If it were known when Kōkan first saw the Dutch illustration that served as prototype for his Hollander, the earliest possible date for the execution of the painting could be ascertained. According to Naruse, who discovered a 1759 edition of *Iets Voor Allen* in the Hirado Museum, Kōkan probably saw the book for the first time during his visit to Hirado, and his painting can therefore be dated after 1788.[36] As previously noted, in the diary account of his interview with Lord Matsu-ura, Kōkan specifically mentioned examining "a number of foreign books."[37] If *Iets Voor Allen* was among them, he saw the illustration at that time.

The fact that the text is now in Hirado, however, is not conclusive evidence that it was there in 1788. A second Dutch source in Hirado provided a prototype for an illustration of the Colossus of Rhodes;[38] though Kōkan did not depict the Colossus until 1803 (Pl. 95), Kitayama Kangan drew a nearly identical illustration for Morishima Chūryō's *Bankoku Shinwa* (New Tales from All Over the World), published at Edo in 1789.[39] It would therefore seem equally possible that the Dutch sources were known earlier in Edo, and it is as likely that Kōkan had opportunity to see them there as in Hirado. Further, figures in Kōkan's paintings are postured similarly to the figures in his etching of a European hospital (Pl. 38), executed around 1784. The Dutch woman is a reverse image of the lady beneath the tree in the engraving; the Hollander on a pier resembles the two figures standing by the river bank; the sailor in the bow of the boat is similar to the gentleman beneath the tree.

The prototype for Kōkan's painting of the coopers (Pl. 69 and 70), in fact, does not appear in the 1759 edition of Abraham's book but only in the 1736 edition. Con-

66. Zeuxis. *1789. Oil on paper. Location unknown.*

67. Johan Ludwig Gotfridi. Zeuxis. *1660. Copperplate etching. Illustration from Gotfridi,* Historische Chronyck.

versely, the prototype of the Hollander on a pier is not included in either the edition of 1717 or 1736, but only in the Dutch edition of 1759 and a German edition of 1711. Therefore, at least two texts were known in Japan, one most probably in Edo. One might go further and speculate that Kōkan himself at some point obtained his own copy of *Iets Voor Allen,* for the illustrations provided motifs for a great many of his paintings executed throughout his life, and actual prototypes for at least four works, one published in a book in 1814, near the end of his life.

In any event, whether the paintings of the Hollander on a pier and the Dutch woman were executed before or after his Nagasaki journey is an academic question. Certainly they may be placed chronologically after his Daruma paintings of the early 1780s and before his painting of Zeuxis, a more accomplished work executed in 1789.

The painting of Zeuxis (Pl. 66) also was based on an illustration in a Dutch book (Pl. 67), though greater departures were made from the original than in his painting of the Hollander. The basic arrangement of figures, furnishings, and layout of the interior—its prominent window opening to the vista beyond—is maintained; by drastically reducing the components of composition, however, Kōkan eliminated what in a Dutch picture contributed most to its character and effectiveness: meticulous attention to the accouterments of the setting. Considering his medium, limited knowledge of Dutch art, and lack of models other than book illustrations, he was incapable of doing otherwise. Working in a viscous medium, Kōkan could not have hoped to imitate the precise delineation of detail achieved in engraved and etched prototypes; and lacking access to Dutch paintings that might have taught him methods of describing and illuminating objects in oil paint, he was forced to simplify his works. For detail he substituted shadow, content to experiment with the effect of light from an open window playing on objects within the room and across the floor.

The subject illustrates the legend of Zeuxis, a Greek artist of the late fifth century B.C. who is said to have depicted grapes so realistically that birds flew through a window and pecked at them. Despite the Grecian theme, Zeuxis resembles Kōkan, and the other two men are pseudo-Dutchmen admiring a pseudo-Chinese grapevine, painted on canvas, in a pseudo-Dutch room.

Kōkan's choice of an interior setting for this and other early oil paintings (such as Pl. 5 and 68) was appropriate, for the broad planes of architecture enabled him to utilize his knowledge of mathematical perspective and to display to maximum effect the "three-face method" of shading he advocated in his writings:

> By employing shading, Western artists can represent convex and concave surfaces, sun and shade, distance, depth, and shallowness. Their pictures are models of reality and thus can serve the same function as the written word, often more effectively. . . . The three-face method of shading in Western art must be studied carefully and understood thoroughly: 1) Keep pure white that part of the painting which is to depict objects in direct sunlight. 2) Paint in pale tones those objects on which the sun shines obliquely. 3) Paint in deep tones those objects that are shaded from the sun and are therefore dark.[40]

Every element of Kōkan's *Zeuxis* reveals a careful structuring of composition. The rectangle formed by the three figures is balanced by the window, the floor area by the ceiling, the bare wall by the chest on which the picture of grapes rests. Straight, gridlike lines of ceiling, floor, and chest, when extended, converge at Zeuxis's hand, a focal point in the movement begun by the raised hands of the figure at the right and continued through Zeuxis's arm, directing attention to the grapes at the left. A diagonal dividing the floor into light and dark areas is repeated in the window-framed landscape; both reflect the compositional arrangement of the fabled masterpiece. Three small birds flying in through the window form a unifying link between the artist's studio and the outside world. Tonal values are effectively used to guide the viewer's attention to motifs pivotal to the story: the figure of Zeuxis, window area, and painting of grapes. Lack of texture contributes to the quiet, ordered atmosphere, animated only by the gestures of the figures.

That Kōkan was able to create this tour de force at all, and to master the exceedingly difficult composition, perspective, and shading, must certainly have been a source of great satisfaction and pride: for the first time he inscribed the Western date on one of his oils: 1789. Further, as if to suggest that his work might compare favorably with that of Europe, he signed his name in roman letters on his rendition of Zeuxis's painting.

The same engraving used as a model for *Zeuxis* provided inspiration for Kōkan's version of *Scholars in Conference* (Pl. 5). In fact, such aspects as the more complex and integrated figure grouping and the seaport vista seen through the window are closer to the Dutch prototype than are those found in *Zeuxis*. Nevertheless, the characteristics noted in the previous painting are equally evident here, with the important exception of more complicated patterns of light and color. An additional light source introduced from the lower right creates shadows across floor and wall. There is a discrepancy in the patterns of shadows at the joining of the two panels, suggesting they have been cut down in size. The figures are lighted in such a way as to create intense color contrasts within the group; here Kōkan has not relied solely on the juxtaposition of ungraded areas of dark and light tonality, but has attempted to model with light, making use of

68. The Pewterer's Shop. *Color on silk. Courtesy of the Kobe City Museum of Namban Art.*

halftones and highlights, particularly in the figure with the compass. The gestures of the figures and the red and orange of their clothing provide an area of animation within an otherwise totally static composition, and also display a degree of technical maturation on the part of the artist. Once arrived at, Kōkan exploited this solution again and again; each of his oil paintings is distinguished by figures arrayed in contrasted coats of red, blue, and yellow, providing a focus within the grey-brown setting of interior or landscape.

Iets Voor Allen also provided Kōkan with a model for his depiction of *The Pewterer's Shop* (Pl. 68), stocked with an array of European plates and vessels. The painting is not executed in viscous *doro-e* but in Japanese tempera, a more fluid medium permitting a freer handling of lines and forms. Muted color tones are limited to soft browns and blue-greys except for the figures, predictably in bright coats of red, blue, and yellow. By expanding his composition from the detailed Dutch depiction to include a wider view of the room, Kōkan was obliged to fill the empty areas with motifs of his own invention; consequently, one segment of the picture is filled with European details taken from the original, the rest composed of broad areas of blank walls in deep shadow with a large urn at left set beside a vessel of the Chinese *tsun* type, which in this context might also be interpreted as a Dutch spittoon.

Whereas the perspective of the section copied from the Dutch illustration appears accurately rendered, in the extended areas inaccurate perspective opens the room to an illogical degree, the right wall rising above the ceiling and the left relating uncertainly to the rest of the composition. Chiaroscuro effects are stated so strongly that they appear almost as tangible as the architectural setting. Light streams through the open doorway and two window areas of the rear wall (though it fails to penetrate the mullioned windows above), illuminating the myriad pots and plates and plunging into deep shadow the sides of counters and unlit wall areas. The urn and spittoon at left are reversely shaded so that the dim light striking them appears to come from a separate source beyond the left border of the paint-

ing. The European motif of a curtain across the upper right corner—not included in his model—glows with its own illumination. In the wall area at left is a garbled Dutch inscription; literally translated it reads: "The pewterer seeks a precious treasure of the most beautiful container."[41]

One of the most interesting of Kōkan's genre scenes depicts an open courtyard with coopers engaged in making barrels (Pl. 69). This subject, too, derived directly from an illustration in *Iets Voor Allen* (Pl. 70), provided opportunity to display his virtuosity and acquaintance with Western themes, artistic techniques, and technology. He first made a sketch of the European etching, carefully copying the details of the original, but shifting motifs farther back in the composition to effect greater depth.[42] In his painting, he reversed the background buildings, rearranged the figures, and added to the foreground the tree motif employed so frequently in his paintings. He defined the foreground by placing objects in large scale at the lower edge: a scattering of logs, boards, a barrel, and an ax. Other boards lying on the ground farther back become progressively smaller as they recede toward distant workmen. This method creates the illusion of depth, reinforced by the placement of figures forming a wedge into space, their arrangement, in turn, echoed by the larger triangle of curtained doorway, tree trunk and branches, and lines of architecture in diminishing perspective. The effectiveness of this scheme can be seen by comparing it with the Shên Nan-p'in–derived manner of representing space by setting massive objects in the immediate foreground against a low-background landscape. The latter

◁ *69.* The Coopers. *Oil on silk. Courtesy of Mori Hiroyuki, Yokohama.*

70. Abraham van St. Clara. The Cooper. *1736. Copperplate etching. Illustration from Abraham,* Iets Voor Allen.

method merely creates a dichotomy—two paintings rather than one. Kōkan's system of integrating foreground and background through linear perspective, if achieved only through faithfully copying original source material, results in a more coherent solution.

The figures themselves, in their bright clothing, though as anatomically uncertain as those in Kōkan's other oils, here, in their own curious way, manage to express plausible action. Proportional relationships are more carefully integrated, and the placement of volumes in apposition creates tensions and a sense of momentarily suspended motion; the viewer, from his own experience, is asked to read these illustrative gestures as movement.

In general, Kōkan's figures can be reduced to a few standard types, reappearing from one painting to the next. Each is a series of geometric cubes, arms piled on a blocky torso, supported by thick, truncated legs and profiled feet. Strong highlights playing over the clothing create distinct patterns of dark stripes wedged between folds, too unvaried to connote either the texture or draping of cloth, and too commanding in their volume to indicate human anatomy beneath. These static and anatomically impossible figures, unlike the ideal figures of Western painting—if only too like the prototypes provided him—convey no action through the expansion and contraction of musculature. They bear even less relation to the traditional Japanese method of creating a sense of lifelike movement through active, tensile line.

Iets Voor Allen, which provided models for at least three oil paintings—the Hollander,

71 (above). The Basketmaker. *Woodblock print. Illustration from* Keijō Gaen. *Courtesy Waseda University, Tokyo.*

72. Abraham van St. Clara. The Basketmaker. *Copperplate etching. Illustration from Abraham,* Iets Voor Allen.

the pewterer, and the coopers—also contained the prototype (Pl. 72) for several sketches of a basketmaker (Pl. 71).[43] The skill Kōkan was able to display in his native medium of brush, ink, and wash results in a freedom of expression and a vitality that his oil paintings never achieved. The assured handling of brushwork that distinguished his *sekiga* has here been allied to a familiarity with Western-style painting. He contributed the picture in 1814 to *Keijō Gaen* (Kyoto Garden of Pictures), a collection of works by famous artists.[44] The inscription in Dutch means "basketmaker."

It is only to be expected that Kōkan would have used his early training in the Shên Nan-p'in manner to create bird-and-flower compositions in oil. His extant paintings of this type reveal also the influence of the Akita school in the inclusion of low-lying background landscapes. Among these are *Turtledoves on a Peach Branch,* in the collection of Kikukawa Kyōzō, Tokyo; a seascape depicting a shell in mammoth scale on a foreground beach, owned by the Tenri Library; a still life of fruit, flowers, bird, and butterfly set before an open landscape of fields and farmhouse, in the private collection of Uchida Rokurō; and a study of a white-fronted goose (Pl. 73).

Kōkan's handling of the traditional seasonal symbol of approaching winter—the goose in an autumnal landscape—reveals a deftness often absent from his more ambitious projects in the oil medium. The lone goose before withered autumn reeds stands on a sloping bank, creating a traditional Far Eastern one-corner composition; fingers of land projecting into a marshy landscape effect the illusion of recession toward a horizon low in the picture plane. The bird is enlarged to a degree that permits the artist to work in the same simplified planes that characterize his figure compositions. The subject of a bird in profile, however, requires only the minimal description of plumage and alertness of stance to result in an expressive portrayal of a living creature. Its aliveness is enhanced by contrast with the airless, textureless surroundings. Kōkan's characteristic palette of steel-grey, blue, and brown is appropriate to the autumn theme.

Another painting of this type, more unusual in compositional arrangement, is *Willow and Waterfowl in Winter* (Pl. 74). A flat screen is established by two birds in giant scale amid foreground landscape elements of willow and knoll, set before the backdrop of a European cityscape. The eastern grey heron poised on the broken trunk of the willow is visually balanced by the Japanese crested ibis occupying the knoll at left; between them a common Indian kingfisher on a peach branch is isolated against the somber sky, providing a secondary accent to the ornithological studies of the foreground. The kingfisher, peach, and willow all formed a part of Kōkan's earlier repertory of bird-and-flower painting derived from Chinese prototypes (Pl. 17 and 18).

In Kōkan's experiments with the oil medium not based on Western models, he wisely chose elements familiar to him, and these segments—particularly the delicate branches of the willow—are sensitively and confidently handled. His composition is more carefully integrated and exacting in detail than are most works of the Akita school; note, for example, the distant birds in the sky and along the shore, the man poling the small boat, and the Dutch ship at anchor near the cluster of foreign buildings. The focus upon rare birds native to Japan is perhaps an indication of Kōkan's far-ranging interests in natural science, as well as art. The painting, then, reveals Kōkan's eclecticism: a theme Chinese in origin placed in a setting derived from Western sources, handled in the Western oil medium, and reflecting interests beyond those of mere decoration.

In the upper left corner the painting is signed in roman letters "Kookan Siba Sun"; there is no signature in Chinese characters. In some of his early oils Kōkan seems to have used only roman letters, which he apparently felt were better suited to his paintings in the Western manner. Other artists, such as Ishikawa Tairō, Kitayama Kangan, and Kawahara Keiga, also signed their works only in roman letters.[45]

Kōkan's chief pride as a painter in the Western style was his landscapes, which, taken as a whole, reveal the same preoccupations as his interior scenes. In many ways, landscape was a more challenging theme, for lacking architectural planes as media for establishing depth, these scenes had to present the illusion of three-dimensional space by an integration of landscape motifs to suggest the extensiveness of nature. Further, landscape painting did not allow him the use of simple flat areas reflecting light and shadow, and demanded that he coordinate natural elements in an encompassing atmospheric space. Kōkan's concern, however, was with a careful study of individual forms, and largely as a result of immature technical proficiency, his compositions lack the tonal gradations necessary to the creation of a unifying atmosphere of light and air.

Kōkan's landscapes are assemblages of isolated segments extracted from nature, seemingly pasted together like cutouts. If his aim was the emulation of Western-style works, he failed; the methods he employed produced instead a patchwork world within a vacuum. Yet his paintings exhibit their own appeal. Stylized they certainly are, but they are admirable in the serenity, rational order, and coherent surface design that are the hallmarks of Kōkan's style at its best. Just as the cooper, machine-like, will wield his mallet for all time in his silent courtyard, the abstract blocks of stone, mirage-like water, and open, quiet vistas that are his landscapes remain strongly impressed in memory, evoking a world belonging neither to East nor to West, but to Kōkan's imagination—a vision of his own peculiar neverland.

A large oil painting showing the shore at Shinagawa (Pl. 6) provides a representative

73. Goose in Autumn Landscape. *Oil on silk. Courtesy Museum of Fine Arts, Boston.*

74. Willow and Waterfowl in Winter. *Oil on silk. Courtesy of Kimiko and John Powers, New York.*

75. Detail of Shichirigahama Beach, Kamakura, *Plate 7. Courtesy of the Kobe City Museum of Namban Art.*

example to introduce Kōkan's landscape style. Enframing and at the same time extending the composition are a small thatched building cut off at left and the ubiquitous serpentine trees rising from a knoll at right. A connecting link between these foreground elements is established by carefully placed figures along the shore, some gathered in an open way station, others scurrying to escape the summer shower, their postures and attitudes reminiscent of figures found in many print designs by Hokusai. Diagonal washes in tones of black and grey over a luminous sky represent the heavy downpour. Despite the human activity, blown trees, and drenching rain, a strangely quiet mood prevails. Kōkan has obtruded upon nature by a laborious intellectual balancing of motifs, a too careful brush, and a blandness of texture and tonality inappropriate to the specific content of his theme.

Kōkan's largest work in the landscape genre, executed in 1796, depicts the Seven League Beach at Kamakura (Pl. 7). The long sweep of beach is seen at right, waves breaking upward on a shore sharply inclined, causing the shoreline to appear as a convex curve adhering to the picture plane, with no foreground established to lead the viewer into the scene. Two oddly proportioned fishermen at lower right, not provided with a logical shelf in depth, seem in danger of sliding out of the scene altogether. Space is handled more coherently, however, in the recession from shore to island to distant mountains. The tension between the rising plane of beach and silhouetted cliffs dominating a small village contributes to the dynamic quality already present in the active shoreline (detail, Pl. 75). Mount Fuji, carefully shaded, contrasts with the nearly flat treatment of Enoshima.

The painting of Shichirigahama was presented to the Atagoyama Shrine in Edo, where it hung for fifteen years, until 1811. Artists of the Tokugawa era commonly dedicated their pictures to shrines for exhibition, a gesture assuring both divine favor

76. Katsu-ura Beach, Shimōsa. *Oil on silk. Courtesy Atami Museum of Art.*

and mundane publicity. Kōkan's offering was also in keeping with his professed intention of revealing to people in Edo the landscapes of other parts of Japan. The possibility of comparing this painting with the actual scene probably contributed to its popularity; the viewer could at least recognize the place depicted, whereas he would have had within his own experience nothing by which to identify or criticize a representation such as *The Pewterer's Shop*. Undoubtedly Kōkan's contribution of the painting was also in defiance of orthodox Kanō painters, who commonly displayed their works in shrines, for he considered Kanō art mere decoration, unlike his own style, which achieved true reality. The painting was removed in 1811 apparently because the priests felt that a work in foreign style might bring calamity upon the shrine. At that time the painting was restored—perhaps by Kōkan himself—and remounted on a larger wooden backing. Above the picture the Edo author and poet Ōta Nampo (Kyōkaen)[46] wrote the following inscription:

> This painting previously was hung in the Atagoyama Shrine south of Edo Castle, but was removed because it is in Western style; it is now owned by Seizandō.[47] Using Western techniques, Kōkan has painted this picture of Enoshima. Within the limits of a single picture he has admirably managed to confine and to catch the feeling of the long, misty, panoramic expanse of beach at Shichirigahama.
>
> —Kyōkaen, 1811

A second commentary, written by the Edo author Nakai Kundō Takayoshi, was composed in the same quasi-poetic spirit:

> The artist, having first plotted his composition carefully, studied the scene diligently, and then executed his painting of silver sand and beach. Mount Fuji rises in the sky beyond the richly detailed landscape of the foreground. Looking at

77. Futamigaura. *1798. Oil on silk. Private collection, Japan.*

the painting, I feel as though I were viewing the actual scene. —Kundō Takayoshi

Although the votive offering of Shichirigahama is not as markedly European as his interior views, Kōkan considered it one of his great artistic triumphs. Among the many other representations that he executed of this scene, three were major works included in his list of eight paintings offered to shrines throughout the country.[48]

The theme of fishermen on a beach was used by Kōkan in other compositions as well, such as *Katsu-ura Beach, Shimōsa* (Pl. 76), with the volcanic island of Ōshima, Izu, at far right silhouetted against the sky.[49] The two figures and tree motifs establish a shallow foreground plane, but transitions between landscape elements are too abrupt to portray a convincing recession into depth; waves, rather than breaking on the shore, form a hard-edged line above it. The characteristic harsh shading, lack of texture, and patchwork assemblage of elements are apparent in both foreground and distant mountains—and even in the diagonal streaks of clouds intended to suggest atmosphere.

On his way to Nagasaki in 1788, Kōkan stopped to visit the site of the famous Wedded Rocks at Futamigaura; ten years later he executed an oil painting of the scene (Pl. 77) based on the sketch in his diary (Pl. 78).[50] This painting provides a particularly expressive example of the stark simplicity and quiescent mood typical of Kōkan's oils. The sea is perfectly calm, waves forming flat, scallop-edged patterns on the shore. Rocks are barely blocked out structurally; their contorted forms are like splintered chunks of glass casting shadows as though on sand and emphasized by dark tones contrasted against brilliant sky. Rocks and boats are scattered at regular intervals across the horizon—an optical balance contributing to the measured, calm impression and fundamental to the decorative effect. At the same time, there is dramatic content

78. Futamigaura. *1788. Woodblock print. Illustration from* Saiyū Ryodan.

in the slash of mountain cutting into the composition at right and the two towering rocks jutting from the sea like silhouetted claws. The sketch from Kōkan's diary depicts the scene from the cliffs above—the position from which one normally views the Wedded Rocks; the painting adopts a low vantage point that stresses the grandeur of the rocks, greatly accentuating their impact.

At the top right, in addition to the inscription, signature, and date in Chinese characters (Kansei 10, i.e., 1798) his name appears in roman script with the mistaken Western date of 1789. The same Dutch phrase appearing on many of his paintings repeats: "Eerst Zonders in Japan."

Only two votive offerings by Kōkan survive. The first, of 1796, has been discussed above (Pl. 7); the second, a large painting executed in 1800, depicts *The Shore of Kisarazu* (Pl. 8). Kōkan's design is one of fine optical balance distinguished by a masterful harmony between the aloof, dominating cone of Mount Fuji and the closely viewed foreground pier. Proportional relationships within the picture, however, are poorly established. Ambiguity of scale can be seen by comparing the sparrow on the tall pole to the man who stands at its base, and the man relative to the boat behind him. Attention is devoted to details, such as the morning-glory vine entwined about the base of the post on which the bird perches, several people gathered inside the boat (Pl. 79), and on the distant shore at far left, a small *torii* gate before which appear two wraith-like figures with outstretched arms, a basket placed between them (Pl. 80).

A comparison between the handling of the sparrow in *Kisarazu* (Pl. 81) and a small study of a sparrow probably executed earlier (Pl. 82) illustrates the difference between his method learned from Sō Shiseki and his more European approach. In his essay on Western art he writes:

In drawing hair and beards, the Japanese

79. Detail of The Shore of Kisarazu, *Plate 8. Courtesy of the Itsukushima Shrine, Miyajima.*

artist draws every single strand of hair individually. The Western technique of drawing hair, however, is to suggest the hair in a few brush strokes, so that the resulting appearance is one of real hair, not a mere mass of lines.[51]

The painting of the single sparrow suggests his youthful training in the Shên Nan-p'in mode of meticulous nature studies. Despite Kōkan's disparagement of this style, the sensitivity and correctness of rendering have produced a spirited creature, revealing not only Kōkan's facility in handling a natural form less complex than the human body, but his ability to skillfully depict nature when provided with adequate models and instruction. Released from such demanding requirements as foreshortening and modeling in the round, he was able to work within the limitations of a simple profile view, creating a naturalistic image through painstaking, specific illustration of the textures and tonal contrasts of plumage. By contrast, in the later conception washes are used to define the basic shape of the sparrow while eliminating the specifics of plumage or anatomy characteristic of a nature study. It is, rather, an abstraction from nature, the forms so well understood that the artist was able to quickly grasp and reproduce the definitive features necessary to convincing naturalistic imagery. The assurance reflected in this abrupt, simplified style represents a spontaneity previously noted in Kōkan's sketches, where he consistently captured the spirit of a scene more directly than in his finished works. The sketchy

80. Detail of The Shore of Kisarazu, *Plate 8. Courtesy of the Itsukushima Shrine, Miyajima.*

handling of the sparrow, due in part to the thick consistency of paint, contributes to the verisimilitude felt in the diagonal thrust of the bird's body and grasping claws; medium and technique successfully combined produce the impression of imminent flight.

In painting Mount Fuji from Kisarazu, Kōkan's intent was to represent an exact likeness of the mountain, in emulation of the Western method of correctly portraying the outer appearance of forms in nature. In his journal, he clearly asserted that the unique beauty of Fuji could be captured only by techniques of realistic representation:

> Because I have followed Dutch methods and used oils to color my pictures, they bear a close resemblance to reality in the depiction of the valleys and the places where snow still lingers unmelted, while the clouds emerging as from the mouth of the mountain or the sun shining on the snow look rather like silver.
>
> There are different schools of artists in Japan—Tosa, Kanō, and, of late, the Chinese. None of them knows how to draw Fuji. Kanō Tan'yū painted many pictures of Fuji, but they do not in the least resemble Fuji because he relied exclusively on "the spirit of the brush" and "the force of the brush." As for the Chinese-style painters, they are incapable of drawing the famous mountains and celebrated scenes of Japan. They paint nameless mountains and call them landscapes. For that matter, they do not show this particular scene or that particular famous mountain in China. These paint-

81. Detail of The Shore of Kisarazu, *Plate 8. Courtesy of the Itsukushima Shrine, Miyajima.*

ers draw mountains and water in whatever way strikes them as interesting, giving free play to their brush. This is exactly the same thing as drawing a dream. Wouldn't it be proper to say that neither the viewer nor the man who painted the picture has the least idea of what it depicts?[52]

Kōkan donated his painting of the mountain he so admired to the Itsukushima Shrine, where it is still located. The inscription to the left states it was "presented in October, 1800, by Yamagata Futanosuke Shōshin of Hirado Han." This probably indicates that a certain Yamagata was permitted to donate the work to the Itsukushima Shrine, Kōkan receiving money from him for including his name on the picture.

The fragile medium of chalk pigments mixed with oil has badly disintegrated. Clumsily executed restoration, with patches of the silk haphazardly replaced on the wood backing, has further damaged what was surely one of Kōkan's finest works of Western inspiration.

The same year Kōkan painted the votive offering of Mount Fuji, he held an exhibition in his house in Shiba-mon, Shinsenza, sending out the following announcement:

> Master Kōkan is an artist of the Western style. It required many years to learn the techniques, but now that he has mastered them, a great many persons are demanding his paintings. Lately, many imitations of his work have appeared. How very stupid people are not to be able to tell the difference between Kōkan's originals and imitations!

One day Kōkan said to me: "When I was a young man I greatly enjoyed traveling, and have visited places all over Japan. Now that I am over fifty, I do not expect to live much longer. For the benefit of future generations, I should like to

82. Sparrow. *Color on paper. Courtesy of the Kobe City Museum of Namban Art.*

leave behind many pictures of the innumerable places and things I have seen during my life. Already I have produced over one hundred." I asked him to show me these pictures. They are seascapes with bright, blue sky or violent, pounding surf; mountains seen at different seasons and at different times of day—dawn, noon, twilight, and evening; and studies of flying insects. All who have seen them agree that they are perfect representations of reality.

Anyone interested in seeing these works is welcome to inspect them. They will be offered for sale. Kōkan will be free to receive visitors on August 27 and September 8. Kindly honor us with your presence at that time. His residence is in Shiba-mon, Shinsenza.

Summer, July, 1800
Written by Shiba Kōkan's assistant[53]

It is interesting to note that even in Kōkan's own lifetime forgeries of his work were so numerous he indignantly repudiated his imitators. It might be expected that his egotistical nature would have found imitations the sincerest form of flattery, but his ultimate concern was public recognition of his talent; failure to perceive his skill was unpardonable. After his death, forgeries of Kōkan's works were made in even greater quantity, a tribute to his fame and indicative of his importance as a forerunner of Western painting in Japan.

Six years later, in 1806, Kōkan announced his retirement from the painting profession, an occasion marked by an exhibition at the Mampachirō Restaurant in Yanagibashi, Edo. He divided the works exhibited into three categories: oil paintings, water colors, and copperplate engravings. In the first part of the announcement, Kōkan asserted his independence in mastering the Western style; his paintings were then listed by an assistant, Shiba Kōnan:

In my youth I showed promise of artistic

83. The Ōi River, Shizuoka. *Color on paper. Courtesy of the Tokyo University of Arts.*

talent and studied painting. During my middle years I became interested in Western oil painting, but European paintings are of such superb workmanship that I was unable to copy the technique successfully. I searched for someone to instruct me, but could find no one. Then I acquired a Dutch book on European art from a Hollander and finally mastered the technique perfectly. This year I have turned sixty, and my physical strength and ambition have declined; I plan, therefore, to retire and turn my practice over to my assistant, Kōnan. On May 25, I shall hold an exhibition of my works at the Mampachirō Restaurant at Yanagibashi, Edo. I hope that you will all note the date and honor me with your presence at that time. —Spring, 1806. Kōkan Shiba Shun.

Works exhibited:

1. One hundred Dutch and Japanese landscapes (mountains, rivers, seas, and so forth) painted in oils
2. One hundred Japanese and Dutch landscapes and figures painted in monochrome ink and watercolors[54]
3. Copperplate engravings of pictures and maps, all engraved by Kōkan himself

The above works will be offered for sale. Other artists will also be present to make impromptu paintings. —Kōnan[55]

"One hundred oil paintings" and "one hundred watercolors" are round numbers not to be taken literally, but clearly, he produced landscapes of both types in vast quantity. An example of a watercolor in the European manner is the painting of the Ōi River in Shizuoka prefecture (Pl. 83). It affords a panoramic view of a nearly dry riverbed. The foreground is distinguished

by small boats ferrying people over the water and tiny figures threaded across the sand, their minute scale contributing to the impression of vastness. The delicacy of pattern is particularly effective, for the line of human activity establishes a link between foreground and mountains, alleviating the otherwise unbroken recession into depth. The perspective of converging lines is reminiscent of works by Hiroshige, though the latter never succeeded in expressing so prodigious a space. Kōkan's success is due largely to a just integration of Far Eastern and Western methods of landscape painting. The land recedes according to a Chinese system of overlapping promontories extended into the water, and the loose brushwork and light coloring of trees and mountains in varying tones of green and ink washes are reminiscent of *bunjinga*. Far Eastern formulas are contained, however, within a rigid scheme of Western one-point perspective that increases their capacity to evoke depth and atmospheric effects.

A final painting in watercolor making use of European techniques to accurately portray a Japanese scene (Pl. 84) was executed during the later years of Kōkan's life.[56] Although the inscription gives his age as seventy-five, he was actually only sixty-five at the time. The work displays a cautious modeling of pale blue, grey, and pink tones, illustrating Kōkan's enduring commitment to Western shading and perspective, though without allowing the ideals of didactic and realistic art to overshadow his sympathetic response to Fuji.[57]

In Kōkan's sketch on the same theme, *Mount Fuji from Yoshiwara, Suruga* (Pl. 85), greater spontaneity of brushwork imparts a fresh, lively appearance not unlike *bunjinga* style. It is executed in monochrome ink, with color added only in spare washes. Outlines are sharp, nonessential detail

84. Mount Fuji Viewed from Kashiwabara, Suruga. *1812. Color on silk. Courtesy of the Kobe City Museum of Namban Art.*

85. Mount Fuji from Yoshiwara, Suruga. *Color on paper. Collection of Kaneko Sensui, Tokyo. Reproduced with permission from* Kokka, *No. 667.*

eliminated, forms tightly integrated, and spatial recession handled coherently. The close correlation between the two works suggests that the sketch may have served as basis for the finished painting of 1812, just as Kōkan's diary illustrations provided models for many of his later paintings and copperplate engravings.

Soon after Kōkan's exhibition at the Mampachirō Restaurant, he traveled to Kanazawa, where he visited Zeniya Gohei, a wealthy shipping merchant and haiku poet. A certain type of cherry tree known as *kikuzakura* (chrysanthemum cherry), found only in Kanazawa, was blooming at the time, and Kōkan executed an oil painting of the tree, depicting Gohei and himself beneath the blossoms.[58] Gohei had in his possession a European oil painting of a full moon and the Milky Way attributed to Rembrandt (Pl. 86). At the bottom, Kōkan added his authentication in red paint. On what basis he founded his identification is uncertain, unless he had access to reproductions of the master's works through Dutch sources at Nagasaki. More probably, he knew nothing of Rembrandt beyond his name and supported the attribution in order to validate his reputation as a connoisseur of Western painting. In any event, it is extremely unlikely he ever saw an original Rembrandt.[59]

86. Rembrandt, attributed. The Full Moon. *Oil on canvas. Collection of Michigami Toshii, Kyoto. Reproduced: Michigami, "Watashi no Remburanto."*

Kōkan did not give up painting altogether in 1806, even though he announced his official retirement; in fact, he continued to paint until the last years of his life. In 1809, he completed a votive offering no longer extant showing the Kintai Bridge at Iwakuni, mentioned in an announcement distributed at that time. The announcement also lists eight other major paintings presented to shrines throughout the country:

> As everyone knows, Shiba Kōkan is a painter of realistic landscapes in the European manner. In recent years, many persons in Edo, Kyoto, and Osaka have been selling paintings in his style and make their livings by dealing in these forgeries. They are not his disciples and know nothing of the true Western techniques, but simply produce poor imitations of his work.
>
> Kōkan, now an old man, recently contributed to the Kannon Hall of the Asakusa Shrine his final painting: a picture of the Kintai Bridge of Iwakuni. The Kintai Bridge is as beautiful as the bridge over the West Lake in China.[60] It is 250 yards long and has five spans, the middle three having no supporting posts beneath them. Kōkan spent eight days in Iwakuni studying it carefully. Undoubtedly many persons in Edo have never seen the bridge; for that reason he made a painting and hung it in the Kannon Hall for all to see. . . . Other paintings by Shiba Kōkan are:
>
> 1. Shichirigahama Beach, Kamakura
> Located: Atagoyama Shrine, Shiba, Edo

2. Mount Fuji from Suruga
Located: Kagura Hall, Gion Shrine, Kyoto
3. Shichirigahama Beach
Located: Yakushi Hall, Ikutama Shrine, Osaka
4. View of Ishinomaki
Located: Shiogama Shrine, Sendai
5. Maikogahama Beach, Hanshū
Located: Warei Shrine, Uwajima [Shikoku]
6. Shichirigahama Beach
Located: Tenjin Shrine, Kōchi [Shikoku]
7. Mount Fuji from Kisarazu in Kazusa
Located: Itsukushima Shrine, Hiroshima-ken
8. Beach at Kamakura
Located: Kurume Tenjin Shrine, Fukuoka

The above-mentioned paintings are all large works. Smaller paintings by Shiba Kōkan may be found all over Japan. —1809. Written by Shiba Kōkan's disciple[61]

The painting of Kintai Bridge undoubtedly was based on the diary sketch and preliminary drawing for his etching (Pl. 45 and 46). *Mount Fuji from Suruga* probably resembled his sketch, copperplate, and scroll painting (Pl. 41, 40, and 42). The view of Maikogahama Beach was removed from the shrine and given to the Datè family of Uwajima; if it survives, its location is unknown. Only two of the paintings listed—numbers one and seven (Pl. 7 and 8)— remain today as evidence of Kōkan's votive art. The disappearance of the others is due mainly to two factors. First, extremely perishable materials could not withstand the test of time and neglect. The chalk paint mixed with oil dried out and crumbled, and as the fragile paper and wood used as backings disintegrated, the paintings fell to pieces; even the two extant paintings—both considerably restored—have lost most of their brilliance. Perhaps if Kōkan had followed the practice of other painters of votive pictures and painted directly on wood, the paintings would have lasted better. Second, shrines and temples, to which such votive pictures were given, are built of wood and very susceptible to fire. Hence the majority of Kōkan's votive paintings have long since turned to dust or ashes.

Kōkan never founded his own school of painting, nor did he instruct any disciple in his Western methods. This seems hardly surprising in view of his attitude toward his fellow artists. Even major figures of his time, such as the Kyoto painter Maruyama Ōkyo, received no praise from Kōkan. Although Ōkyo did not work strictly in the Western manner, he exerted the first creative effort to assimilate the aesthetic of Western art into the Japanese tradition by incorporating Western elements of perspective and shading in his paintings. His stress on realism and insistence upon drawing from nature became the basic tenets of the Maruyama school he founded. Despite Ōkyo's wide acclaim and the popularity of his art, however, Kōkan had his own opinion of his significance:

> In Kyoto, there was an artist named Ōkyo. He was born in Sasayama, Tamba province. He went to Kyoto and created his own style, neither Chinese nor Japanese, but a new method of drawing. His style was admired and imitated by many artists, and became a popular fashion, but now people have grown tired of his pictures.[62]

Who indeed would have been capable of following in Kōkan's footsteps? The 1806 notice of his retirement states that he planned to turn over his practice to Kōnan. But Shiba Kōnan never seems to have taken up painting in the Western manner. His extant Chinese landscapes in the Kobe City Museum of Namban Art indicate that he was, moreover, an artist of undistinguished merit. Nothing else is known of his career, and it is difficult to believe that Kōkan would have bequeathed his life's work to so amateur a painter.

Kōnan may be the person Kōkan referred

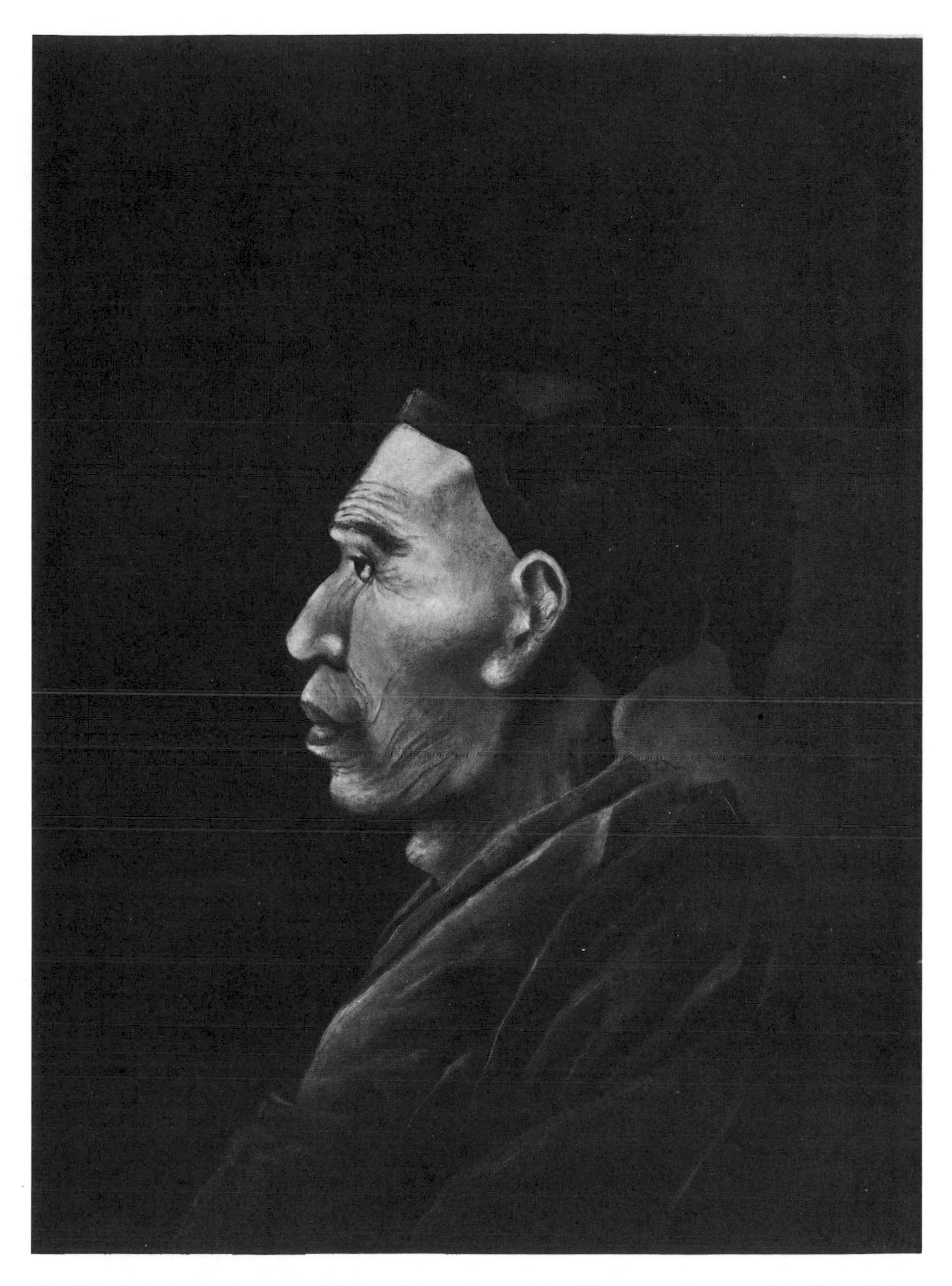

87. *Takahashi Yuichi.* Portrait of Shiba Kōkan. *Circa 1875. Oil on paper. Courtesy of the Tokyo University of Arts.*

to as Minwa in a letter written July 9, 1813, to Yamane Kazuma, or the name may refer to the Kyoto artist Aikawa Minwa, though the latter did not paint in the Western style either and there is no evidence that he studied under Shiba Kōkan. In any case, the letter reveals Kōkan's disenchantment with Minwa's ability, and his decision not to appoint him successor:

> I returned from Kyoto to Edo with Minwa, who became my assistant. Most persons called him Kyōjin meaning a man from Kyoto, and when we got to Edo he really became *kyōjin* [insane]. Kyoto people are timid, and when he came to Edo and saw many warriors walking about with weapons as though about to engage in battle, he was so frightened he went quite out of his mind. This means I still have no follower to take over my work.
>
> After that experience I named another man, a doctor, as my beneficiary, renounced the world, built a new house in Meguro, and changed my name to Mugon Dōjin. His name is Ueda Tazen, and he lives in Shiba-Shinsenza, where I formerly lived. Occasionally, I visit his residence.[63]

The physician Ueda Tazen seems an unlikely successor; nothing more is known of him beyond one other brief mention in a later letter:

> My heir, whose name is Tazen, is forty years old and very honest, but not particularly a man of refinement.[64]

The artist Matsui Keichū apparently claimed Kōkan as master, for he wrote on his painting of a Hollander the inscription: "Painted by a direct pupil of instructor Shiba Kōkan. —Keichū."[65] The significance of this statement is unclear, for no evidence beyond this inscription supports it. Matsui Kenzan, who wrote the above under his art name Keichū, was a Nagasaki artist of the Araki school, believed to have been the successor of Matsui Genchū (Kōzan), and so far as is known, he had no personal connection with Shiba Kōkan. He seems, therefore, to have been a self-appointed disciple.

But though Kōkan had no immediate successors, his indirect influence was pervasive. This is particularly apparent in the impact he had on later scholars of Western culture such as the nineteenth-century artist and theorist Takahashi Yuichi. As Haga Tōru has pointed out, Takahashi's views on art expounded in his *Statement for the Painting Division* are remarkably similar to those contained in Kōkan's *Seiyōga Dan* (Discussion of Western Painting).[66] A direct historical link undoubtedly existed between the two men. The relationship suggested by the close correlation of the texts is borne out by Takahashi's expressed deference to Shiba Kōkan as a pioneer in Japan of painting in the Western manner.

Strongest evidence of veneration is the oil portrait of Shiba Kōkan (Pl. 87) executed by Takahashi around 1875, presumably based on Kōkan's *Self-portrait* (frontispiece). In both drawing and painting one is struck by the expression of energy throughout, and by a countenance more Western than Japanese: sharp profile, prominent bone structure, aquiline nose, bright staring eyes, thick garrulous lips, an unusually large ear with hairs growing from it, sharply angled jaw, and protruding Adam's apple. Every facial feature is indicative of his personality: determined, proud, ambitious, and even a trifle amused by his own strong character. Kōkan is revealed as a man of firm conviction, fully capable of carrying out his self-aggrandizing, proselytizing role—a pioneer implanting the principles of Western art within his nation's culture. Considering the long-established Buddhist tradition of a disciple's honoring and acknowledging his master by painting his portrait, it may not be too fanciful to detect in this portrait by Takahashi an act of similar intent.

CHAPTER EIGHT

SCHOLAR OF WESTERN SCIENCE

RESTLESS AND INQUISITIVE by nature, Shiba Kōkan always was eager to investigate new fields of scholarship. Though he pursued a painting career throughout his life, his avocation was the acquisition of any and all Western learning, particularly in the disciplines of science. He himself never became a creative scientist, but he fulfilled an important function in transmitting scientific information to his countrymen, bringing an awareness of the world outside Japan and of the technological advancement of Europe.

For European maritime traders in the Far East, knowledge of geography was inextricably linked to study of the stars, indispensable to navigation. In his writings, Kōkan too made no real distinction between geography and astronomy. His early books on science were focused on geography, and only gradually, as he became more familiar with astronomy, did he direct attention to that discipline. From the beginning, however, he set down whatever scientific information was available to him; his explanations became clearer as he himself attained deeper understanding of Western science. Astronomy was the most difficult discipline to comprehend, but it must be remembered that violent disputes concerning the nature of the heavens had long raged in Europe, and information available to him derived from conflicting sources. A brief examination of the notions of astronomy that evolved in Europe may be helpful in considering the progress made by Japanese scholars.

Prior to the introduction of a heliocentric theory, Western man had conceived of the universe in terms set forth by the Greek philosophers Aristotle and Ptolemy. Aristotle postulated a spherical, motionless earth at the center of a revolving universe, composed of a series of crystalline spheres containing the sun, moon, planets, and stars. These revolved according to a system of complex linkages; the outermost derived its rotation from the Divine source. The innermost sphere, belonging to the moon, divided the universe into two distinct parts. Outside it, including the moon, the heavenly bodies were made of changeless and incorruptible matter; all celestial matter moved serenely and eternally, with uniform motion, in a cricle. Inside the sphere bounded by the moon, all matter was composed of four elements: earth, air, fire, and water, and all was subject to change and decay.

Ptolemy's system was vastly more complicated; its complexity accounted for every known irregularity in the heavens. He too placed a stationary earth in the center of the universe, but he explained the orbits of the sun, moon, and planets by a system of eighty epicycles, thus solving the inconsistencies evident between Aristotle's theory and actual observation. When Alfonso the Wise of Castile was introduced to the Ptolemaic system, he remarked: "If the Almighty had consulted me before the Creation, I should have recommended something simpler."[1]

For nearly fourteen hundred years after Ptolemy published his theory in the masterpiece of astronomy known as the *Almagest,* there were no significant changes or new ideas in the field. Thus it happened that the first Western astronomical concepts introduced to Japan were based on the geocentric theories of the Greek philosophers—theories strongly supported by the Roman Catholic Church. By this time in Europe, however, men accustomed to the belief that the earth was the central element in the universe were presented with a new concept that seemed to disrupt the Divine order of Creation: in the universe decribed by Copernicus, the earth's central position was replaced by the sun.

Copernicus's intention was not to establish an entirely new system, but rather to improve on Ptolemy's mathematical techniques. In the course of his work he revived the ancient, rejected theory of Aristarchus of Samos, who believed the rotating earth revolved around the sun in company with the planets. By assuming that the earth rotated on its axis and also revolved with the planets around the sun, Copernicus claimed he could reduce Ptolemy's eighty epicycles to thirty-four. Ultimately, however, his system became so involved and contained so many inaccuracies that the resulting calculations offered little improvement over Ptolemy's; he was obliged finally to introduce forty-eight epicycles, whereas the Ptolemaic system, brought up to date in the fifteenth century, required only forty. Because of its mathematical weaknesses, in addition to its fundamental attack upon the foundations of Western thought, his theory was at first received with little enthusiasm; before the beginning of the seventeenth century there were in Europe few convinced Copernicans. It required the scientific insight of men of genius like Galileo and Kepler to realize the superiority of the Copernican system over the Ptolemaic.

That Copernicus's theory was not immediately accepted even by leading scientists of his day is evidenced by the writings of his successor Tycho Brahe. Although Brahe's theory was mathematically the equivalent of Copernicus's, he rejected the notion that the earth was capable of movement and asserted that it remained stationary in the center of the universe. According to his theory, the sun circled the earth, while Mercury, Venus, Mars, Jupiter, and Saturn—the only planets known to European astronomers until the late eighteenth century—revolved around the sun.

The Copernican theory was not established until the publication in 1632 of Galileo's *Dialogue Concerning the Two Chief World Systems—Ptolemaic and Copernican.* Thanks to the invention of the telescope, Galileo also could provide men with the awareness that the universe contained many more heavenly bodies than were visible to the naked eye. New horizons in the field of science were opened, and astronomy became the topic of the day in Europe. Since these new concepts met with bitter opposition from the Church, however, it was not until after the expulsion of the Christain missionaries that Japanese scholars became aware of Copernican astronomy.

One of the first Europeans to introduce

concepts of Western science to Japan was the Englishman William Adams, a ship's captain who arrived in 1600 after a two-year voyage from Rotterdam around the southern tip of South America. Adams—known to the Japanese as Miura Anshin—enjoyed great prestige as a foreign adviser to the government. He taught geometry and mathematics to the first Tokugawa shogun, Ieyasu, and explained the phenomenon of comets to the second shogun, Hidetada. Later, when relations became strained, he attempted to return to England but died in Hirado in 1620.

The scientific instructions of Will Adams might have remained no more than mere diversions had the Japanese themselves not exhibited intellectual curiosity. Reactions to the new science, however, were not always positive; Western astronomical theories opposing orthodox beliefs occasionally elicited indignant responses. In 1606, for example, when Hayashi Razan, a brilliant Confucian scholar and adviser to Ieyasu, was presented with a globe by Fukansai Fabian, one of the Jesuits' most capable Japanese converts,[2] Razan was shocked by the notion of a round earth. In reply he wrote the essay *Hai Yaso* (Against Jesus) repudiating the global theory on the grounds that it did not accord with the Confucian teachings of Chu Hsi, which claimed that the dome of heaven rose above the terrestrial square. Though Fabian had discarded this time-honored belief, he was, ironically, equally inhibited by the dogmatic requirements of his faith. As a good Catholic, he was heir to the astronomy studied by missionaries, who insisted on a geocentric system and restricted their scientific inquiries to the bounds set by the Church. Japanese Christians adopted the solar calendar and theories associated with its creation to establish a chronology of Church events; thus, in 1591, the lunar calendar generally used in Japan was rejected by converts for pragmatic reasons rather than out of any real scientific conviction.

Nevertheless, Japanese Christians contributed most to the continued study of astronomy. A group in Nagasaki maintained lively interest in the field, publishing a number of books; the founder, Hayashi Kichiemon, had attracted a large following by the time of his martyrdom. One of his most talented pupils, Kobayashi Yoshinobu, published in 1667 a two-volume work on natural science entitled *Nigi Ryakusetsu* (Explanation of Heaven and Earth). The order of the universe he described followed Aristotle's theory of the sphere of fixed stars revolving around the central earth. The range of Yoshinobu's researches, however, was far-reaching; he further expounded the existence of universes outside our own, a concept derived from theories of the ninth-century Arabian astronomer Tobit Ben Korra, and perhaps also influenced by ancient Buddhist theories of infinite universes.

The study of Western science was not looked upon favorably by the Japanese government, and in 1630, as part of its plan to block the circulation of foreign ideas, a prohibition was decreed on the importation of books. Primarily, the intention was to exclude books advocating Christianity, but the Christian content of some prohibited works was extremely slight. Thirty-two categories were prohibited: twenty-one concerned Christianity and eleven related to pure science, astronomy, and mathematics. The latter were forbidden because the books were written by missionaries and therefore might indirectly be dangerous. The ban was directed not so much against works in European languages imported from Europe as against Western books translated into Chinese, or against books compiled in China by scholars deriving information from Jesuit missionaries. Few Japanese could read European languages, but books in Chinese advocating Christianity could reach a more extensive audience.

As a result of the prohibition of foreign books and the subsequent expulsion of all foreigners except Dutch and Chinese merchants, Japanese were cut off from Western scientific information for nearly a century. No encouragement was given Western studies until 1720, when the eighth shogun, Yoshimune, lifted the ban on all works but those dealing directly with Christianity. More recent European scientific discoveries could thereby be investigated, though even then myths and misconceptions often were linked with verifiable facts.

Of paramount interest to many scholars was the field of Western medicine, pioneered by Maeno Ryōtaku and Sugita Gempaku. They witnessed an autopsy in 1771, comparing the revelations with drawings in a European anatomy text. Gempaku recorded the discouragement he and his colleagues felt at their lack of medical information and practical experience:

> What a shame it is that we have all this time attended lords as doctors without knowing the real construction of our bodies, which is really the basis of the medical profession. Unless we practice medicine with knowledge of the truth about the body based upon actual experiments, we have no excuse whatever in living as doctors.[3]

Despite tremendous obstacles, the two men set about learning the Dutch language, and in 1774 they published *Kaitai Shinsho* (New Book on Anatomy), the first openly circulated translation of a Dutch text.[4]

Government officials, curious despite their scorn or affected indifference to Western scholarship, commissioned the more proficient interpreters at Nagasaki to translate European scientific texts. One of the ablest of these was Motoki Ryōei,[5] who translated eleven Western science books, greatly stimulating the study of astronomy. His third translation, appearing in 1773, contained the first statement of the Copernican theory in Japanese.[6] His ninth work, completed in 1793 in seven volumes, constituted his most extensive explanation of astronomy.[7] The words Ryōei coined for planet, parallax, satellite, et cetera, are still used today.

Many Japanese scholars of astronomy—including Miura Baien and Honda Toshiaki—derived information chiefly from the translations of Motoki Ryōei. Shiba Kōkan in particular was indebted to him; the scientific words he used in his own writings were borrowed largely from Ryōei's ninth translated work. Nevertheless, Kōkan wrote of himself: "I have always had a great interest in astronomy and geography. It was I who first introduced the heliocentric theory to Japan."[8] Strictly speaking, his statement is false, but in a broader sense, there was much truth in what he claimed.

As an interpreter-translator sponsored by the government, Ryōei was carrying out official duties. Unlike the Edo *rangakusha,* he had no urgent desire to enlighten his countrymen on European science; after his death his name and accomplishments were virtually forgotten until he was rediscovered during the present century.[9] Moreover, his translations were never widely published or freely circulated, but remained copybook manuscripts, read by those who commissioned them and by interested scholars. As such, they provided the basis for the research of nearly all other astronomers in Japan, but outside that elite circle, were completely unknown. Kōkan not only adopted the heliocentric theory, but disseminated his knowledge throughout the nation. Even in his own time he seems to have been generally recognized as having introduced Copernican astronomy. The scholar and astronomer Katayama Shōsai praised him as "the father of the heliocentric theory in Japan."[10] Kōkan was not a man modestly to repudiate such praise.

The period of Kōkan's activity as a popularizer of Western science was relatively short, spanning only twenty-four years—from his first publication on world geography in 1792, when he was already forty-five years old, to his last book on astronomy in 1816. Evidence prior to that time, however, indicates his interest in European scientific discoveries. As we have seen, he first learned of copperplate engraving and of oil painting from Hiraga Gennai; it was Gennai too who introduced him to scientific studies of nature. Gennai's interest in metallurgy led him in 1773 to investigate the possibilities of mining in the Chichibu mountain range. Kōkan, then a youth of twenty-six, accompanied him in a search for precious metals, a bizarre pursuit he later recorded in his journal:

> Gennai told me that mountains containing gold, silver, copper, or iron have special projections on their peaks such as crags or rocks, and the technique of finding metals lay in distinguishing these shapes. I joined him in the search, but it was a terrible mistake, and I soon regretted my part in it and gave it up.[11]

Continuing evidence of Kōkan's early interest in science is found in his illustrations, executed in 1787, for Morishima Chūryō's *Kōmō Zatsuwa;* included are pictures of a microscope, and insects, flowers, and seeds viewed through the lens, as well as Adam's Peak, the mountain sacred to Buddhism in Ceylon.[12] That same year, when he journeyed to Nagasaki, he mentioned several times in his diary unusual plants and medicinal herbs he discovered—another interest undoubtedly due to Gennai. Most significantly, he delivered during his journey many lectures on geography and European inventions.

Among the foreign curiosities Kōkan had to show his various hosts was a world map, several of which, printed in Europe, were in circulation in Japan at that time. His account of a typical demonstration illustrates his ability to impart information in terms understandable to even the most uneducated listeners, and further points out the mixture of fact and fancy involved in his "scientific" explanations:

> September 10. . . . I took out my map of the world and explained it. A woman of about thirty-six who was listening drew closer to me and said that she understood from my explanation where the historical Buddha Shaka lived in India, but wanted to know where Paradise was, for she hoped to go there while still alive. In that area of the country, many people belong to the Monto [Shin] sect of Buddhism, which teaches that everyone can go to Paradise after death, but she felt that priests would be embarrassed by a request to be taken to Paradise during life. I thereupon explained why no one can go to Paradise while alive. I said that this world is spherical, that there are many other globes like ours in space, that the space between globes is what we call the sky, and no living person can fly through this space unless he becomes a deity. The woman understood, and her faith in Buddha became all the more devout. Later, she sent me cakes and other food in a tiered box. She is the daughter of the family, and is now a widow living in the neighborhood. Her only wish is to go to Paradise.[13]

Beyond frequent mentions of displaying and explaining his world map, Kōkan gives no further information in his diary about it. Both Sugita Gempaku and Ōtsuki Gentaku possessed maps, and Kōkan might have borrowed Gentaku's, though it seems unlikely that Gentaku would have permitted him to take so valuable a treasure on a long journey across the country. Probably Kōkan had his own, either of foreign make or a copy he drew himself. In any case, it was no accident that three years after his return from Nagasaki, Kōkan executed a copperplate map of the world. Obviously, he had been planning this for some time, and his interest in world geography had been heightened by his travels:

> During my leisure hours when I was not painting, I made sketches of various articles and pictures imported from Holland. Some time ago I learned the Dutch method of copperplate engraving and have already exhibited many pictures that I produced by the new method. Then I conceived the idea of making a copperplate map of the world, using as a model a map made in the West, and recently I completed the task.
>
> There are very few persons in Japan today who know anything about other

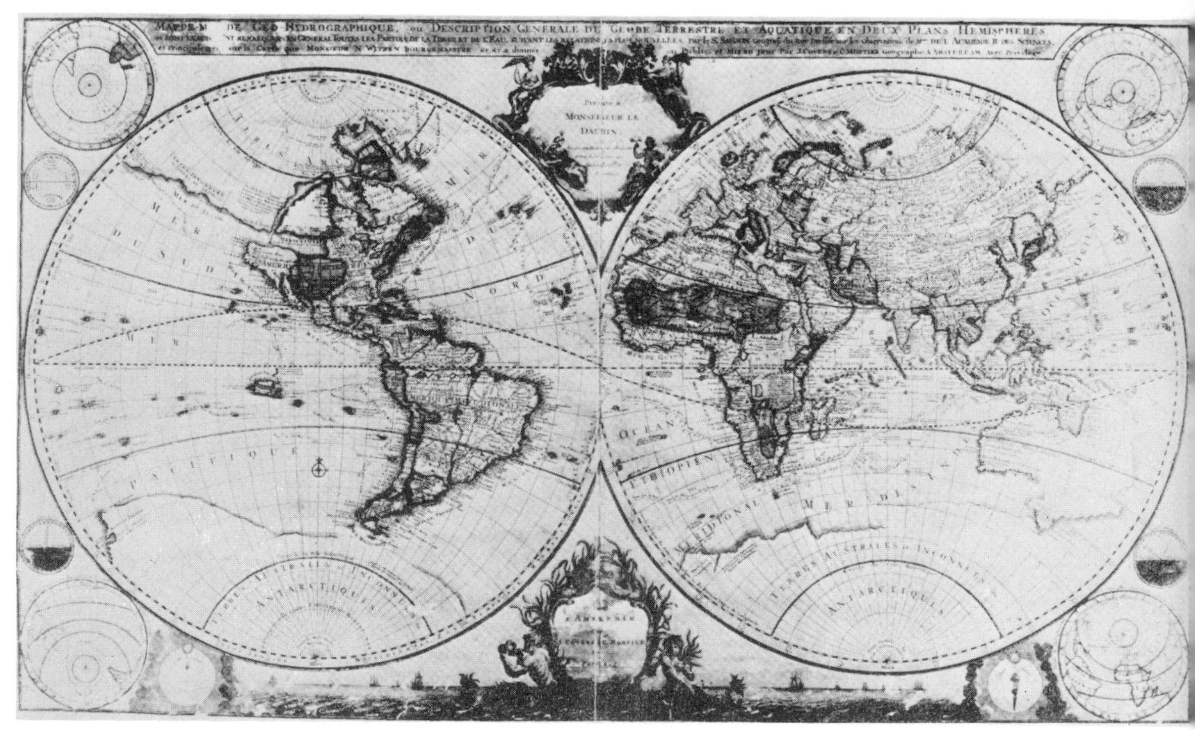

88. Covens and Mortier. Map of the World. *Copperplate etching. Reproduced: Ayuzawa,* Sakoku Jidai.

countries of the world, and I sincerely hope that by looking at my map people will learn something of the world's great size. The details may require revision by someone better informed than I, but my humble ambition is simply to inform the people of Japan about the world. For the same reason I have written an explanation that I hope will prove useful in affording a more comprehensive understanding of the map.[14]

The map Kōkan took to Nagasaki probably was inadequate to serve as a model of his etching. For this he borrowed Gentaku's, as mentioned in the preface Gentaku wrote for Kōkan's geography text.[15] The European model (Pl. 88) was designed by Covens and Mortier, printed in Amsterdam, and written in French, a language virtually unknown in Japan.[16] In order to avoid incorrect readings of place names, Kōkan used the Japanese *kana* syllabary rather than the traditional method employing Chinese characters:[17]

Place names on European maps are given in languages unfamiliar to Japanese, and therefore no one in Japan can read them. I have used as a model a map from the West and have made my map according to the Western method, but have translated the place names into Japanese *kana*. I have made no changes in the irregular contours of the land, and though it was impossible to give in complete detail the names of all the mountains, rivers, and capital cities, I have indicated the positions of the major countries.[18]

Ōtsuki Gentaku's foreign map provided the model for both Kōkan's world maps, entitled respectively *Yochi Zenzu* (Complete Map of the Earth) and *Chikyū Zenzu* (Complete Map of the World). Both bear the date Kansei 4, 2nd month (March, 1792), but the latter must be incorrectly dated, for

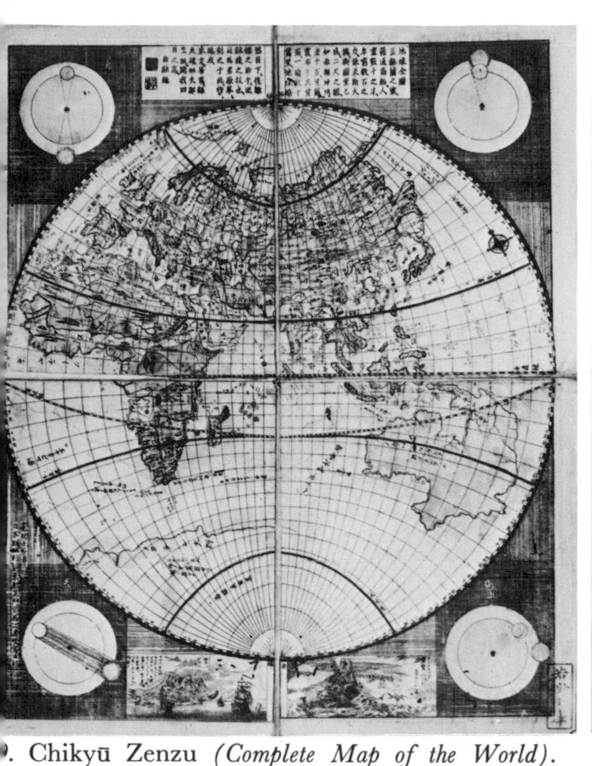

·. Chikyū Zenzu *(Complete Map of the World). '93. Copperplate etching. Courtesy of the Kobe City 'useum of Namban Art.*

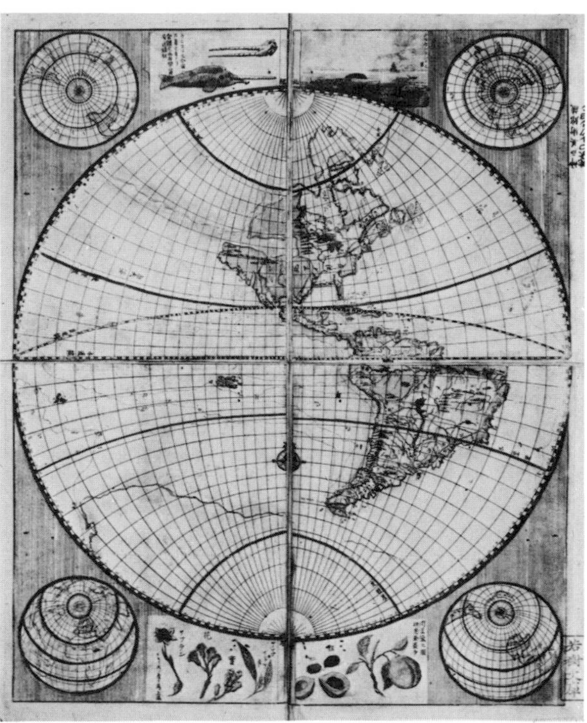

90. Chikyū Zenzu *(Complete Map of the World). 1793. Copperplate etching. Courtesy of the Kobe City Museum of Namban Art.*

considerable time must have been needed to make the revisions it contains. Kōkan acknowledged the aid received:

> Recently Mr. Ba Shin'yō was commissioned to repair the globes in the astronomical observatory. I asked him to correct any mistaken place names on my map, and thanks to his assistance, have been able to add information to it.[19]

Chikyū Zenzu (Pl. 89 and 90) is more carefully executed, with several place names added to the globes, six pictures included in the margins, and an inscription printed above the Afro-Asian hemisphere. Logically, the first map was followed by the publication of its accompanying text *Yochi Ryakusetsu* (Brief Explanation of the Earth), dated autumn, 1792; the second was followed by its text *Chikyū Zenzu Ryakusetsu* (Explanation of the Complete Map of the World), dated March, 1793. When revising his map, Kōkan apparently used the same copperplate, simply adding data. Since the 1792 date was already engraved on the plate, he left it as it was, not bothering to note that the revised printing took place one year later. The supposition that *Chikyū Zenzu* was published in the spring of 1793 is substantiated by extant letters written by Gentaku and Kōkan.[20]

It is significant to note that though Kōkan's later works on geography were published for all to read, his world maps were not intended for public distribution. A map containing such vital information about the world was necessarily reserved for government perusal, and even required official sanction before it could be printed. Any work dealing with foreign knowledge had to pass government censorship before publication; in 1774, for example, Sugita Gempaku and Maeno Ryōtaku had been obliged to obtain official approval before publishing their text on anatomy. Kōkan wrote:

91. Adam's Peak, Ceylon. *1793. Copperplate etching. Detail of* Chikyū Zenzu, *Plate 89. Courtesy of the Kobe City Museum of Namban Art.*

> My world map was printed after I obtained permission from the lord of Shirakawa [Matsudaira Sadanobu], with whom I privately consulted. It cannot be offered for sale. Only important persons are permitted to have it, and the price is therefore irrelevant.[21]

Had Kōkan not abided by the government stipulation, his work might well have been confiscated and destroyed. The same year that Kōkan published his first world map, Hayashi Shihei sought permission to publish his text *Kaikoku Heidan* (Military Discussion on a Maritime Country); Sadanobu not only denied him permission to publish, but confined Shihei to house arrest.

Yochi Zenzu and *Chikyū Zenzu* were each printed on two separate sheets of paper, one half depicting Asia, Africa, and Europe; the other, the Americas. In the four corners of the halves illustrating the Afro-Asian hemisphere are diagrams explaining the geocentric earth and the positions of the sun and moon during solar and lunar eclipses. The earth seen from different angles appears in the four corners of the Western hemisphere. The route of Magellan's circumnavigation is shown by a dotted line, and on the Eastern hemisphere, a lightly dotted line indicates the route taken by traders from Holland to Java and Japan. The continent of Australia is labeled both Nova Oranda and Shin Oranda and is joined with New Guinea (called Nova Guinea), in the manner depicted on the map by Covens and Mortier. Although Kōkan claimed he copied the European original exactly, he improved on at least one detail. Japanese geographers had to rely on foreign maps for information about the rest of the world, but concerning their own country's topography, they had better knowledge than did Europeans. The original map showed Hokkaido as part of the Asian mainland, a mistake Kōkan rectified.

Additional illustrations on *Chikyū Zenzu* depicted, on the Western hemisphere, whale fishing off the coast of Greenland; a narwhal; the stalk, flower, and seed of a saffron plant and a poppy; and the branch, fruit, and seed of a peach tree. Depictions of plant life certainly indicated Kōkan's continuing interest in botany, and perhaps were used symbolically as well, the peach, for example, connoting longevity. Inspiration for these themes derived from the Dutch book by François Valentijn, from which Kōkan also copied illustrations on the Afro-Asian hemisphere of Dutch ships in the waters off the Cape of Good Hope, and Adam's Peak in Ceylon (Pl. 91 and 92).[22] As noted, Kō-

92. *François Valentijn.* Adam's Peak, Ceylon. *1726. Copperplate etching. Illustration from* Oud en Nieuw Oost-Indiën.

kan previously had drawn Adam's Peak for Chūryō's book *Kōmō Zatsuwa*. The inscription above the globe expressed his admiration for the achievements of the West:

> How wonderfully skilled the Dutch are in traveling all over the world in ships! They use all their knowledge and brainpower and the accumulated knowledge of thousands of past generations. That is how they are able to produce maps such as this one. This map is but two feet square, yet by studying it, you can understand even small facts about very tiny countries, illustrated as clearly as stars in the sky. At one glance you see before you on this map the entire enormous surface of the earth. Furthermore, what a magnificent technique is the art of engraving! It is a technique from Europe, and has been mastered in Japan by Shiba Kungaku.

Other world maps had been printed in Japan before Kōkan's, but his represented an important advance. Whereas earlier maps were printed with woodblocks, Kōkan's was a copperplate engraving, setting a precedent for all subsequent detailed charts. Later men adopted the new medium Kōkan had proved superior—although it may be noted that rarely were other engravers also scholars and originators of their own maps.[23] In his desire to enlighten the Japanese on world geography, Kōkan reflected the spirit of his age, but his use of a copperplate indicates his initiative in applying for scientific purposes a medium previously confined to artistic ends. He realized the inadequacy of traditional woodblock printing for accurate depiction of scientific details.

Yochi Zenzu's accompanying text, *Yochi Ryakusetsu,* described a geocentric universe, with the earth in the center circled by the sun, moon, and planets. Kōkan also discussed the seasons and the length of day and night relative to the earth's Torrid, Temperate, and Frigid zones; the difference between solar and lunar eclipses; and the earth's five continents. Following these explanations, he commented:

> Most Japanese, even if presented with a world map, would ponder little over its importance, but keep it merely for amusement. But European people, especially the Dutch, do not think of maps as amusing playthings. Maps are essential to navigation; that is why Western maps must be accurate. Also, Europeans are extremely clever in manufacturing scientific instruments; all precisely made articles that Asians use are made in Europe. . . . In Japan, very little is known about countries of the world other than Holland, yet all peoples live on the same earth under the same heaven. It is truly a great misfortune that Japanese know so pitifully little about the heavens and the earth we live on.[24]

Chikyū Zenzu Ryakusetsu also described the universe in geocentric terms, explaining the movement of the sun around the earth and the reason for day and night as the sun travels along its ecliptic. It might appear strange that having made a copperplate map of the world and written an explanation, Kōkan should have followed his work only a year later with a second map and a similar explanation. Between February of 1792 and the spring of 1793, however, he devoted much of his time to the study of geography, accumulating facts to add to his map and text. More important, between the publication of the first and second book, Kōkan became aware of the heliocentric theory. *Yochi Ryakusetsu* posited only a geocentric universe, whereas *Chikyū Zenzu Ryakusetsu* described both the geocentric and heliocentric systems. The theory contained in the earlier book was stated first:

> All the stars describe great circles around the earth, which is globular in shape and located in the very center of the heavens.

Following this statement he added:

> Up until this time, the explanation of heaven and earth has stated that the earth is in the center of the heavens and the sun and moon move in a circle around it. But there is another theory that

> the earth too moves clockwise and the sun is at the exact center. The earth, then, revolves in the heavens! The moon is also a world that travels around the earth. This theory further states that the five planets are all worlds. The apparatus constructed to show the complete phenomena is called an "orrery"; there is a drawing of it in a book written by a man named Buys.[25] An acquaintance of mine, Matsubara Josui, is planning to make a model of this apparatus.[26] Because this explanation represents an extremely new and overwhelming concept, men who are not wholeheartedly devoted to scientific investigation are sure to consider it a falsehood.[27]

The new astronomical discovery, together with added information Kōkan had collected on geographical details, sufficiently justified his decision to revise the plates of *Yochi Zenzu* and publish a second text.

Chikyū Zenzu Ryakusetsu apparently enjoyed considerable popularity, for it was reprinted in 1797, with a new section describing in some detail the countries of the world. This edition was again published in 1800. Much of the added text was concerned with establishing conterminous borders and identifying rivers and capital cities; in his studies of world geography, Kōkan proved himself a meticulous and thorough scholar. Included in the topographical information were accounts of foreign peoples and their countries. Concerning England, for example, Kōkan wrote:

> The capital, London, is far more beautiful than any other city in Europe, having numerous palaces and towers both within and outside the city walls. The Thames River flows through the city, and over the Thames there is a stone bridge about 656 yards long. On the bridge, houses stand in a row like chessmen, forming a market area. The watches, glass, and various other wonderful things of the world's finest quality that Holland has introduced into Japan are made in this country.[28]

A brief discussion of Asian and African countries followed the section on Europe. Information on North America included Mexico ("a possession of Spain, rich in gold and silver, with strange flora and fauna unknown in Japan") and Florida ("a land of ignorant and primitive natives who rob indifferently because they have no conception of morality"). There is also, he wrote, a land to the west known as California.

Kōkan derived information for his book from both Buys's encyclopedia and Valentijn's geography, but he depended most heavily on Japanese sources. There was a wealth of material he could draw upon, for many studies of geography had been published in Japanese before Kōkan wrote his first text.[29] One author copied another, adding to each new book bits of information obtained on his own.

A fourth undated edition of *Chikyū Zenzu Ryakusetsu* was published in three volumes, the first two containing the complete text of the 1797 edition. Volume Three elaborated on the descriptions of countries, replacing factual geographical detail with extraordinary and often bizarre tales of the customs and mores of foreign peoples. Kōkan, however, did not write the last volume; the literary style is quite different, and the flights of fancy are more than he would have indulged. The fourth edition contained the earlier illustrations of a couple from Greenland and two men from Coromandel, though redrawn and crudely executed, and included six new ones, among them foreign soldiers and an American steamship. The text of Volume Three must have been written after 1815, for it mentions the defeat of Napoleon. In any case, this republication with supplement added indicates the developing interest in foreign countries among the Japanese, and the continuing reputation of Shiba Kōkan as a geographer.

In 1805, Kōkan published his third and final map entitled *Hinkai Zu* (Map of Navigation; Pl. 93), together with the text *Oranda Tsūhaku* (Dutch Navigation) explaining the map and adding facts about the world. Technically superior to his earlier endeav-

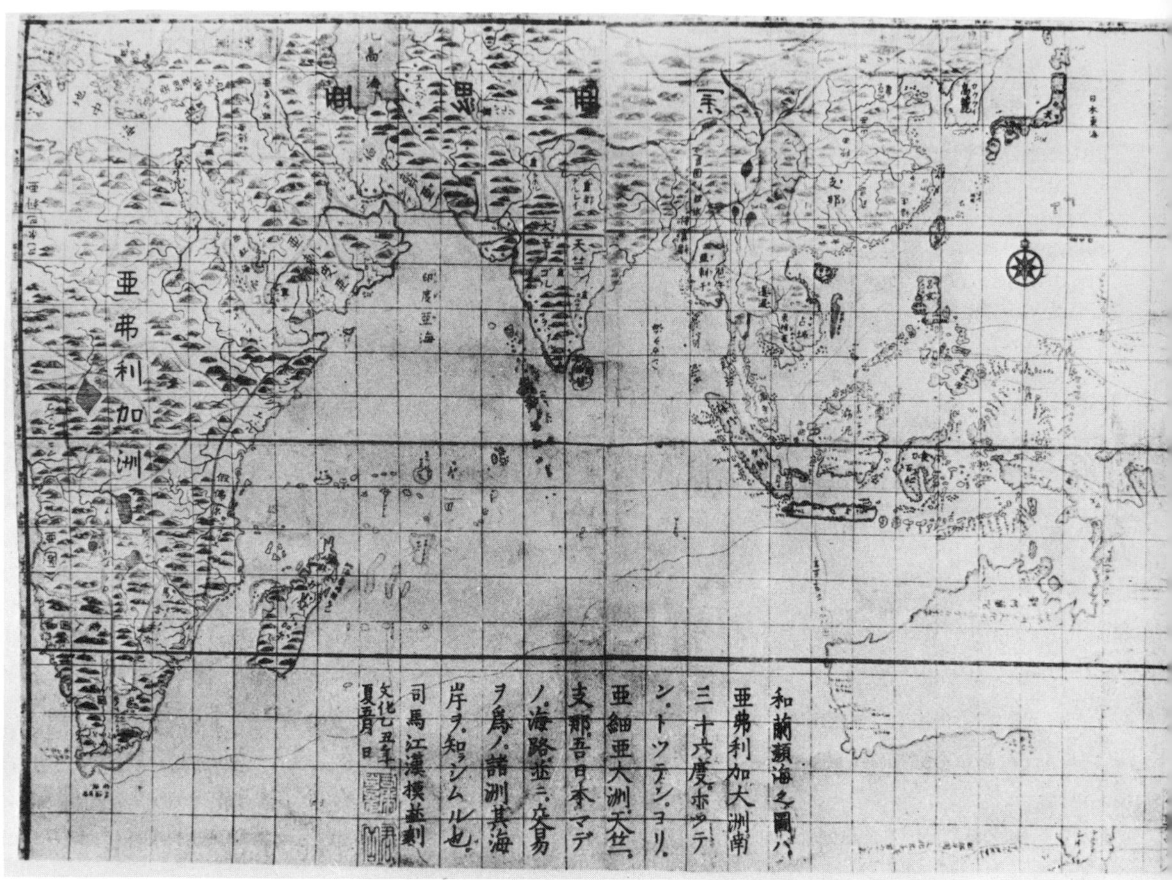

93. Hinkai Zu *(Map of Navigation). 1805. Copperplate etching. Collection of N. H. N. Mody. Reproduced, with permission of Charles E. Tuttle, Co., from Mody,* A Collection of Nagasaki Colour Prints and Paintings.

ors, the map was limited in scope to the routes between Europe and Japan. Kōkan divided the area with lines of longitude and latitude, explaining his method in the preface of *Oranda Tsūhaku*. The preface also stated the reason for the new map and revealed Kōkan's pride in his accomplishment and progress:

> Although previously I attached a brief explanation to my copperplate engraving called *Chikyū Zenzu*, the entire map is limited in detail, and I outlined only generally the shapes of the various states and countries. Now again I have copied a map brought here by a Dutch ship and have finally completed a new map of my own. Compare this with *Chikyū Zenzu*![30]

Oranda Tsūhaku was printed in two volumes, the first presenting a summary of the five continents; the second, specific details. Information, stated somewhat haphazardly, followed a general outline beginning with a description of Europe and progressing eastward, covering Africa and the Asian countries. Some of his material, Kōkan wrote, was taken from Valentijn's geography text. Most of his account and even his phrasing, however, are reminiscent of the manuscript written by Katsuragawa Hoshū in 1786—in turn, a translation of the Dutch text accompanying the world map by Johan Blaeu.[31] Katsuragawa's manuscript was not published during his lifetime, but undoubtedly Kōkan had opportunity to examine it.

Miscellaneous facts concerning foreign peoples and customs are more numerous in *Oranda Tsūhaku* than in the previous *Yochi*

Ryakusetsu or *Chikyū Zenzu Ryakusetsu.* After some opening remarks, Kōkan presents a brief history of astronomy from Ptolemy to Copernicus. He then takes up the explorations of the Portuguese and Vasco da Gama's journey around the Cape of Good Hope in 1497; next, he mentions the survey of the Siberian coast by Russia in 1740, returning to a general discussion of European society. His comments include an often curious mixture of fact and fancy, representing a Utopian image of the West distinguished by virtues traditionally associated with ancient China:

> Europeans are all very fond of literature. The king establishes a school in each district and selects the most able from among thousands of people to become teachers. European learning stresses natural science. Astronomy is studied first, then the student may take up whatever subject most interests him. Everywhere in Europe there are institutions supporting widows and widowers, aged persons who have no children, and orphans. There are also poor houses and hospitals.[32]

The discussion progresses from the customs of Europeans to the countries of Asia, including China, India, Persia, Arabia, and Judea—"the cradle of civilization." Kōkan describes Tartary as a vast cold land in northern Asia, mentions many of the islands in the Indian Ocean, and concludes with a brief explanation of America and a land at the south pole discovered by Magellan, "which may be a continent but is still largely unknown."[33]

In Volume Two of *Oranda Tsūhaku,* Kōkan refers to the arrival in Japanese harbors of foreign ships, the sizes and types of Dutch cargo vessels, and the method and materials used in building Dutch houses. Much of his information on Holland, he states, came from his study of European copperplate pictures. Undoubtedly he derived his observations on navigation and geography from works by contemporary Japanese scholars, rather than delving directly into foreign sources. In 1795 Miura Baien had written:

> Europeans use a globe for charting their navigation routes. Before setting out on a journey over the seas, they observe the sun, moon, and stars, check the season in each place by observing the degree of latitude, observe the land topography of mountains and rivers and the roughness of the sea waves. Only then do they set sail. This is entirely different from Japanese sea trips to Osaka or sailing on rivers.
>
> Mr. Matsumura Kunki has written a book about the sea voyages of the Dutch from their capital at Amsterdam to Nagasaki. The book, *Oranda Kōkai Ryakuki* [Outline of Dutch Navigation] explains as follows: "Before a Dutch ship sets out to sea, the sailors measure the height of the sun many times with an octant. Therefore they know at every moment the location of their ship and how many degrees they are from the equator by calculating the movements of the heavens. They are able to adjust their position whenever they stray too far or too close to the equator. For a sailor this study is of paramount importance, and there are many methods involved, but I shall not describe them here."[34]

One geographer borrowed from another; Kōkan was not unusual in repeating what he had learned from others.

Again Kōkan traces the route from Holland to Japan, adding information about the countries en route. He is particularly impressed by the generosity, humane practices, and charity of the French; the images he presents are distinctly designed to portray a superior moral order, which Kōkan apparently believed the natural result of Western scientific inquiry and technological processes:

> French people are kindhearted and polite, and many display great interest in astronomy, surveying, and physics. They are also courageous, and always maintain an army prepared for any emergency, but are careful to avoid wars by treating other countries with extreme courtesy.

Therefore, France justly deserves to be the great, cultured nation she is. Both the high- and the low-born work together to maintain perfect harmony within the country.

In the north, on the banks of the Seine River, is the great city of Paris, where the grand and beautiful palace of the king is located. The city is thirty-seven miles in circumference, has seventeen gates, and more than sixty thousand houses. There are over one hundred monasteries, called "cloisters," as well as churches both large and small. There are also asylums providing for widows, widowers, old persons without children, and orphans. Each asylum has a workshop to train people to use whatever powers they have: the blind are taught to use their hands and feet, the crippled to train their eyes and ears. In this way each person learns to make the most of his ability, and no one is left to become a worthless person. There are institutions for children where infants are taken in, so that poverty does not force parents to desert their offspring on the street or to throw them into a ditch.

There are many hospitals for those who are too poor to afford medicine or who suddenly become ill while traveling. Hospitals are divided into sections for treating various illnesses, such as plague or other contagious diseases. All kinds of medicines are carefully dispensed by responsible persons, and excellent doctors in every hospital see to their patients' needs daily. Hospitals further offer such facilities as clothing, beds, curtains, etc., and there are also nurses (generally old women). Those who have recovered from illness are given money, clothing, and food to help them begin life anew. There are thirty of these hospitals in France.

When a man finds money or anything else of value on the street, he immediately puts up a notice of what he has found on the church gate. These valuables are of course returned to the person identified as having lost them. In the event that they are unclaimed, they are offered in charity to the poor or contributed to asylums. All charitable institutions are established by the government, a practice followed in other European countries as well. From my examination of the asylums depicted in copperplate pictures brought to Japan, I have discovered that the walls are made of stone with glass set in the windows. The buildings are seven or eight stories high, and of indescribable size and magnificence.[35]

94. Pyramids of Egypt. *1805. Woodblock print. Illustration from* Oranda Tsūhaku. *Courtesy of the Kobe City Museum of Namban Art.*

As French intellectuals of the eighteenth century used the image of the Oriental sage and the harmony and humanity of the social order in China to criticize their own

95. The Colossus of Rhodes. *1805. Woodblock print. Illustration from* Oranda Tsūhaku. *Courtesy of the Kobe City Museum of Namban Art.*

society, Japanese used such descriptions as these to point out through implication the failings of Japan by exaggerating the superiority of the West. In discussing the charitable institutions of France, Honda Toshiaki wrote that if France were not located so far from Japan, Japanese would surely go there to escape poverty in old age.[36]

Other countries of Europe are treated less extensively. Kōkan's criteria for judging the greatness of a nation rests largely on whether its scholars studied astronomy and its merchants carried on foreign trade. Spain and Portugal, as colonial powers engaged in commerce, are highly lauded. Africa, he writes, consists chiefly of great plains where fantastic animals unknown in Japan abounded. His information deriving ultimately from Dutch sources, he considers the natives of Africa "black, foolish, wicked, and savage," except along the northern coast where Europeans had settled. The Egyptians, he asserts, were civilized people who studied both astronomy and medicine. They built huge composite stone statues, half-woman and half-lion, and also great towers 250 steps high. Kōkan includes a picture of the "towers," obviously not copied from a Dutch engraving (Pl. 94). He flanks the pyramids with pillars topped with winged angels, and on the summit of each adds a Christian cross, apparently inspired by church steeples he had observed in European pictures. He mentions also the Valley of the Kings and the ancient method of embalming mummies.

Kōkan traces the trade route around the southern tip of Africa—the land of the Hottentots who were "so stupid that they scarcely seem like human beings at all." When conditions were favorable, he states, it took one month to make the voyage from Holland to the Cape of Good Hope, and three months from the Cape of Good Hope to Batavia in Java, where the main base of the Dutch East India trading company was located. All Dutch ships that called at Nagasaki came from Batavia.

Kōkan describes Java as a tropical land rich in fauna and flora. Islands near Java included Sumatra and Borneo, primitive cultures with rich, fertile soil where grains grew well. The staple food there was sorghum, a flat-tasting food with no nutritive value—quite unlike the sweet and nutritious rice produced in Japan. There is, he writes, with a touch of national pride—typical of Japanese even today—no rice in all the world as delicious as that of Japan.

After describing Indonesia, Kōkan continues northward along the trade route to Nagasaki, then follows the coastal route westward again to Holland, describing the countries along the way. He reports on the Mediterranean Sea and some of its islands. On Rhodes, he writes, there was once a huge bronze statue 105 feet high—so gigantic that a man could walk between its fingers. It was built astride the harbor, standing atop two flights of stone steps, and ships could easily pass beneath the statue. In its left hand the colossus held a torch; in order to light it, a man entered at the toe and climbed up a spiral staircase. The statue took ten years to construct and was considered one of the Seven Wonders of the World. Twelve years after its construction, however, it was destroyed by an earthquake.[37] Kōkan illustrates the Colossus of Rhodes (Pl. 95), basing his portrayal on the depiction in the Dutch book by Gotfridi,[38] which followed the sixteenth-century belief that the monument had been constructed straddling the harbor. As noted, sixteen years earlier, in 1789, Kitayama Kangan had copied the illustration in Gotfridi's book to include in Morishima Chūryō's *Bankoku Shinwa*.[39]

Kōkan traces a third sea route north from Holland to the Arctic Ocean. Ever since the discovery of the route to India by way of the Cape of Good Hope, English and Dutch seamen had been searching for an alternate passage to Cathay northeast around Siberia, and by the time Kōkan's book was written, the Dutch had made considerable explorations in Arctic waters. He mentions whaling activity carried on in the Arctic region where "unicorn whales" (narwhals) were numerous, and describes the natives of Novaya Zemlya, who were only three feet tall. The common European myth of arctic midgets had long been known in Japan, and many of the earliest Japanese pictures depicting peoples of foreign lands included them.[40]

Oranda Tsūhaku concluded with a description of Russia and Siberia. Moscow, Kōkan writes, was an impressive city with beautiful palaces, but Russia itself, despite its vastness, was not nearly as beautiful as Holland or England. The Russian people had tried to educate the ignorant natives to the east, but the land was frozen most of the year and covered by dense fog. Nothing grew, and Japanese rice could be sold there for ten times the price realized in Japan.

The main purpose of *Oranda Tsūhaku* was to explain the geography of the world by adding greater detail to the previous *Chikyū Zenzu Ryakusetsu*. It represented a summation of Kōkan's study of world geography and was his last major work dealing exclusively with the subject. Undoubtedly it was written partly to satisfy his own curiosity about the world, but he had also a less direct motive for its publication. The timing was appropriate, answering a current demand in Japan for knowledge of foreign countries—a demand that arose concurrently with a tension in international relations. Although the Tokugawa regime had isolated the country from the outside world, other nations were becoming increasingly interested in trade with Japan, and in October of 1804, the Rezanov mission arrived in Nagasaki harbor from Russia. After months of uncertainty and hesitation, the Japanese government, despite opposition from some of the more enlightened leaders, finally denied the mission the trading agreement it sought. Kōkan stated his own opinion on the matter several years later in *Shumparō Hikki*:

> In April of 1805 [*sic*], a Russian ship entered Nagasaki harbor. The chief ambassador, Mr. Rezanov, brought with him a letter signed by Empress Alexander [*sic*],[41] which stated: "Although our country is far distant from yours, we have colonies nearby. We therefore desire to establish friendly relations, exchange diplomatic envoys yearly, and engage in trade with your nation. We extend our sincere respect and felicitations to the king of Japan." The Japanese government, however, kept the Russian ambassador waiting in Nagasaki harbor for half a year and would not even permit him to set foot on Japanese soil. Moreover, acting in complete disregard of his proposals, the Japanese sent a disgracefully discourteous and haughty reply.

96. A Western Studio. *1794. Copperplate etching. Courtesy of the Kobe City Museum of Namban Art.*

> Russia is located far to the north, where no crops can grow well, and is a second-rate nation, but the country is vast and has many colonies. Did we not treat them as though they were savages? Mr. Rezanov came here as a representative of his sovereign.[42] Is there any difference between their sovereign and ours? The first requirement among men, from the ruler on down, is courtesy. To give an analogy, it is as though a gentleman, dressed in his finest, most decorous attire, were to be greeted by a person stark naked. Certainly the Russians must think that we are animals![43]

Despite an abhorrence of foreign contacts stemming from fears for national security, the Japanese government could no longer afford to remain ignorant of other countries. Russia's demand for trade, though not a direct inspiration for Kōkan's map and text, may well have stimulated him to his labors.

One other small volume remains as evidence of Kōkan's geographical studies: *Ryōjusen Zusetsu* (Explanation of Adam's Peak), published in February, 1808. As stated in the text, information in this book was obtained from François Valentijn's *Oud en Nieuw Oost-Indiën.* Kōkan described in detail the sacred Buddhist mountain in Ceylon; his depiction of Adam's Peak, already printed in Chūryō's *Kōmō Zatsuwa* and on Kōkan's world map (1793), was omitted in favor of six other woodblock illustrations.[44] He concluded his account with typical self-recognition:

> Many strange tales are related of Ryōjusen, but none of them is true. The statements in the book by Valentijn, however, are all correct, for the author actually went to Ceylon and wrote a firsthand account. The illustrations contained in the original book are printed by the Dutch etching method and are extremely realistic. By looking at these one can obtain a clear impression of the actual places and things depicted. All the pictures are exquisitely printed with copperplates. Very few persons in Japan understand the etching technique, but I have been producing etchings according to the Dutch method ever since 1783, when I made the first copperplate ever executed in Japan. For my own publications I have produced *Tenkyū Zu, Chikyū Zu, Hinkai Zu,* and other maps of foreign countries.[45]

As Kōkan's knowledge of European science broadened, he turned his attention increasingly from the study of geography to an investigation of the heavens. A curious etching of 1794 depicting an artist in a Western studio (Pl. 96) seems to symbolize his energy and ambition during this most active phase of his life. This may have been his last copperplate executed for artistic intent rather than for scientific illustration. The artist, seated before an easel in the center of the room, is creating a picture reminiscent of Kōkan's portrait of a Hollander (Pl. 63). The architecture of both the room and the buildings glimpsed through the open window is European, an indication that the scene was inspired by Western works.

Similarities between Kōkan's conception of the studio and the Western Renaissance notion of the artist as a scholar of all branches of learning seem hardly coincidental. Among the vast collection of objects in the foreground are a world globe, a disarray of books, right angles, triangles, compasses, and brushes—exactly those objects associated with Western interpretations of the artist-scientist, perhaps best known in Albrecht Dürer's engraving *Melancholia I*. Moreover, the activities within the studio echo numerous European illustrations of the processes of print-making, from Jost Amman to Thomas Rowlandson. Kōkan has used Western symbols to connote his personal development; he has crammed into one picture objects representative of his extraordinary variety of interests. Within the panel at bottom is the inscription: "In September, 1783, the first copperplate etching was made by Shiba Kōkan. August, 1794."

Kōkan's first book directed primarily to the complex subject of astronomy was titled *Oranda Tensetsu* (Explanation of Dutch Astronomy), published in January, 1796; the following month, he produced accompanying charts of the heavens called *Tenkyū Zu* (Planisphere; Pl. 9 and 10). In dealing with geography, Kōkan had published his world maps before their accompanying texts, but he undoubtedly realized that a planisphere would have little meaning to the Japanese without an explanation, and therefore published the text first. In the preface of *Oranda Tensetsu* he stated:

> Previously I executed a map of the world, and now, using the same method employed before, I have taken a map of the heavens brought to Japan by a Westerner, etched it on a copperplate, and completed a new engraving. . . . The Dutch are accustomed to trading in all countries of the world, and they travel everywhere. When they go by sea one degree away from the land, even mountains are lost from sight; therefore, they must plot the course of their ships by the stars. For this purpose, a map of the stars is of utmost importance and no mere plaything. Westerners make clear, concise maps of the heavenly bodies.[46]

Several foreign charts of the heavens had been imported to Japan by the time Kōkan produced *Tenkyū Zu*. The two he perhaps copied were depicted in the top corners of Johan Blaeu's world map of 1639, housed at the Edo observatory—the one reproduced here (Pl. 97) is shown upside down to facilitate comparison with Kōkan's corresponding chart (Pl. 10).[47] In drawing his planisphere, Kōkan again may have received assistance from Ba Shin'yō, who earlier had aided him in correcting his world map. Some information also may have been obtained from Motoki Ryōei, whom Kōkan met in Nagasaki in 1788.

Tenkyū Zu is divided into two hemispheres, subdivided into twelve sections each, with the signs of the zodiac illustrated within the circles. Outside the circumferences are depictions of Saturn, Jupiter, the moon, and various instruments used in measuring the heavens. In the margin Kōkan writes:

> On the original Dutch celestial map, names of animals and humans are used to indicate constellations. Though each name has a special significance for Westerners, I have not translated all of these names on my map, but only those of the twelve main constellations. The constellation known in Japan as *Hokuto-shichisei*, for example, is called the Bear because the seven stars form the figure of a bear. Other names are given in the same way. The constellations on the ecliptic are called the twelve zodiacal signs, similar

97. Johan Blaeu. Celestial Chart *(Planisphere). 1639. Copperplate etching. Detail of Blaeu's* Map of the World. *Location unknown.*

to the twenty-eight constellations used in connection with the lunar calendar.[48]

On the margin of the other hemisphere is the inscription:

> Etched and printed by Kōkan Shiba Shun of Edo, the first man to make copperplates in Japan. Spring, 1796. Revised by Honda Saburōemon.

The inscriptions were added with woodblocks, and not all extant copies contain the statement "revised by Honda Saburōemon." Kōkan's relationship with Honda Saburōemon (better known as Toshiaki) is unclear, but from this statement we may assume he provided Kōkan with information and assistance; Kōkan's world map *Chikyū Zenzu,* reprinted in 1796, also bears the inscription "revised by Honda Saburōemon."[49] Among other accomplishments, Honda Toshiaki was a scholar of navigation and astronomy. In his *Seiiki Monogatari* he refers to Kōkan's celestial map:

> A man named Shiba Kōkan has recently made copperplate maps of the earth and the heavens. If you examine these maps, you will understand that the heavenly bodies were charted more than six thousand years ago in Egypt. You will also understand that the earth is a sphere, and on the sphere are many countries large and small, all shown on his map. The globe called "Earth" is only one of the smaller stars. Look at his maps and you will understand.[50]

Of the sources used for *Oranda Tensetsu,* the chart's accompanying text, Kōkan provided the cryptic acknowledgment:

> In compiling this explanation, I have selected the best statements of Seiju and Shiroku; in addition, I have used an explanation in a Dutch book.[51]

The unspecified Dutch source may have been the *New and Complete Dictionary of the Arts and Sciences* by Egbert Buys. The term *seiju* (Western scholar) was an honorific title given to Matteo Ricci, the well-known Jesuit missionary in China from 1582 until his death in 1610.[52] Kōkan mentioned him by his Chinese name in *Tenchi Ridan:*

> There is a book on natural laws called *T'ien-ching Huo-wên.* Japanese people are becoming interested in astronomy, but until recently there has been no book on the subject. Now, many have the *T'ien-ching Huo-wên.* This book appeared at the end of the Ming dynasty during the Wan Li era [1573–1620], when a man named Li Ma-tou brought to China for the first time a map of half of the world. This man lied and said he was a Westerner, but actually he came from Goa in India. The book is a compilation by the Chinese of his teachings.[53]

The Chinese book, called in Japanese *Tenkyō Wakumon,* was compiled about 1600 by

Yu I, also known as Tzŭ Lu, or in Japanese, Shiroku, and was based on the astronomy expounded by Matteo Ricci.[54] The identity of Seiju and Shiroku therefore becomes clear.

The *T'ien-ching Huo-wên* was smuggled past the watchful censors in Nagasaki sometime between 1630 and 1680. Perused at first in secret, it gradually became widely recognized among Japanese scholars, receiving more acclaim than it ever enjoyed in China. In 1730, it was published in Japan with diacritical marks added by Nishikawa Seikyū to facilitate reading,[55] and reprinted in 1794. Kōkan probably derived his information from the annotated edition.[56] Widely read and disputed, the book became the subject of commentaries and refutations for the next hundred years.[57]

Kōkan's knowledge of astronomy was extremely elementary in 1792, when he published his first book on world geography. He had not yet heard of the heliocentric theory, and his *Chikyū Zenzu Ryakusetsu* of the following year gave no more than a summary of it. By 1796, however, increased familiarity with Western theories enabled him to present in *Oranda Tensetsu* his first comprehensive statement of astronomy. He explains both the geocentric and heliocentric theories, concluding with an avowal of his preference for the heliocentric. The book follows a logical progression, beginning with a description of the earth and proceeding to clouds, fog, rain, and dew, a mention of solar and lunar eclipses, and the calendars devised to predict them. Next, he gives the basic method of surveying the heavens by dividing the circumference of the planisphere into units and calculating the meridian lines. The surveying technique, he explains, employs a device called a quadrant, and he includes a drawing of the instrument. He then discusses the five planets, giving their relative sizes, the yearly revolutions of Jupiter and Saturn, and the distances between each planet and the earth.

Finally, he arrives at what was actually the main point of his text—the solar system, or heliocentric theory. He describes it by opposing the theories of Brahe and Copernicus, including a diagram to illustrate each respectively:

> According to the explanation by a man named Tycho Brahe, the moon travels around the earth, which remains in the center, and the five planets travel around the sun, which circles the earth. Three planets, Saturn, Jupiter, and Mars, travel slowly in the heavens, and two, Venus and Mercury, travel rapidly.
>
> According to another explanation by a man named Copernicus, the sun is in the center of the heavens and revolves in place, and while the moon travels around the earth, the earth makes one complete revolution each day, causing day and night. In one year the earth makes one revolution around the sun and revolves three hundred and sixty times.[58]

He also describes the theory given in the *T'ien-ching Huo-wên* (*Tenkyō Wakumon*):

> Yu I claims that if the earth were to revolve several thousand miles as on a boat journey, people would have great difficulty in leading their daily lives. We can eat and sleep easily because heaven moves around the earth's circumference, which is 26,352 miles, and thus forms day and night. Very definitely it is the heavens that move and revolve around the earth; the earth itself is still.[59]

Yu I argued, as had Ricci and Ptolemy before him, that the rotation of the earth was too incredible to consider seriously. It was felt that if the earth were to go hurtling every twenty-four hours over a distance of some two million miles, all the while spinning around eastward at up to one thousand miles per hour, it would fly to pieces under the stress of centrifugal force; the atmosphere would be left behind; and there would be a continuous, violent wind sweeping clouds and birds away to the westward.

Nevertheless, the concept of a revolving earth was scarcely more difficult to comprehend than the problem presented by a rotating universe. It was realized that the

98. An Orrery. *1796. Copperplate etching. From* Tenkyū Zenzu. *Courtesy of the Kobe City Museum of Namban Art.*

stars are at a vast distance from the earth, and should the universe revolve completely every twenty-four hours, the speed at which the stars travel would be stupendous.

After presenting the divergent theories, Kōkan concluded: "The sun is in the center and moves, while the stars and the earth surround the sun and revolve around it. . . . I have chosen as my basic source Copernicus's explanation."[60]

Oranda Tensetsu does not deal exclusively with pure astronomy, but takes up other topics concerning meteorology and natural phenomena, such as weather, meteors, rainbows, mirages, earthquakes, tides, and water veins. The book, in short, shows a marked advance in Kōkan's scientific studies over his earlier geographies. It contains his first clear expression of the heliocentric theory, and though much of his discussion is general and somewhat vague, it indicates he had concrete knowledge of the heavens and the astronomical instruments used in measuring them. His coverage of natural phenomena other than pure astronomy is treated more carelessly, but reveals his expanding interest in all phases of natural science.

In the autumn of the same year that *Oranda Tensetsu* and *Tenkyū Zu* appeared, Kōkan produced a set of ten etchings entitled *Tenkyū Zenzu* (Complete Illustrations of the Heavens), and for each wrote a paragraph of description. These pictures, now in the Kobe City Museum of Namban Art, seem to have been intended for the never-published *Shumparō Gafu*. The announcement of *Shumparō Gafu* at the end of Kōkan's essay *Seiyōga Dan* listed the etchings that would appear in Volume Three, entitled *Temmon Chiri* (Astronomy and Geography); this list is nearly the same as the titles on the extant series. Impressive both as scientific diagrams and as works of art, the copperplate illustrations are finely executed and hand-colored.

The ten etchings, and excerpts from Kōkan's accompanying explanations, are:

1) An orrery (Pl. 98)[61]

An orrery is a globe illustrating the heavens, and was first constructed by Copernicus of Poland. The sun is in the center, and the earth revolves around it. The entire order of the heavens can be understood by examining an orrery . . . and one can ascertain the truth of the heliocentric theory. The universe is blue and boundless, and since it is without end, one cannot describe its shape, but one can mark the sun as its central point. The sun is 360 times as large as the earth, and has been shining since time immemorial. It exerts more influence on the things of earth than one can ever describe. Only those with a sincere interest in science can understand these things.

2) The sun (Pl. 11)

True shape of the sun. I have copied this picture from a Dutch book. At dawn, when the sun is rising over the sea, one can see its shape by viewing it through a dark mirror. The edge resembles the spray of sea waves blown back by a strong wind. The sun appears to revolve in the ether; in a north wind, it seems to revolve to the right, and in a south wind, to the left. At high noon there is no apparent movement. Without the special mirror made by the Dutch, one cannot see the sun clearly at all.

3) The moon (Pl. 12)

Selenograph. I have copied this picture from a Dutch book. Some time ago, I observed the full moon through a telescope, but it did not look like this picture, and I felt that the illustration was false. Recently, however, I again had an opportunity to study the moon through a telescope for two hours, and gradually I was able to distinguish the dark and light areas, and afterward again examined the picture carefully. The true shape is exactly as depicted even to the smallest detail! The Dutch illustration is such an amazing, admirable work that I have made this copy of it. From the illustration alone I realize how precisely and thoroughly Westerners study natural science.

4) The elliptical earth

5) The heliocentric and geocentric universes (Pl. 13)

According to the *T'ien-ching Huo-wên* and other explanations, the sun travels around the heavens and the earth does not move. If, however, one actually surveys the heavens and makes a sound study of astronomy, one will realize that the earth does revolve, causing day and night, and taking one year to completely encircle the sun. The sun is in the center of the heavens and revolves in place. These two explanations are not so very different, but somewhat resemble each other. Look at the diagram and you will understand.

6) The earth in space

7) The ebb and flow of the tides

8) Snowflakes seen through a microscope

Snowflakes have six, twelve, or twenty-four points—all multiples of six. . . . Holland is more than fifty degrees north latitude and is a very cold country; therefore, one sees snowflake patterns there never encountered in Japan.

99. A Dirigible Balloon. *1797. Blue and white porcelain plate. Courtesy of Capt. and Mrs. Roger Gerry, New York.*

9) Insects and seeds (Pl. 14)

Insects seen through a microscope. One can see clearly the eyes, ears, etc., of insects through a microscope. Insects have muscles, and feelings of joy, fear, and worry just as humans have. How interesting life is!

a) Ant. b) Gnat. c) Deathwatch beetle. d) Plantain seed. e) Sesame seed.

1) Millet seed. 2) Poppy seed. 3) Seed of the beefsteak plant.

10) Mosquito larvae

The range of subjects Kōkan treated in his scientific etchings pinpoints his diverse interests; in short, anything relating to European knowledge became his concern. An illustration on a blue and white ceramic plate (Pl. 99), executed the year following the completion of his series of etchings, depicts a subject of considerable interest at that time to Europeans: two men steering their course through the heavens in a *luchtschip*—a dirigible balloon not unlike that in which Jean Pierre Blanchard and John Jeffries made the first aerial crossing of the English channel on January 7, 1785. The earliest balloon ascension had occurred in 1783, but Blanchard's was the first airship to attempt to achieve dirigibility by using a kind of rudder; Kōkan's depiction of the craft must have been inspired by one of the several European engravings depicting Blanchard's departure from Dover.

The year 1808 was the climax of Kōkan's astronomical studies. It was in that year that he completed his most thorough statement of the Copernican theory: *Kopperu Temmon Zukai* (Illustrated Explanation of Copernican Astronomy). Shortly before the book appeared in December, he also published a booklet explaining the Copernican system entitled *Chitengi Ryakuzukai* (Illustrated Explanation of the Celestial Globe), which included a diagram composed of several free-moving parts to explain the revolutions of the earth, moon, and planets. Whereas in his earlier works he had referred to Saturn, Jupiter, Mars, Venus, and Mercury by the term *gosei* (five stars), he here referred to them as *wakusei* (planets)—a word coined by Motoki Ryōei in his book *Taiyō Kyūri Ryōkaisetsu* (Understanding the Physics of the Sun), Kōkan's probable source.

At the end of *Oranda Tensetsu,* Kōkan had announced the future publication of *Kopperu Temmon Zukai,* indicating that already, while compiling the earlier work in 1796, he had conceived of another book on astronomy broader in scope, with a more extensive explanation of the Copernican theory. *Kopperu Temmon Zukai* is divided into two parts, the first consisting of pictures and explanatory diagrams, the second the main text, more fully describing the drawings. The preface indicates the source of his information:

> The explanation presented here is taken entirely from a Western book. Previously I asked Mr. Motoki, an interpreter at Nagasaki, to let me examine it, and found that it concerned Copernicus's laws on the rotation of the earth.[62]

The book, called *Gronden der Sterrenkunde* (Principles of Astronomy), was a Dutch translation of a text written in 1770 by George Adams. Motoki Ryōei's translation, called *Taiyō Kyūri Ryōkaisetsu* and published in 1793, had not been made when Kōkan visited Nagasaki in 1788, but after Ryōei presented it to the government, both his manuscript and the Dutch text were kept at the astronomical observatory in Edo, where Kōkan undoubtedly studied them. He states that he received further assistance from the *rangaku* scholars of Edo, though the conclusion of his preface suggests he was no longer on intimate terms with them:

> There are a number of scholars in Edo who are engaged in Dutch studies. Secretly I observed them until I was able to get a good idea of what they were about. I then asked one member of the group adept at translation for an explanation of astronomy. Now I have made new illustrations explaining the earth's rotation, though naturally I fear there may still be errors.[63]

At the beginning of the book, Kōkan includes a penetrating self-portrait (Pl. 100), which reinforces the impression already received from his writings of an incisive, alert, and determined individual. He was sixty-one years old, baldheaded, and thin to the point of emaciation, with sharp eyes sunken in bony sockets. The stubble of his beard and hairs growing from his ears and Adam's apple suggest an indifference to personal grooming appropriate to the scholar image. His long, aquiline nose seems more Western than Oriental, and though the landscape in the background is Japanese, the curtain draped above his head is reminiscent of the use of this device to ennoble the sitter in European portraiture.

The main theme of *Kopperu Temmon Zukai* was the heliocentric theory as formulated by Copernicus, though Kōkan incorporated the corrections of Johannes Kepler.[64] Copernicus had envisioned uniform circular motions of the heavenly bodies in the manner of Ptolemy; by failing to recognize that the planets move in ellipses, he was obliged to introduce a complex theory of cycles and epicycles in order to prove his system geometrically. Kepler, by establishing a single elliptical orbit for each planet, was able to eliminate Copernicus's cycles and epicycles. Kepler himself found the concept of elliptical planetary motion distasteful, but Kōkan evinced no surprise or distrust of the theory. He was not an astronomer questioning the work of Western scientists, but an unquestioning transmitter of this knowledge to the Japanese.

Explanations in *Kopperu Temmon Zukai* were stated more systematically and precisely than in *Oranda Tensetsu,* showing that Kōkan's understanding of astronomy had progressed considerably. He omitted entirely the geocentric order expounded in *T'ien-ching Huo-wên,* which he had felt obliged to include in his earlier work. Also, in his former book he established the distances of the planets in relation to the earth, whereas in the later work he discussed the distances between the planets and the sun, giving their respective positions in their elliptical orbits. But though *Kopperu Temmon Zukai* went beyond the elementary level of the previous text, Kōkan never lost sight of his motive in explaining the new science. However complex the subject, his discussion never became overly technical; he was writing for an audience essentially ignorant of Western scientific principles, not for trained astronomers.

Kopperu Temmon Zukai was Kōkan's last major work dealing with astronomy, though he published one other short explanation called *Chitengi Shimō* (Enlightenment Concerning the Celestial Globe), a copy of which is owned by the Kobe City Museum of Namban Art. The book is undated, but probably was printed around 1809, certainly after *Kopperu Temmon Zukai,* for mention of the longer work is made in the opening lines. The explanation of the heliocentric theory is similar to that in *Kopperu Temmon Zukai,* and the movable celestial chart made for *Chitengi Ryakuzukai* is elucidated in greater detail.

100. Self-portrait, Age Sixty-one. *1808. Woodblock print. Illustration from* Kopperu Temmon Zukai. *Courtesy of the Kobe City Museum of Namban Art.*

Kōkan was sixty-two years old in 1809, an age at which most men of his generation would already have retired. Three years earlier he had announced his retirement from the painting profession, though he continued to paint, dedicating his final votive offering of Kintai Bridge in 1809. After 1809 he published no other books, but completed several manuscripts and continued his studies of natural science almost until his death. The 1810 essay *Dokushō Bōgen* (Self-laughter and Reckless Remarks) contains observations on natural science, as do *Shumparō Hikki* (Notes by Shumparō, 1811) and *Mugon Dōjin Hikki* (Notes by Mugon Dōjin, 1814). These manuscripts, however, were not primarily scientific works, but collections of miscellanies; they are discussed in the following chapter.

One final book should be noted in conjunction with Kōkan's scientific writings: *Tenchi Ridan* (Discussion on Astronomy and Geography), an unpublished manuscript completed in 1816, when he was sixty-nine. Kōkan's observations here span a wide range, from astronomy to such topics as the reason trees bear fruit, the cause of sore throats, explanations of thunder and lightning, hailstones, earthquakes, snowflakes, rainbows, landslides, tides, meteors, waxing and waning of the moon, salt water, the reason for the light emitted from the eyes of wolves and cats, the greenness of plants, and the various colors of flowers. Many of his explanations represent a kind of home philosophy of little scientific validity. In his observations on fossils and the theory of the earth's creation, however, he displays greater erudition:

> Coal and shell fossils. There is much coal in Chikuzen [Kyushu], mined at the base of mountains, but some of it does not burn. This coal is actually wood that has changed to stone, and in it one can see the wood grain. Sulphur burns underground just as charcoal burns. The unpleasant odor exuded when coal burns is sulphur; when the flame is extinguished, the stone remains and does not turn to ash, for it is only the sulphur that burns.
>
> Before the creation of the world as we know it today, there were other forest lands, which gradually became oceans, while mountain peaks became the basis of mountains. After many aeons, these forests that had been buried turned to coal. Shell fossils have been found on mountain sides at great distances from the sea. Before the creation of our world, these mountain areas were beaches where shellfish thrived, and now the former beaches are mountain tops. Among the shell fossils are other stones formed ages ago from clay and sand.[65]

These views are expanded in Kōkan's later book *Shumparō Hikki*:

> According to a recent Dutch theory, the earth is not perfectly round, but slightly elliptical, due to the collected deep water masses. The water is highest in the great ocean located east of Japan and west of America. There are some small islands in this ocean that, after tens of thousands of years, will gradually increase in size, and Japan may become a part of the American continent. . . .
>
> About three miles from Izu and Atami is the Higane Mountain Range, the highest peak of which is called Maruyama. In the autumn of 1811 I climbed to the top of this peak, where I could look in all directions and see many provinces, islands, and mountains, which all seemed to stretch away into the sea. When I thought about it, I realized that the many creases in the mountain ranges actually have the appearance of having been formed by the eroding action of water. Only Mount Fuji is a self-formed mountain that in prehistoric times burned for many thousands of years and shot forth sand that congealed, formed into masses, and finally became rock. Earth became crags, which after many centuries became harder rock. Water turned to quartz and crystal. All these phenomena occurred before the creation of our present world.[66]

Elsewhere a skillful purveyor of European science to the Japanese public, in *Tenchi Ridan* Kōkan reveals himself capable of original scientific thought based on his own observations. One Japanese scholar, comparing him to Abraham Gottlob Werner, wrote:

> Kōkan's explanation of the aqueous theory is contemporary with Werner's, and further, he wrote of an igneous theory, which was in advance of Werner's. It makes one proud to realize that the East

too can claim a scholar of such foresightedness.[67]

Many of Kōkan's explanations have the charm of slightly bemused wisdom in an old man who has studied science and experienced the rich variety of life. In his last years he awaited death almost impatiently, but even when weary of life, he could marvel at its mystery. Near the conclusion of *Tenchi Ridan* he wrote:

> An embryo forms inside a mother's womb and exists without breathing. When born, the infant breathes air, and grows up just as a young tree grows. He requires food, as a tree requires water taken in through its roots. The growing child can see with his eyes, listen with his ears, smell with his nose, feel cold and hot weather with his body, and the nerves within his body are conscious of pleasure and pain. Life is indeed a fragile, wondrous thing![68]

The subjects treated in *Tenchi Ridan* lack the organization and clarity of Kōkan's earlier explanations of geography and astronomy; nevertheless, the book is a landmark in Japan in the study of natural phenomena. Such works as *Kikai Kanran* (Natural Phemonena, 1825) by Aochi Rinsō and *Rigaku Teiyō* (Summary of Physical Science, 1852) by Hirose Genkyō were inspired by Kōkan's studies. Considering the level of development of natural science in Japan during Kōkan's time, it seems extraordinary that he could have produced *Tenchi Ridan*—the more so when one realizes that he completed his manuscript at the age of sixty-nine.

How successful was Kōkan in fulfilling his purposes in the study of natural science? Certainly he was eminently successful in realizing his primary aim of disseminating Western scientific knowledge, not only among the intelligentsia and scholars, but among interested people of all classes. His contemporary, Katayama Shōsai, asserted:

> There was an artist named Shiba Kōkan, who was also a scholar of Dutch studies. After devoting a great deal of time to the study of astronomy and natural science, he discovered a new theory of the earth's rotation expounded by a man named Copernicus. . . . Kōkan explained this theory in two books, *Oranda Tensetsu* and *Kopperu Temmon Zukai*. These books became very popular, and the people of our country learned for the first time of the earth-rotation theory.[69]

Kōkan's popularization of Western knowledge was accomplished not only through books but through personal contacts as well. His diaries record his tireless efforts to instruct nearly everyone he visited during his year's journey to Nagasaki on the principles of European art and science. *Shumparō Hikki,* as well, records lectures on science delivered before famous lords and other wealthy personages. A particularly revealing account describes Kōkan's interview with the lord of Kishū (present-day Wakayama prefecture):

> Once I was summoned to wait upon the lord of Kishū. His attendants informed me: "Please understand that this is not an audience with the Lord High Councilor. You will converse with us, and His Lordship will, if he chooses, overhear the conversation at a suitable distance." I signified my acquiescence respectfully and went to fetch the charts I had recently made of the celestial and terrestrial globes; these I presented before His Lordship with a deep bow. Thereupon, he said to me: "Kōkan, this is the first time we have met, but I have heard your name many times before." I then explained my celestial and terrestrial globes to the attendants. Presently, His Highness interjected: "I myself have possessed a globe and celestial sphere for some time; please bring yours closer so that I may examine them while you explain the details." I brought them to him and said: "In Japan, no one but myself understands the theory of earth rotation, and therefore, I have made a celestial chart[70] showing the revolutions of the planets." . . . After

discussing astronomy, I painted for him, executing a picture of Wakanoura and several other landscapes. When I had displayed my various talents, I withdrew to a respectful distance. His Lordship, turning to his attendants, remarked: "Seldom have I passed so instructive a day."

I later heard that His Lordship had for many years been interested in astronomy and used to question Mr. Yoshida, Yamaji Saisuke, and others who worked at the astronomical observatory. But they could never answer his questions on astronomy because they were merely low-ranking officials thrown into a panic at appearing before so exalted a personage; even if they had been able, after frantic cogitation, to formulate some kind of answer, they could never have summoned up enough courage to open their mouths before him. Furthermore, their function was to calculate calendars, and they really knew nothing about natural science; rather than answering his questions, they pulled in their necks, bit their tongues, and slunk away. His Lordship has no use for that sort of man. I, on the other hand, was not in the least afraid to speak with His Lordship. In my profession I am quite accustomed to appearing before noblemen; I therefore spoke with him just as I would with one of my colleagues, giving a discourse on the heavens such as has not been heard since the days of Ch'in Fu.[71] His Lordship was eager to have me enter his service, but I was already advanced in years at that time and had managed all my life never to enter another man's employ. I therefore told him that I preferred to keep my remaining powers of mind and body at my own disposition for my own purposes, and I refused his request.[72]

Almost every action of Kōkan's life was devoted to didactic purposes. As a measure of his dedication, all but two of his books on science (*Yochi Ryakusetsu* and *Ryōjusen Zusetsu*) were published by the author, probably at his own expense, under the publishing house name Shumparō Zōkoku. This would suggest that Kōkan continued to earn his livelihood primarily by the sale of his art and that remuneration received from his books was of secondary importance. Certainly, financial gain was never his aim in publishing works on science; rather, his motivation was to expand the intellectual horizons of his countrymen.

His claim that he was the first to introduce the heliocentric theory to Japan was justified. It was hard enough to understand the theory unassisted, more difficult still to render it intelligible to readers completely untrained in mathematics and the scientific tradition. Kōkan, moreover, used his newly acquired knowledge to challenge antiquated beliefs, such as the Buddhist explanation of the cosmos.

Many other scholars derived information from him. Satō Nobuhiro, for example, wrote at the end of his *Rangaku Daidōhen* (Compilation of Dutch Scholarship) that his book was no more than a digest of Kōkan's *Oranda Tensetsu*.[73]

On the other hand, Kōkan was not universally admired by all his contemporaries. One indication of his status is found in a mock playbill composed in 1796 at a party given for scholars of Western learning at the Shirandō, Ōtsuki Gentaku's school of Dutch language. The purpose of the party was to celebrate the Dutch New Year, a practice begun in 1794,[74] and continued thereafter for the next forty-four years, until 1837. Kōkan apparently never attended these festivities. For amusement, the guests compiled a fanciful playbill parodying the current offering at the Kabuki theater on the theme of the famous Soga vendetta. Entitled "The Flourishing Soga Brothers of Dutch Learning," the playbill listed scholars concerned with Western studies throughout the country, assigning to each a part, developed in some cases by additional comments. Two descriptions made Kōkan's role clear:

Monkey Boy: the peddler of foreign pictures

Arrogant Fabricator: the hawker of copperplates

Disparaging as these comments appear, however, it must be considered that they were written in a party atmosphere where sakè flowed and high spirits quite naturally inspired humor and sarcasm. Kōkan's own lack of tact when referring to the activities of his contemporaries was legend; certainly in the atmosphere of revelry, the absent Kōkan provided an ideal target for lampoons. Further, it must be noted that most of the men listed, probably unfamiliar to the majority of guests, received no comments whatever. Kōkan was known to all, and to some he no doubt appeared an enviable figure. At the same party the guests also composed a chart listing scholars under signs of the zodiac and other Western symbols; to Kōkan was assigned "Day and Night," an allusion to his painting during the day and studying the stars at night. Three years later, in 1799, at another such New Year's party, his name was prominent in a mock program of sumo wrestlers as contender number six, opposing the eminent scholar of Western science, Matsubara Uchū.[75] A man of Kōkan's outspoken personality and energetic productivity inevitably became a focus of attention; whatever his personal reputation, his accomplishments could not fail to elicit response.

Certainly Kōkan's place in the world of scholarship is open to dispute. He made mistakes, inevitable in an age of misconceptions concerning Western learning, and it might be said that he yielded too often to a penchant for ostentation, an overwhelming desire to display his learning. This foible often caused his activities to suggest dilettantism rather than a sincere desire to impart knowledge. His reluctance to associate himself with the ruling class did not stem from any lack of desire for official recognition, nor from disinterest in personal advancement or fame; his writings reveal that he had more than his share of ambition, which never was completely satisfied or achieved. Frustration was at least in part responsible for his ostentatious and sometimes contentious display of learning. His restlessness caused him to move from one project to another with extraordinary alacrity. His ego and self-absorption left little room for praise of the activities of others. Even those to whom he owed the greatest debts for assistance in acquiring knowledge of Western scholarship were not immune to his criticisms, evidenced, for example, in his comments previously noted concerning Hiraga Gennai's search for precious metals.

In his criticisms of others, as well as in all phases of his own activity, his approach always was motivated by practical considerations. Even as an artist his obsession with technique and a "true representation of reality" was inspired by the belief that the aims of art were best realized through a precise transcription of visual appearance. Though philosophy occupied his thoughts in his last years, here too his views were pragmatically oriented.

It would be too simple, with the easy infallibility of hindsight, to criticize Kōkan for failing to recognize the importance and potential of the electrical generator; if his foresight was limited, his indignation and impatience with "curiosities" reveal his seriousness of purpose and pragmatism:

> When Gennai went to Nagasaki he obtained a book the Dutch had presented to the shogunate. It had been sent back to Nagasaki as useless, and abandoned in the interpreter's house, getting more and more damaged, until Gennai discovered it and brought it back to Edo. After several days of careful study, he completely mastered the subject, which was the machine we now call the "electer." Daimyo and lesser lords were deeply impressed by his creation and Gennai became a hero. But the electer could do nothing but make bits of paper jump into the air and send sparks flying. It had no practical use whatever for humans. He also had something called a "glass jar," but I am not sure what that is supposed to do. Others were brought from Holland after Gen-

nai's death and exhibited as curiosities, even quite uneducated people coming to look at them.[76]

Pragmatism was at the root of all his criticisms, and more often than not, his targets merited his displeasure. One practice he particularly opposed was the writing of texts in *kambun,* that is, Chinese style—a dislike shared by many of his enlightened contemporaries. Books, he asserted, were written to impart knowledge; to conceal ideas within an obscure writing system known only to a few scholars was to him the epitome of deceit and ostentation:

> The characters we use in our writing are Chinese, and the ancient sages were all from China. In olden times, Japanese could not read Chinese books and knew nothing of their contents. As they began to study Chinese books, they shifted their interest from what the books said to the style in which they said it. Then everyone began writing various things in Chinese. This practice is a great mistake. Even among people who dislike writing and cannot read Chinese, one may find a person having the wisdom of a sage. One should always write in Japanese, which will prove beneficial both to the author and his readers.
>
> Ōtsuki Gentaku is a surgeon for the lord of Sendai, and also a famous scholar of Dutch learning. Recently he wrote a book on the origin of tobacco—and wrote it all in *kambun!*[77] Now, tobacco is a product enjoyed largely by the lower classes, and his book, therefore, was widely ridiculed. There is also a recluse priest of Higashimori in Kyoto named Entsū who wrote a book called *Bukkoku Rekishōhen* [The Buddhist Calendar].[78] In his book he confirmed the Buddhist doctrine of Mount Sumeru and denied that the world is round.[79] He quoted many books and wrote his entire text in *kambun,* for no other reason than to intimidate those who cannot read the Chinese style.
>
> Even among learned men there are some who do not understand the importance of what I say here.[80]

Kōkan unquestionably occupied a unique place in his culture, and has, in fact, been labeled "one of the great thinkers of our country."[81] The *rangaku* scholars, as advocates of progress, were critical of their age, but none showed himself as markedly individual as Kōkan. Though his extremely logical view of the world was shared by many contemporaries, no one member of the group of *rangakusha* listed by Ōtsuki Gentaku in his book *Rangaku Kaitei* (Ladder to Dutch Studies) was as truly progressive in nature as Kōkan. In character, Gentaku and Kōkan seem almost diametrically opposed. Gentaku was an academician, a member of officialdom who enjoyed a brilliant career. Kōkan never accepted office. Gentaku belonged to the orthodox school of Dutch studies.

It may seem paradoxical to speak of "orthodoxy" when dealing with so unorthodox a school of learning, but Gentaku's actions differed little from those of the head of a traditional Confucian establishment, and he strongly advocated government control of *rangaku.* His foreign books and his translations were reserved for a select group of scholars, and he evinced no interest in disseminating knowledge to the Japanese people as a whole.

Kōkan, on the other hand, remained aloof from the clique of dedicated Edo scholars. His books, from the first geography, were unadorned by literary flourishes and published for general circulation; he rejected *kambun* because it was beyond the comprehension of all but well-educated men. He wrote for the general public in a direct, agreeable style, published his books "until the woodblocks wore out,"[82] and then made more. He worked actively and constructively, persisting in his endeavors until his views were accepted as truth by the most progressive men of his age.

CHAPTER NINE

SAGE

In 1809, Kōkan published his last book and dedicated his last votive offering. Writings after that time were not intended for publication and appeared only posthumously. They are notebooks of miscellaneous information and random thoughts, jotted down with little attempt at organization.

During his retirement years he increasingly devoted his energies to religious and philosophical questions. In light of his general interest in European achievements, it might be expected that he would have looked more closely than he did at religious and philosophical systems of the West. In these areas, however, he was sharply restricted by government censorship, for official attitude held that all Western philosophical views represented a threat to the political balance based on the Confucian moral order that had so long provided "peace in our time." Although to extremists, all Western scholarship was considered an insidious instrument of Christianity, to more liberal political leaders, only the religious and philosophical systems of the West presented a threat to national stability, and Western technology was thought at least harmless, if not actually beneficial to Japan, posing no threat in itself to the stability of the nation. The Confucian scholar and historian Arai Hakuseki had early distinguished Western techniques and science from Western religious thought, insisting that the one could be exploited while the other was controlled. Europeans, he had asserted, excel in the concrete, not the abstract. This attitude, generally accepted by Japanese, was naturally adopted by Kōkan, who, in his late years, might well have uttered the famous slogan of Sakuma Shōzan: "Eastern ethics and Western science."

The sharp distinction between Western technology and philosophy resulted in a neglect not only of specifically religious doctrines but of Western achievements in philosophy and in social and political science as well. It is true that Kōkan did consider briefly the question of whether Western religious thought might complement the scientific knowledge of Europe, but the scant information available to him made his investigation necessarily superficial. He was aware of certain Old Testament stories, and in his writings mentioned Adam and Eve, Cain and Abel, Noah and the Flood.[1] He discussed the Christian concept of heaven, which he equated with the Buddhist paradise:

> According to Christian teaching, in the beginning there was Chaos, and from the Chaos of the Universe God created the earth, sun, and moon, and then produced human beings. In later days people began to suffer from their own avarice and desire. Then God pitied them and let them come into his paradise, which provides comfort and happiness. One need not be discouraged in the face of many tribulations, persecutions, or condemnations, for this is but a transient world. At the time of death, one will be born again into a world of comfort, and thanks to God's mercy, men will be immortal as long as God exists. This is the philosophy of Christianity. It is similar to the Buddha's teaching of Mount Sumeru, or to paradise and hell.[2]

Unaware of the more ancient heritage of Buddhism, Kōkan concluded that Christianity, transmitted to the Far East by Sakyamuni, provided the basis for Buddhist doctrines.[3] He dismissed the Christian faith as of no real value to Japan; the West, for all its accouterments of science and art, appeared to offer no more for the enrichment of the Japanese spirit than did Buddhism.

With the exception of Zen, Kōkan rejected categorically the teachings of traditional Buddhism. Scorning both popular superstitions and religious doctrines, he saw the Buddhist belief in an afterworld merely as a method to lead the ignorant along paths of moral righteousness. For the priests who taught these doctrines, and for the malpractices of the clergy in general, he had only contempt:

> Buddhism is a heterodox Indian religion foreign to Japan. It is not suited to our Land of the Gods, and we have delayed too long in prohibiting it.[4]

> Man fears death and wants to live longer even when he has reached an advanced age. This is a common desire among all living things, but there is no elixir of life. Even when it is explained to them, women and ignorant men never can understand this fact. Therefore, they are told that they will go to paradise after death, and that because of their sins while alive they are living in a world of hell. This concept is taught according to a theory of transmigration, which claims that those who did evil in a previous life are born into lowly, poor families or suffer malignant diseases in the present life. Hardships in the present life must be suffered in atonement for evil done in a past life, and should be endured without complaint. If, as the result of suffering in the present life, one performs new evils, he will be reborn in the next life as an ox, and his hardships will increase the more. This teaching is only an expedient used to guide the common man.
>
> Spiritual awakening is a true realization that one comes forth from nothingness and will return to nothingness—that there is neither birth nor death. In the West, priests are government officers whose function is to guide the ignorant masses. In Japan, priests strive solely for their own awakening, and those who achieve even that are very few indeed. Almost none of them is without worldly desires; most are unenlightened. They are a useless and idle lot, not included among any of the classes—warriors, farmers, artisans, or merchants. They have no occupations other than looking after their temples and conducting funeral services.[5]

Most frequently, Kōkan leveled his attack against the inflexible doctrines and outmoded methods of Buddhist scientific investigation:

Buddhist priests who believe in Mount Sumeru[6] know nothing whatever about the order or the movements of the planets and have no conception of the causes of solar and lunar eclipses. Their explanations of these things are sheer nonsense, but Japanese people are deluded simply because they are so accustomed to hearing Buddhist teachings. In Europe, on the other hand, a sound knowledge of the heavens is basic to all scholarship.[7]

Nor was neo-Confucianism, the foundation of the Tokugawa social order, immune to Kōkan's criticism. Basically, he accepted the Confucian ethical code and believed firmly in the established class system as a logical and harmonious whole. Though he advocated no radical change, he attacked the misuse of power within that system and registered his indignation with the injustices of a rigidly stratified society that prevented men of ability from achieving their goals. His chief concern was with closing the gap between the professed Confucian moral order and existing transgressions:

> A genius born into a farmer or merchant family can never realize his talent and it will be wasted. Even a fool born in the nobility or into a warrior family will prosper and appear intelligent.[8]

> Men who govern the country should cease luxurious living, should economize, give aid to the poor, and encourage farming. If they did, all people would benefit. Those who have all the necessities of life but fail to help others are the real criminals.[9]

> Some time ago when I visited Iwakuni . . . I saw a young girl of five or six who was carrying a three-year-old child on her back. I was told that the children had been abandoned by their parents and had no relatives. They had a place to live, but had to wander about begging for table scraps. Such unfortunates as these ought to be aided by the local rulers. Although I was told that the lord of that province was a wise and learned man, his mercy certainly did not extend to helping those children. Many people in our country have the notion that anyone who appreciates Chinese things and has refined tastes is a true scholar and gentleman, but I say that such standards are absurd.[10]

For Confucian scientific practices Kōkan has as little sympathy as for Buddhist methodology:

> Recently, Confucianists have been writing absurd things about science. Not one among them has any real knowledge of the subject. The things that those "Scholars" claim are all fallacious, and the only scholars are Westerners. Yet befuddled Confucianists are so numerous that no one can say any more how many of them there are. If these uninformed "scholars" are so numerous, one can imagine the ignorance of the common man in Japan! If one does not understand natural science, how can one pretend to know anything else![11]

Toward the native religion of Shinto Kōkan adopted a more favorable view: "Ours is the Land of the Gods, and there should be no other creed here but Shinto."[12] His writings, however, nowhere reveal that he found in the teachings of that faith anything of specific value.

Though he frequently chastised verbally the priests of the Zen sect for their worldly concerns with rank, fame, and wealth,[13] and though he cautioned others to avoid Zen practices until late in life, he himself, as will be seen, at last turned to Zen for self-awakening. The Chinese religio-philosophy of Taoism, analogous to Zen in many ways, also inspired him, and the journals of his late years are filled with references to the Taoist sages. The scientific studies so optimistically pursued in earlier life lent credence to his philosophical conclusions. Interest in geography had awakened him to the vastness of the earth; European astronomy had revealed the smallness of this planet within the universe. The more he speculated on the insignificance of the individual, the less he viewed man in terms of worldly accomplishments. He concluded finally that all men—rich and poor, good and bad, high born and low, intelligent and ignorant—devote their lives to striving, and all arrive at the same final void. Here he recognized the seeds of Taoism and gradually cultivated his appreciation of that philosophy.

At the bottom of a hanging scroll executed in 1809, Kōkan drew a peach, two chestnuts, and a globe, symbols of the three chief influences in his life at that time.[14] The peach was a Chinese Taoist symbol of immortality; the chestnut, significant for its simple, rough exterior with kernel inside, was associated with Zen Buddhism; the globe denoted European science. The signature, Dōjin, a name he was to use for the remainder of his life, signified "one who follows the Way," that is, the Way of a Taoist.

Most of the scroll is devoted to a lengthy inscription covering a range of Kōkan's philosophical views. The same comments are included in the opening paragraphs of *Dokushō Bōgen* (Self-laughter and Reckless Remarks), a text Kōkan completed one year earlier:

> Man is foremost among all living things on earth. Although the ox and the elephant are greater in size, they lack the one great treasure of human beings—wisdom. A man born with little natural intelligence, however, can never achieve great wisdom no matter how assiduously he may strive for it. Such a man may attempt to gain wisdom by reading books and studying the ways of the ancient sages, but all his efforts will be in vain. If he is not favored with innate intelligence, he must learn to govern his activities according to his own capabilities.
>
> Anyone who has studied astronomy and geography can look into the heavens and feel the vastness of the universe; the earth by comparison seems but a tiny grain of millet. Men who dwell upon this minute, revolving world are like microscopic particles of dust. A person who fails to realize his insignificance, who presumes to consider himself great, simply demonstrates how very little he knows of the world.
>
> The life of a man passes in a twinkling. Life is a running white horse seen through a chink in a door. Man's existence is but a dream, or, as the poet Saigyō[15] wrote, "one night's lodging at an inn, dreaming dreams within a transient world of dreams." It is a dream seen in half sleep—restless, seldom at peace, fraught with countless dangers and surprises.
>
> In the course of a year there may be five or six beautiful days of happiness, never more than ten. The other days bring wind, rain, heat, cold, or clouds—changes as numerous as the griefs men endure.
>
> Our eyes see a range of colors, our ears hear things that delight or anger. These senses that permit us to see and hear are nerves like oil in man's body. Nerves are present not only in man, but in all living things, from man to the smallest insect.
>
> The life of a gnat expires in two hours. For a cicada life lasts eighty or ninety days, from summer to autumn; the following year when summer returns, a new cicada thinks he has found a newly created universe. Man sees the changes of the seasons and the revolutions of the stars many times, but if he thinks because of that he is a great being, he is only a fool.
>
> Ten thousand years from now this earth will decline, and the empires of Japan, China, and India will fall to ruin, just as we know of the earth's former changes from shell fossils found in the mountains. Meanwhile, there will be wars, for men will always fight with one another. Even during times of peace men will fight each other for fame and fortune, those with higher intelligence rising to the top, those less endowed falling to a lower status.
>
> Viewed from heaven, mankind appears without rank or distinction. Today's no-

bility, however, are heirs of clever and intelligent ancestors. The foolish man can survive in times of peace but will be destroyed in wartime. The intelligent man has courage; his intelligence is congenital and is a gift from heaven inherited through his ancestors—the only way it can be obtained. Therefore, if you would achieve a happy life, never desire more than your intelligence is capable of encompassing. This is the moral way of life, difficult indeed for a young man to understand. Many an old man as well, though he may grasp the general principle, never achieves complete comprehension. Try your utmost to understand.[16]

In an analogy between man and the ant, Kōkan goes on to lament man's limited capacity to comprehend his universe:

> All creatures on earth, even the tiniest insect, have nerves, ears, eyes, and limbs just as humans have. The ant is like the most able of men in his intelligence and courage. In summer, crowds of ants emerge from their holes and walk ten, twenty, or thirty yards—perhaps even farther than a hundred yards. They plan how to obtain food, which they store up in their holes for use during the winter months. . . . An anthill is built by the concerted efforts of tens of thousands of ants. It is like a castle or a building many stories high and has an exquisite form. Ants may indeed be cleverer than men. . . .
>
> Among the world of ants there was once a great sage who was known as Priest Ant. He might be likened to Confucius or Buddha in the world of men. He was cognizant of the infinite universe and the vastness of the earth. Because he possessed great knowledge and did no evil, he was respected and worshiped as a saint.
>
> One fine day when the wind was still, Saint Ant gave a sermon to his 3,300 billion ant believers. . . .
>
> "There is above us another stratum known as the human world. In that stratum lives a creature called man, who is similar to us, having limbs, a nose, and eyes. His life span is 100 billion ant years, and his height 26,352 ant miles. . . .
>
> "Man considers heaven, earth, and human beings the three powers in the universe. . . . [Here, Kōkan describes the earth, sun, moon, planets, and stars, and explains the Copernican theory.] The vastness and height of the stars are beyond human knowledge. The stars in the heavens are like the sun. . . . The greatness and boundlessness of the heavens are wonderful and scarcely comprehensible to human beings, much less to tiny ants."
>
> When the sermon ended, every one of the listening ants, wise and dull alike, burst into laughter at their leader's words.
>
> The worm in a peach is a peach worm,
> The worm in a chestnut a chestnut worm,
> The worm that lives on the earth is man.
> World worms, from the noble on down, eat, copulate, and crepitate.[17]

A recurrent theme in Kōkan's late writings is that the cosmos is made up of two basic elements—fire and water—through whose interaction all things are created, sustained, and transformed:

> The Dutch book *Groot Historie* contains an account of the beginnings of the world. Before heaven and earth were separated there were no men and we therefore have no means of actually knowing what existed. We can only guess, and it is such guesses that the Dutch book contains. In the beginning the wheel of the sun appeared in the sky, and the essence of the sun produced the essence of water, which became solid and turned into this earth. . . .
>
> Man is made of water. When fire is applied to water it becomes hot, and this brings about life. The essence of the sun is fire. When the sun's essence mixed with water it formed earth's essence, which the

Dutch call "thin water" or "air." Man, breathing this air, sustains life. Just as man breathes "thin water," fish breathe thick or undiluted water. It is the air that preserves the fire in man's body; it is food for the body just as kindling provides fuel for a fire. This is the reason man is a living being. Death is like a fire whose kindling is exhausted and whose flame dies; at the time of death, the fire in the body returns to the heavens. The phenomenon is the same, whether the person be great or humble.[18]

Kōkan's theory, though not indicating a direct cross-cultural influence, is reminiscent of that of the Greek philosopher Heraclitus, who "visualized the world not as an edifice, but rather as one colossal process; not as the sum total of all *things*, but rather as the totality of all events, or changes, or *facts*":

> In the case of Heraclitus, the emphasis upon change leads him to the theory that all material things, whether solid, liquid, or gaseous, are like flames—that they are processes rather than things, and that they are all transformations of fire; the apparently solid earth (which consists of ashes) is only a fire in a state of transformation, and even liquids (water, sea) are transformed fire (and may become fuel, perhaps in the form of oil). "The first transformation of fire is the sea; but of the sea, half is earth and half hot air." Thus all the other "elements"—earth, water, and air—are transformed fire.[19]

Hiraga Gennai also wrote of the primary function of fire as "the source of all creation," asserting that "fire, water, earth, and air fill all the space between heaven and earth."[20] Another scholar, Tominaga Nakamoto, claimed that the Buddhist theory of Four Elements was ultimately of Western origin, presumably Aristotelian.[21] The important difference between Kōkan's theory and those of Gennai and Nakamoto is that Kōkan reduced the basic components of the universe from four to two.

The fundamental structure of his thinking, however, is little more than a logical revision of traditional Eastern beliefs. Japanese Shintoists, realizing the primal nature of fire, had made the sun their chief goddess, Amaterasu, and Buddhists too identified their central deity, Dainichi, with the sun, source and sustenance of life. Moreover, the concept of two primal forces, yin and yang, is a major element in Chinese cosmology going back to the *I-ching,* one of the five Confucian classics. Yang denotes fire, heaven, sun, heat, dominance, male; yin refers to water, earth, the moon, cold, sustaining, female. As each force reaches its extreme it produces its opposite, and the two continue to succeed each other in a never-ending cycle. Yin-yang ideas were adopted by Han Confucianists, and Kōkan's philosophy reflects the writings of the Early-Han-dynasty philosopher Huai-nan Tzŭ:

> The hot force of the accumulated yang produced fire and the essence of the fire force became the sun; the cold force of the accumulated yin became water and the essence of the water force became the moon. The essence of the excess force of the sun and moon became the stars and planets. Heaven received the sun, moon, and stars, while earth received water and soil.
>
> Heaven is said to be round and earth rectilinear. Round things are bright, and brightness gives off energy; fire, therefore, is an expanding element. Dark things absorb energy, making water a contracting element. Fire the giver, water the receiver; through interaction, the active element gives, and the passive is transformed.[22]

Huai-nan Tzŭ's explanation of the creation was used as a preface to the earliest national history of Japan, the *Nihongi.* Kōkan read the account in *Huai-nan Tzŭ T'ien Wên Hsün* (Huai-nan Tzŭ's Explanation of the Cosmos), a book he referred to frequently in his *Mugon Dōjin Hikki.*

The document most revealing of Kōkan's life, criticisms, and philosophy is *Shumparō*

Hikki, completed in November of 1811. The text, already quoted extensively, includes comments on natural science, art, events of Kōkan's day, poems and tales that struck his fancy, remembrances of past events, advice to younger men, and his thoughts on the meaning of life. He continues to inveigh against the Buddhist clergy, and expresses disillusionment with the policy that had kept the nation closed to the outside world. In general, however, the book is not one of social protest. Kōkan explains:

> Now that I am an old man living in retirement, I no longer take pleasure in the ways of men nor find them of interest. I am writing down my thoughts at random, just as they occur to me. Men of future generations who share my feelings and may have occasion to read my works will understand.[23]

Much of the book's appeal lies in its random scattering of incidental notation. Among the miscellany, for example, Kōkan discusses the smoking of tobacco, and offers his own Draconian method for breaking the habit:

> The first time a person smokes he feels dizzy because there is nicotine in the smoke of tobacco. If a bird or insect were to eat this nicotine inadvertently, it would die immediately; you can see from this how strong tobacco poison really is. . . . It is claimed that bean curd is an effective antidote for tobacco poison, and if you eat bean curd you will not suffer any ill effects from smoking. I don't really believe, however, that eating bean curd would prove sufficient to counteract the ill effects of smoking. You had better give up smoking entirely if you don't want to get sick. . . . One good way to abolish smoking would be to enforce the following law: from now on, all men are forbidden to smoke, and anyone caught selling smoking equipment is to be punished severely. If a boy smokes, his parents must kill him without delay. Were the government to promulgate such a law, within thirty years there would not be a single smoker left.[24]

Kōkan's view of man's insignificance is expressed often in *Shumparō Hikki.* In a section entitled "Things I Regret," he admits:

> I had a passionate longing for fame and wealth; in pursuing these two things I squandered many years of my life. Now I see that if a famous person commits the slightest indiscretion, the whole world immediately knows, whereas if an obscure person does the same thing, no one hears about it. I realize what a mistake fame is, and wish I had never pursued it. What does it all really amount to? Heaven and earth will go on forever. One may succeed in being famous for a few centuries, but what is that set against ten, a hundred thousand years? All the ambitions and strivings of my youth were vain.[25]

Equally basic to his thinking, however, was his conviction that, given man's condition, striving was natural and even desirable:

> As a youth approaches manhood, he becomes increasingly ambitious to excel and never lag behind others. This is a natural result of man's interest in fame and fortune. A few people, it is true, have no interest in such material gains but take refuge in high mountains in order to escape the din and bustle of this world. They are not, however, truly enlightened, but simply prefer seclusion. . . . If you have some natural talent, use it for the betterment of the world. Benefit both your country and yourself; by so doing you eventually will establish your fame, which will be remembered by later generations.[26]

The aging Kōkan, caught between these two beliefs, attempted a reconciliation by dividing the span of man's life into two distinct stages:

> Enlightenment as realized through Zen philosophy is a true understanding that

> all creation begins and ends in nothingness. This doctrine, however, is far too difficult for the average man to understand. If you truly wish to comprehend it, you should not make the attempt until you are over sixty. Were you to learn it in your prime, your life would be worthless and you could accomplish nothing.[27]

The solution he stresses most frequently is moderation, a basic tenet of Confucian doctrine:

> I believe that people bring about their own destruction by attempting to accomplish more than they are capable of. . . . Understand the limit of your capabilities. If you can work and earn profit, do it; if you can become famous, do all you can to achieve fame. But know your limits and do not attempt that which is impossible for you. Do not overindulge. That which you like, do not like too much. In all things be moderate; the middle way is the best way.[28]

One of the reasons Kōkan gives for the evils of his society is that "there has never been a tradition of scientific investigation in Japan or China, and that is why Japanese people are ignorant."[29] He continues:

> We Japanese have no proclivity for scientific investigation. We concern ourselves with the writing of fine, elegant phrases in an attempt to appear cultured, though what we say has no bearing on reality. We have the minds of women. All women are confused, believe anything, and have no sense of fact.[30]

Lack of scientific tradition was due, he felt, to the relatively short time that had elapsed since the civilization of Japan, a notion he repeated many times in his writings.[31] The assertion of the superiority of Europe based on her more ancient culture was made not only by Kōkan, but by Honda Toshiaki and many other scholars of Dutch learning. Keene has pointed out:

> The early *rangaku* scholars had demonstrated that Dutch learning was of value. Later men had disputed China's claims of being the centre of the world, and by Honda's time there were some who elevated Europe to the position of Japan's model in all things. But before an examination of the intrinsic superiority of Western achievements might be undertaken, it was necessary for the friends of European civilization to prove the great pedigree of the Western nations. In so doing they afforded an interesting parallel to those of their European equivalents who wrote admiringly of the timeless antiquity of China. Timelessness, however, was not the point emphasised by these lovers of European science and precision; most sought to state exactly how much older Europe actually was. "Which of the nations of the world was first to become civilised?" asked Honda, and himself replied that it was Egypt, whose civilization dated back over 6,000 years. China, he added, was only about 3,800 years old, while Japan could boast of a mere 1,500 years since the Emperor Jimmu founded the country. He therefore concluded that it was only to be expected that young nations like China and Japan failed to exhibit the same perfection in their institutions that Europe had long ago attained.[32]

In lamenting the inadequacies of his country, Kōkan often reveals a remarkably progressive attitude:

> Because the civilization of Japan is so recent, Japanese are very superficial in their knowledge. In *Ika Kinkan* [Casebook for Medical Practitioners] and in a Western book the method of vaccination is described. When this method is employed, deaths do not occur, there are no scars on the face, and no incurable disease results. When an epidemic breaks out, those who have a large quantity of the poison in their bodies die. But even those born with large quantities of the poison in their systems can lessen it by vaccination, which must be given twice. If the poison is not lessened in this way, at the

time of an epidemic the person will die. Even a congenitally weak person should not avoid vaccination. Some relatives of mine have a small child. I told them about inoculation, but they would not consent because they said it was like asking for the disease. I insisted it was foolish to avoid such a slight discomfort, finally managed to have the child vaccinated, and he quickly recovered from his illness.[33]

Another reason for Japan's backwardness, Kōkan asserts, was that the country had been closed too long to outside influences:

Our country is not sufficiently civilized and the people take no interest in science. They are concerned only with their own small lives and want to live in peace, never considering the fate of their descendants. Recently I went to Bōshū province to see the peach blossoms, and while there I noticed a dog by the roadside who was suffering from some peculiar illness: he was eating his own legs and couldn't walk. Japan has been a closed country for such a long time that we know nothing about medical science.[34]

Japan was nearing the end of an era. Political and social reforms were needed, and Kōkan asserted prophetically:

The products of Japan are insufficient to fulfill the needs of all individuals. People, finding their desires frustrated and hopes futile, turn instead to idle pursuits and frivolous amusements. In the end, all this is bound to lead to great trouble for our nation. The signs already are apparent. As pleasure seeking becomes the goal of the people, the poor become poorer and their lives more wretched. Eventually there will be an internal uprising in the nation, and when that happens foreign nations will take that opportunity to invade us. Before we know it we are going to be involved in serious trouble.[35]

To his notes he confides his belief that it would be of great benefit to Japan to foster interchange with foreign nations through trade:

Huai-nan Tzŭ wrote: "One does not sell firewood in a forest or vend fish by a lake. That is because there is more than enough on the spot."

Japanese rice cannot be found in other countries. If we were to load big ships with rice and sell it to Russia and elsewhere, we would benefit by obtaining goods from other lands, such as medicines and valuable manufactures, that we do not possess here.[36]

In recent years the price of rice has become so cheap that warriors no longer realize any profit from it. Anyone who still believes that we should not trade it in Russia is a fool. . . .

The lord of Shirakawa[37] is a very clever and intelligent man, but he still has something to learn about geography. Nagasaki is a thousand miles from Russia, whereas if Ezo [Hokkaido] were opened for trade, that area would develop naturally. Furthermore, I see no reason for all this fear of Christianity. . . . Even if the Russians were to propagate their religion in Japan, no one would be likely to believe it.[38]

Had these statements been published during his life, Kōkan might well have found himself explaining such views to government authorities. But he was not one to seek out trouble deliberately and entrusted his most controversial thoughts to his private journals.

Kōkan had long planned to spend his last years in Kyoto.[39] In the spring of 1812, he put up for sale his house in Shinsenza, Edo, and left the city that had been his home for sixty-five years. Upon his departure on April 1, he was given a farewell party at a restaurant in Shinagawa, Edo, and from there set out to visit the famous cherry-blossom area of Yoshino, omitted during his journey to Nagasaki. After three days spent enjoying the mountains and the trees in full bloom, he continued on to Nara, Osaka, Suma, and Maiko Beach. During his journey he kept a diary entitled *Yoshino Kikō* (Account of a Journey to Yoshino).[40] At Maiko the diary ends, with a promise to write later of his activities in Kyoto; unfortunately, no later record exists, but his *Mugon Dōjin Hikki,* completed in 1814, contains several references to his sojourn in Kyoto. This book and personal letters furnish information concerning Kōkan's strange and restless last years.

He arrived in Kyoto on May 11 and took lodging at an inn on Nijō Street, where he seems to have been relatively content:

> In the area where I lived in Kyoto the houses were so close one could hear people talking in the neighboring houses. I couldn't help noticing the soft gentle quality of their voices, particularly of women and children, and it was a great pleasure to hear them. At the time of this writing I am back in Edo, staying in the teahouse attached to Mr. Ōgawara's home. In the alley beyond the garden there is another house, and from it I can hear voices of other women and children. They come from some province near Edo, and their speech and the words they use are so vulgar I can scarcely bear hearing them.[41]

For a man of his years, he lived an active life, visiting friends, participating in a scholarly society,[42] and making trips into the mountains near Kyoto. A marginal note in *Saiyū Nikki* refers to these trips and shows that Kōkan was still as active and adventurous as ever.[43]

Although he at first enjoyed his popularity and many friends in Kyoto, life there eventually became too hectic, and before the end of 1812 he decided to return to Edo.[44] Another factor prompted this move: he received word that his relatives were spending the money he had entrusted with them.[45] Late in December he arrived in Edo and, finding that his house in Shinsenza had still not been sold, took up residence there again:

> Being old and weak and unable to work as in former days, I had to think how I might manage to live comfortably. Then an idea occured to me: there was a rather countrified man from Shinano named Sanai who used to visit me occasionally. . . . I told him about the money I was unable to collect and said that if he were successful in recovering it, I would entrust it all to him on condition that he provide for me until the end of my life. . . . He forced everyone to pay and managed to recover nearly all of the original sum. Then he lent the money out again at a high interest rate, built a small retreat for me, and paid me sufficient money to live on each month.
>
> Sanai's business practices, however, are certainly not ethically commendable. Personally, I feel that people from Shinano are basically boorish, even though they are usually very hard workers and show considerable integrity. Unlike Kyoto people, they are always doing something stupid. . . . The other day, for example, Sanai tried to mend a broken table leg only eight inches long by driving a four- or five-inch nail into it; the nail, of course, came out the other side. This one incident is indicative of his whole personality. He is an uncouth fool but, strangely enough, has tremendous perseverance in collecting his bills. He can collect money where the average man would be sure to fail.[46]

A man of Sanai's character, whatever financial assistance he gave Kōkan, must have provided unrewarding companionship. Kōkan's only confidant during his years of retirement appears to have been Yamane Kazuma, a member of the warrior class employed as a government official in Saga Han. He had lived in Edo for eight years, from 1803 to 1811, and it was probably during this period that Kōkan first made his acquaintance. In a series of letters,

Kōkan confided to him his thoughts and interests:

> There is no relief for mankind during his time on earth. The other day I attempted to write with a pen an essay entitled "Peace of Mind," but it was not easy and I gave it up. You and I share the same feelings, and I know that you too desire to live in peace; but so many things are happening everywhere that it becomes quite impossible to find relief from the complications of living.
>
> An old man made of wood and string,
> Skin like the cock's comb, bald like the crane;
> Fashioned in a moment, played with capriciously,
> Discarded, forgotten.
> This is man's life—the dream of an instant.
>
> I wrote down the above poem, drew a picture beneath it, and sent it to a friend.
>
> The fire burns,
> Knowing not whence it comes, where it goes;
> While it is burning
> We must do our best.
>
> A man who labors for his master, his wife, his children, or his brothers is unable to perceive the true meaning of life. One truly seeking perception would do well to become a Zen priest; but after one has mastered all passions and abstained from eating meat and fish, one still will have difficulty finding relief from this world short of death. Even priests doubt the veracity of their perception and feel they know the meaning of life only at the time of death. Other bonzes know nothing of Buddhahood, entertain self-doubt, lose their way among the many things of life, and are ignorant of true perception. . . . July 9, 1813.[47]

The painting mentioned in this letter is extant (Pl. 101), the two poems written above the illustration. The first poem was composed by the T'ang-dynasty poet Liang-huang,[48] the second presumably by Kōkan himself. The rooster is a symbol of success, literary spirit, courage, and fidelity; the crane, of longevity and immortality;[49] the puppet, of worldly success in this illusory existence. He stands before the crane, the vehicle of the Immortals, awaiting release from this world.

The painting is signed Mugon Dōjin. *Mugon* (no words) was inspired by Lao-tzŭ's doctrine of *mui* (inaction), more specifically by the phrase: *Iu mono wa shirazu; shiru mono wa iwazu* (Those who speak know nothing; those who know say nothing). From this phrase Kōkan also derived the name Fugen.[50] "Dōjin" signified "one who follows the Way of the Tao."

Weary of life, unable to find peace of mind, Kōkan left Shinsenza in August of 1813 and went to Kamakura. Despite his dislike of the Buddhist clergy, he became the disciple of the Zen priest Seisetsu at the Engaku-ji temple.

From Seisetsu he received the name Tōgen, derived from the Chinese proverb: "Though the peach and the apricot say nothing, men will beat tracks to them."[51] He also used the name Fugen Zenji (Zen teacher Fugen), indicating that he was assuming the role of a priest; the signature appears on a chant he composed entitled *Hōgo Mariuta* (A Buddhist Sermon Chanted to the Rhythm of a Child's Ball-bouncing Song), written in the spirit of Zen philosophy:

> If you ask where are the far-off corners of the world,
> You will be told China, India, or even Holland;
> But the earth is round like a dumpling kneaded with water.
> Do not ask whether Mount Sumeru is round or square,
> Like an insect it comes from the earth;
> Meditation, Perception, Enlightenment —all are useless.
> Smash the Buddhist images, warm your groins by the fire,

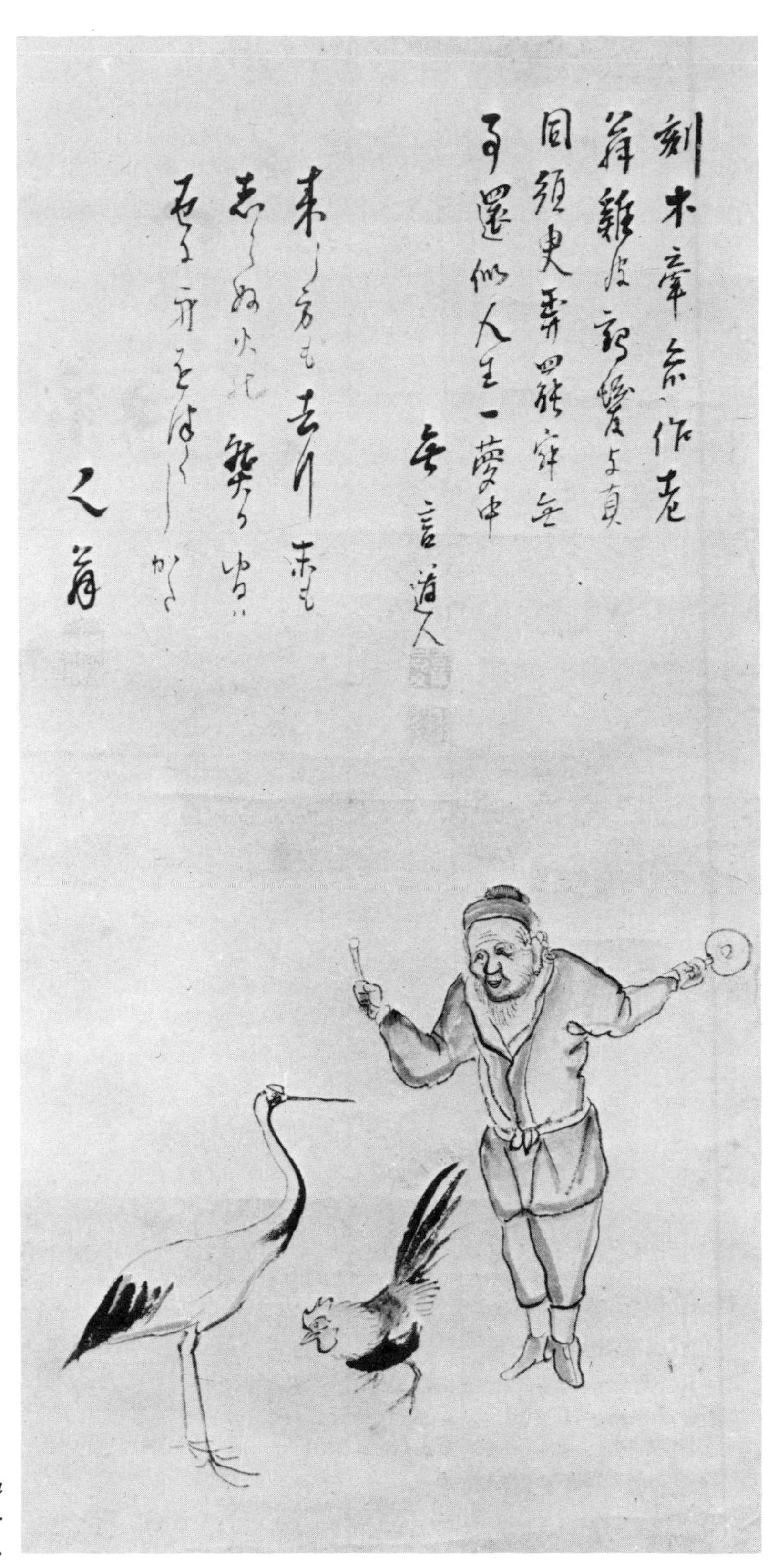

101. The Puppet. *Circa 1813. Color on paper. Courtesy Waseda University, Tokyo.*

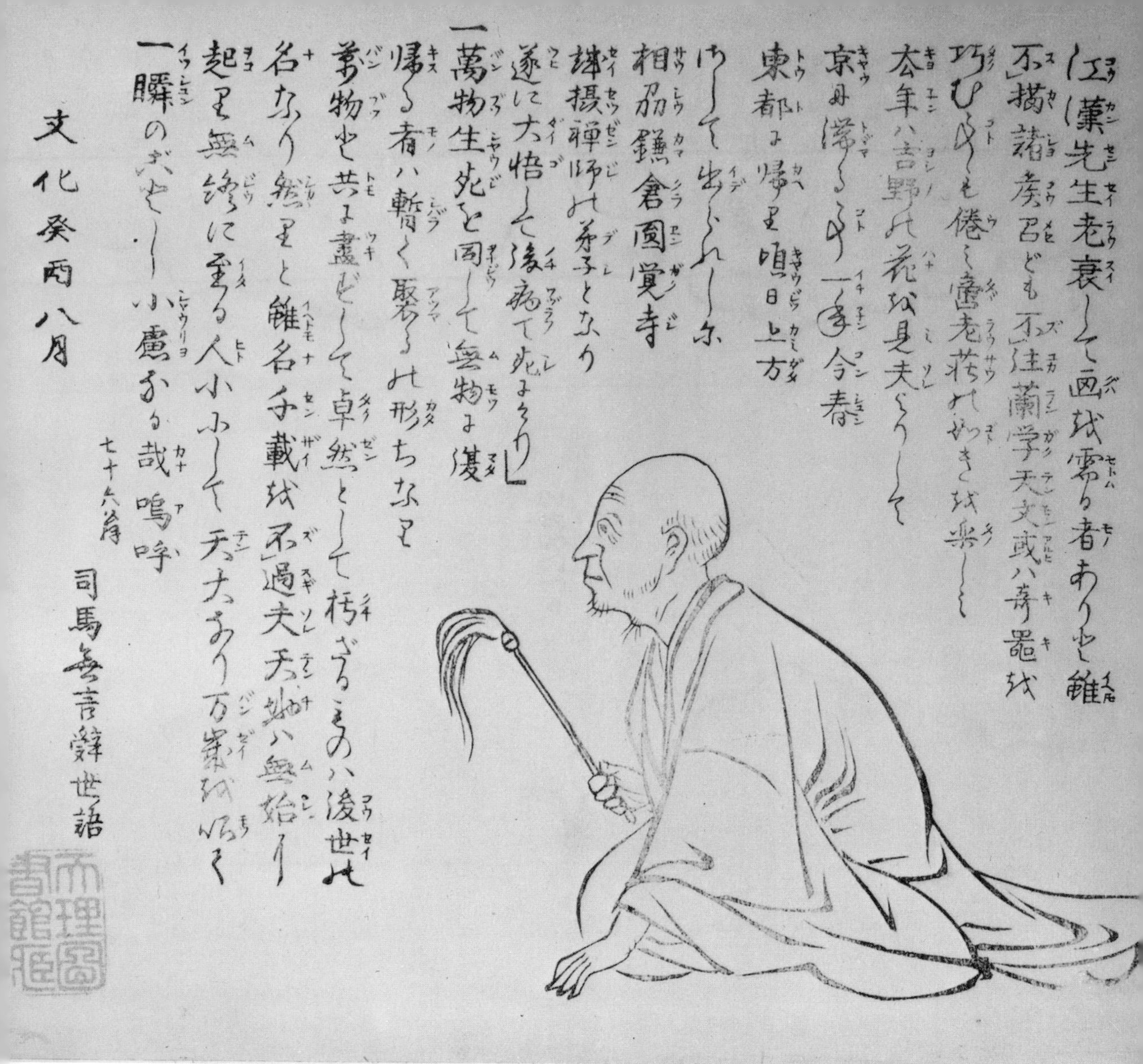

102. Obituary *(Jisei no Go). 1813. Woodblock print. Courtesy of the Tenri Library, Nara prefecture.*

In an instant Buddha's image will be ashes;
Let it be ashes—it should be so.
All things of this world have sprung from the earth.
And all must then return;
Knowing this is Buddhahood.[52]

Soon after he arrived in Kamakura, Kōkan wrote his own obituary, sketched a self-portrait on it, and sent copies to acquaintances throughout the country (Pl. 102):

Master Kōkan grew old, and would no longer paint pictures even when requested. Though summoned by great lords, he would not attend. He wearied of Dutch scholarship, astronomy, and the making of foreign instruments and sought pleasure only in the ways of the Taoists Lao-tzŭ and Chuang-tzŭ.

Last year, after seeing the cherry blossoms at Yoshino, he went to Kyoto where he stayed for one year. In the spring of this year he returned to Edo. He then went to Engaku-ji in Kamakura, where he became the disciple of the priest Seisetsu, finally attained Enlightenment, and died.

All things of this world must perish. Only fame lives on, but though it does not decay with the body, it lasts no more than a thousand years. The universe is without beginning or end; man is but a microscopic particle in an infinite cosmos. Ten thousand years are like the blinking of an eye. What deluded things men are!

Words of farewell by Shiba Mugon,
Age 75[53]
August, 1813

His announcement signifying his death to things of this world seems to have been prompted by the desire to escape from mundane society. Two months later, in October of 1813, he commented in his journal:

In August I printed notices that I had died at Engaku-ji in Kamakura and sent them to all my acquaintances. After that, no one came to visit me. But news spreads quickly in the city, so I decided to leave Kamakura and hide out in Atami. . . .

About forty-five years ago I visited Kanagawa, and . . . met a priest who spent his time alone in a hermitage copying Buddhist scriptures. The hermitage was in a garden and faced the sea; beyond, in the direction of Kanagawa, one could see Mount Fuji. It was an exceptionally quiet and peaceful place where no visitors came. Only one man prepared the priest's meals and swept the garden in the mornings. I myself am utterly weary of the world and feel great respect for that priest's way of life and for his character. It is extremely difficult to sever all desire for fame and fortune as he has done.[54]

A legend associated with Kōkan's life at this time seems peculiarly appropriate to the old man:

Kōkan announced to the world that he had died, then went to Shiba in Edo to live in secret. One day, an old acquaintance saw him on the street and hurried up to him calling his name. Kōkan fled, the other person shouting in pursuit. Finally, Kōkan whirled round and snapped: "How can you expect a dead man to talk to you?"[55]

In December, four months after writing the spurious death notice, Kōkan reported to Yamane Kazuma:

I am now retired from active life and live comfortably and in peace, with no concern for the daily problems of living. I went to Kamakura to study Zen and became the follower of the Zen priest Seisetsu. I wore the simple, rough robes of a priest and found great satisfaction in helping others to understand the meaning of life. I have given up my studies of astronomy and Dutch scholarship.

While in Kamakura I announced my death and sent out death notices to people in Edo, Kyoto, and Osaka. Many persons believed the obituary and sent money and gifts in memory of the deceased, but others did not believe it. A great many people know my name and consider me something of an eccentric; opinions, therefore, varied as to whether I had died or not. Even after sending out my obituary, I still visit close friends. . . .

This past autumn I went to the hot springs at Atami, Izu, and took a trip to various hot springs in Hakone. I spent about forty or fifty days traveling and am now feeling healthier than I have for a long time. I made the entire journey through the mountains and valleys of Hakone on foot and feel exceptionally healthy. My loss of appetite you so kindly inquired about in your last letter improved greatly after my journey, and I am still feeling fine. . . .

Thank you very much for the picture of the elephant you drew for me. It is so realistic that I am certain you carefully observed the living elephant; I regret that it was not brought to Edo.[56] A few years ago, an elephant was brought to Nakano. At first a great many persons went to see it, but after a while people stopped going, and finally it was left to starve to death; now there are only bones

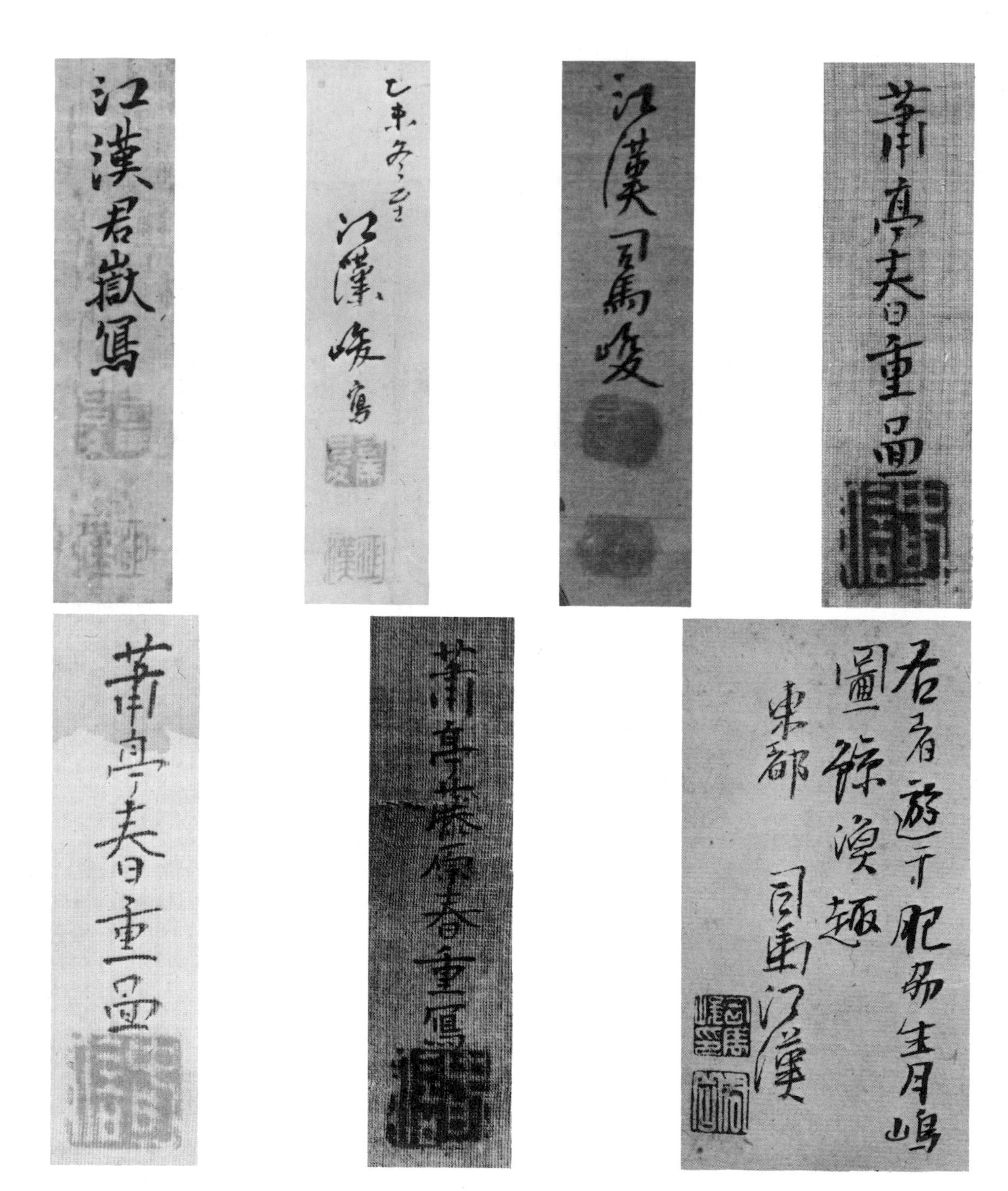

103. Signatures and seals of Shiba Kōkan. Left to right, top: Grapevine, *circa 1769 (Pl. 15), private collection, Japan;* Kingfisher and Willow, *1775 (Pl. 17), reproduced with permission from* Kokka, *No. 838;* Turtledove and Willow, *1775 (Pl. 18), reproduced with permission from* Kokka, *No. 838;* Summer Moon, *circa 1775–81 (Pl. 2), courtesy of the Freer Gallery of Art, Smithsonian Institution, Washington, D.C.; left to right, bottom:* Winter Moon, *circa 1775–81 (Pl. 3), courtesy Museum of Fine Arts, Boston;* Enjoying the Cool of the Evening, *circa 1775–81 (Pl. 31), courtesy of the Kobe City Museum of Namban Art;* Picture Scroll of Whaling, *circa 1793–94 (Pl. 53, 55, 56, and 58), courtesy Tokyo National Museum.*

104. Signatures and seals of Shiba Kōkan. Left to right, top: Daruma, *circa 1780 (Pl. 60);* Priest Kensu, *early 1780s (Pl. 62); left to right, bottom:* Hollander on a Pier, *mid-1780s (Pl. 63);* Dutch Woman Beneath a Tree, *mid-1780s (Pl. 65);* The Pewterer's Shop *(Pl. 68). All courtesy of the Kobe City Museum of Namban Art.*

remaining. I consider that a terrible disgrace to our country. . . .

My time now is precious, and I treasure each moment I have left of life. I think I shall study poetry again, perhaps go to Kyoto to visit the poet Seikei, whom you know. I shall send you a picture I drew in my spare time. . . . Written December 3, 1813[57]

Kōkan continued to add to his journals. *Mugon Dōjin Hikki,*[58] written piecemeal between 1812 and 1814, contained, in addition to information on his personal activities, stories, maxims, and fables drawn from a variety of sources. Some were taken from Chinese literature and from the writings of Taoist and Confucian philosophers; others derived from *Aesop's Fables,* first translated by the Jesuits in Nagasaki in 1593, but, with the subsequent suppression of all Christian books, virtually unknown in Japan when Kōkan discovered it.[59] By August, 1814, he completed a manuscript devoted exclusively to Western fables and Chinese tales entitled *Kummō Gakai Shū* (A Collection of Fables, Interpreted and Illustrated).[60] Each is written first in Chinese, then in Japanese transliteration with Kōkan's interpretation and illustration. The tales he selected were ideally suited for expressing his criticisms of society and human weakness, and he attached to them his own moral lessons.

A letter to Yamane Kazuma in 1815 provides a last informal glimpse of Kōkan's life and thoughts:

> Now I am old and unwell and cannot walk more than a few miles. As I wrote you in my last letter, I have built a small house in Azabu and live there with an old woman who takes care of me. But it is a hilly area and very cold in the winter and spring; it has snowed twenty-one times, and the roads are as muddy as rice paddies. My fire keeps me warm, however, and the other day I was able to go out for a little while.
>
> I have indeed had a long life in this world of fire, and now that I am old and suffering, I am eager to escape this life of pain and go to paradise as soon as possible. It is easy for the aged to survive in summer, but very difficult in winter when the weather is so cold. I am planning to move again before the year is over.
>
> Ever since I announced my death last August, no one has come to visit me. But recently people have begun to realize that I did not die, and soon I shall have visitors again. I feel resuscitated by this thought; just as in the old days, I shall associate with writers, painters, and other men of the arts, but never again shall I have anything to do with feudal lords or people of high official rank. Henceforth I shall associate only with persons of similar interests. No man can live without hardships; therefore, I have learned to tolerate my pain, and even find ease in my suffering. . . .
>
> Now that you have moved to Imari in Arita, I should appreciate your sending me a simple present such as a paperweight inscribed with the words: "To Shiba Kōkan of Edo, from Arita-yama, Matsuura-gun." I am over seventy and should be very grateful to receive something from you that will remain after my death and can be admired and cherished by posterity. If you will have the date inscribed on it, it will be even better. I should prefer to have some sort of writing equipment for my desk rather than a tea bowl.
>
> I myself still paint now and then, for my only desire is to leave behind paintings that can be seen by posterity, so that my fame will live on. . . .
>
> Shiba Tōgen
> April 29, 1815[61]

There is no evidence that Kōkan ever left Azabu. Although he wrote he was unwell and ready to die, he was also working on the revision of the records of his Nagasaki journey and preparing the new manuscript *Saiyū Nikki*. The following year he returned to his scientific studies, and in April, 1816, he completed his final manuscript on natural science, *Tenchi Ridan*. To the very last, he continued to paint.

Kōkan's writings testify to an intense preoccupation with recognition of his personal achievements. Nevertheless, the recognition he sought did not take the form of material wealth or professional status. He sought rather to be immortalized as an enlightener of mankind, famous for having imparted knowledge to others and for having contributed significantly to his nation's progress. This obsession inspired his inquiries into copperplate engraving, painting in the European manner, geography, astronomy, and the fundamental laws of nature.

Unlike other scholars of his era who studied the national culture or Shinto religion, Kōkan never took the strongly nationalistic position that Japan was a uniquely blessed country. His vision always was broader; his intent was to make his people understand that the countries of Europe were indeed superior technologically and that Western knowledge must be absorbed in the Japanese culture. Both rational and humanitarian considerations influenced his thinking. Working diligently to make known his beliefs, he achieved a surprisingly

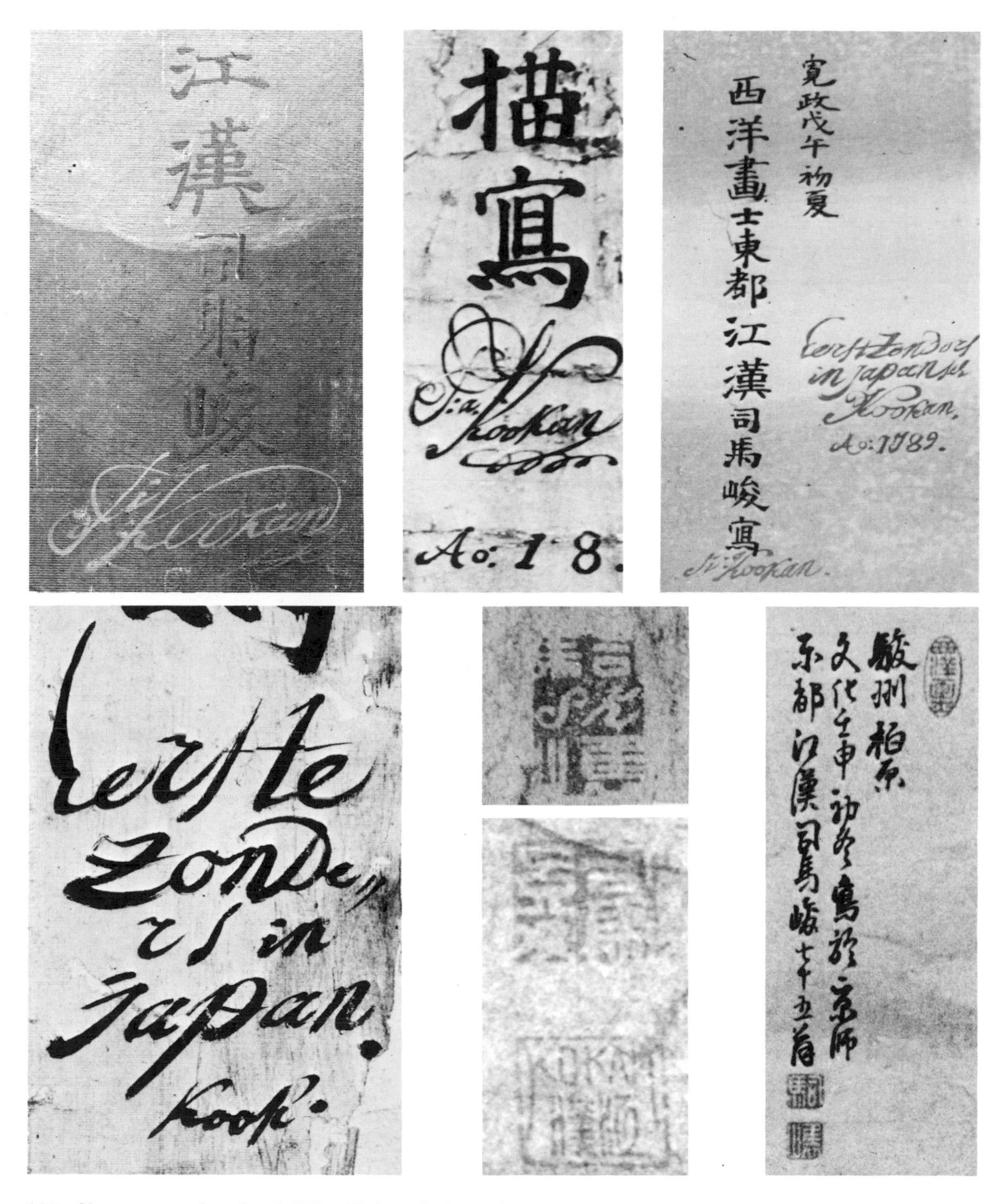

105. Signatures and seals of Shiba Kōkan. Left to right, top: The Shore at Shinagawa, Edo *(Pl. 6), courtesy Museum of Fine Arts, Boston;* Shichirigahama, Kamakura, *1796 (Pl. 7), courtesy of the Kobe City Museum of Namban Art;* Futamigaura, *1798 (Pl. 77), private collection, Japan; left to right, bottom:* The Shore of Kisarazu, *1800 (Pl. 8), courtesy of the Itsukushima Shrine, Miyajima; (above)* Sparrow *(Pl. 82), courtesy of the Kobe City Museum of Namban Art; (below)* The Ōi River, Shizuoka *(Pl. 83), courtesy of the Tokyo University of Arts;* Mount Fuji Viewed from Kashiwabara, Suruga, *1812 (Pl. 84), courtesy of the Kobe City Museum of Namban Art.*

sound understanding of science and published his knowledge for the benefit of others, though Japanese tradition had for a thousand years dictated the transmission of learning only to chosen disciples. He mingled with scholars, noblemen, all manner of people, always remaining aloof, determinedly living as he chose, following no prescribed path to scholarship or high position.

The last two years of his life were finally quiet; he died on November 19, 1818, and was buried at Jigen-ji temple in Edo.[62] Later, his remains were moved to the Kōshinzuka Cemetery in Nishi-Sugamo, Tokyo, where they lie today. Kokan's posthumous Buddhist name is Tōgen-in Kaiei Juenkoji.

Kōkan did not live to see the full impact of Western learning on Japan. The ideals that he embodied continued, however, to exert their influence. Just fifty years after his death, in 1868, the Tokugawa regime crumbled, the nation opened her doors to the rest of the world, and Japan's modern era began.

APPENDIX I

CHRONOLOGY OF KŌKAN'S LIFE AND RELATED EVENTS

1747: Shiba Kōkan born in Yotsuya, Edo. Family name: Andō. Given name: Kichijirō. Names after marriage: Tsuchida Magodayū, Tsuchida Katsusaburō. Pen and art names: Kungaku, Harushige, Shōtei Harushige, Suzuki Harushige, Shun, Shumparō, Rantei, Seiyō Dōjin. Names assumed later in life: Tōgen, Mugon, Fugen Dōjin, Mugon Dōjin. Posthumous name: Tōgen-in Kaiei Juenkoji.

Sō Shiseki:	age 32
Suzuki Harunobu:	age 22
Maruyama Ōkyo:	age 14
Hiraga Gennai:	age 13
Motoki Ryōei:	age 12
Honda Toshiaki:	age 3

1748, age 1: Aōdō Denzen and Satake Shozan born.

1749, age 2: Odano Naotake and Ōta Nampo (Shokusanjin) born.

1751, age 4: Tokugawa Yoshimune died, age 67.

1752, age 5: Kōkan copied designs of sparrows.

1756, age 9: Kōkan drew pictures of Daruma.
Ōtsuki Gentaku and Yamane Kazuma born.

1758, age 11: Sō Shigan arrived in Nagasaki.
Matsudaira Sadanobu born.

1759, age 12: Haruki Nanko (Monya) and Wakasugi Isohachi born.

1760, age 13: Tokugawa Ieharu became the tenth shogun.

1761, age 14: Kōkan studied in the Kanō school.
Kōkan's father died.

1762, age 15: Sō Shiseki became Kōkan's art teacher.
Kōkan studied Chinese classics and poetry under Karahashi Sesai and took the names Kungaku, Shiba, Kōkan, and Shun.
Ishikawa Tairō born.

1763, age 16: Hiraga Gennai published *Butsurui Hinshitsu* (Classifications and Different Materials), illustrated by Sō Shiseki.
Tani Bunchō born.

1764, age 17: Hiraga Gennai made asbestos.

1765, age 18: Harunobu perfected multicolor woodblock printing.

1767, age 20: Tanuma Okitsugu became Grand Chamberlain under Shogun Ieharu.

1769, age 22: Tanuma became Senior Councilor.

1770, age 23: Suzuki Harunobu died and Kōkan began executing forgeries of his woodblock prints.

1771, age 24: Maeno Ryōtaku and Sugita Gempaku witnessed an autopsy and began their translation of *Tabulae Anatomica.*

1772, age 25: Kumashiro Yūhi died, age 59.

1773, age 26: Kōkan accompanied Hiraga Gennai to the Chichibu Mountains in search of precious metals.
Gennai met Odano Naotake in Kakudate, Akita.
Naotake went to Edo in December.
Motoki Ryōei completed *Tenchi Nikyū Yōhō* (Directions for the Use of the Two Charts of the Heavens and Earth), the first statement of the Copernican theory in Japanese.

1774, age 27: Kōkan ceased making ukiyo-e prints.
Maeno Ryōtaku and Sugita Gempaku published *Kaitai*

Shinsho (New Book on Anatomy), their translation of *Tabulae Anatomica.*

1775, age 28: Until around 1781 Kōkan executed ukiyo-e paintings, using the signatures Harushige and Shōtei Harushige.

1776, age 29: Ikeno Taiga died, age 53.

1777, age 30: Odano Naotake returned to Akita in December.

1778, age 31: Odano Naotake went again to Edo.
Satake Shozan wrote *Gahō Kōryō* (Discussion of Painting).

1779, age 32: Hiraga Gennai died, age 45.
Odano Naotake returned to Akita.

1780, age 33: Kōkan met Isaac Titsingh in Edo in 1780 or 1782, and may have received *Groot Schilderboek* from him.
Odano Naotake died, age 31.

1781, age 34: Kōkan drew *sekiga* for the lord of Sendai.
Kōkan's mother died, age 72, and he married into the Tsuchida family, taking then his wife's surname and assuming the names Magodayū and Katsusaburō.

1782, age 35: In April, Isaac Titsingh made a second journey to Edo.
Mitsui Shinwa died, age 82.

1783, age 36: Ōtsuki Gentaku assisted Kōkan in translating the section on etching in Chomel's encyclopedia, and Kōkan produced his first copperplate etching, *View of Mimeguri, Edo.*
Ōtsuki Gentaku published *Rangaku Kaitei* (Ladder to Dutch Studies).
Yosano Buson died, age 67.

1784, age 37: Kōkan constructed a camera obscura and produced the etchings *Ochanomizu, Oyaji Teahouse at Hirō,* and *Shinobazu Lake, Ueno.*

1785, age 38: Kōkan produced the etching of a leather tanner.
Satake Shozan died, age 37.

1786, age 39: Kōkan drew an illustration of a mermaid for Ōtsuki Gentaku's *Rokubutsu Shinshi* (Record of Six New Items), using as model the picture in François Valentijn's *Oud en Nieuw Oost-Indiën.*
Kōkan produced the etching of Toranomon, Edo.
Sō Shiseki died, age 71.
Shogun Ieharu died, and Ienari became the eleventh shogun.
Tanuma Okitsugu resigned, and Matsudaira Sadanobu became Prime Minister.

1787, age 40: Kōkan drew illustrations of a microscope, insects and seeds, and Adam's Peak for Morishima Chūryō's *Kōmō Zatsuwa* (Miscellany of Dutch Studies).
Kōkan produced the etchings *Schichirigahama, Ryōgoku Bridge,* and *Mimeguri.*

1788, age 41: Kōkan departed for Nagasaki May 28. Met Kimura Kenkadō in Osaka. Arrived in Nagasaki November 7. Left Nagasaki for Hirado December 11. Went to Ikitsuki-shima December 30.
Motoki Ryōei appointed Chief Translator (*Daitsūshi*) of Dutch at Nagasaki.
Tanuma Okitsugu died, age 69.

1789, age 42: Kōkan left Ikitsuki-shima January 29, visited Kimura Kenkadō again in Osaka, returned to Edo May 7.
Kōkan executed the oil painting *Zeuxis.*

1792, age 45: Kōkan published his first copperplate map *Yochi Zenzu* (Complete Map of the Earth) and geography *Yochi Ryakusetsu* (Brief Explanation of the Earth).

1793, age 46: Kōkan published *Chikyū Zenzu* (Complete Map of the World) and *Chikyū Zenzu Ryakusetsu* (Explanation of the Complete Map of the World).
Motoki Ryōei completed *Taiyō Kyūri Ryōkaisetsu* (An Explanation of Solar Physics), a translation of *Gronden der Ster-*

renkunde (Principles of Astronomy) by George Adams.
Hayashi Shihei died, age 55, after being confined to house arrest by Matsudaira Sadanobu for publishing *Kaikoku Heidan* (Military Discussion on a Maritime Country).
Watanabe Kazan born.

1794, age 47: Kōkan published *Saiyū Ryodan* (Account of a Western Journey).
Kōkan executed the *Picture Scroll of Whaling,* an oil painting of whaling, and the etching *A Western Studio.*
Ōtsuki Gentaku and his group of *rangakusha* celebrated the Dutch New Year by the solar calendar (Kansei 6/11/11).
Motoki Ryōei died, age 59.

1795, age 48: Maruyama Ōkyo died, age 62.

1796, age 49: Kōkan published *Oranda Tensetsu* (Explanation of Dutch Astronomy), *Tenkyū Zu* (Planisphere), and *Tenkyū Zenzu* (Complete Illustrations of the Heavens).
He presented his oil painting *Shichirigahama* to the Atagoyama Shrine, Edo.
The mock playbill deriding Kōkan was composed at Ōtsuki Gentaku's New Year's party.
Ishikawa Tairō and his brother executed their copy of the floral still life by Willem Frederik van Royen.

1797, age 50: Kōkan published the revised and enlarged edition of *Chikyū Zenzu Ryakusetsu.*

1798, age 51: Kōkan's manuscript *Oranda Kokudan–Oranda Zokuwa* (Tales and Anecdotes of Holland) copied Kansei 10/2/18.

1799, age 52: Kōkan published *Seiyōga Dan* (Discussion of Western Painting) and completed *Shumparō Gafu* (Illustrations by Shumparō).
The mock program of sumo wrestlers listing Kōkan as contender number six opposing Matsubara Uchū was composed at Ōtsuki Gentaku's New Year's party.

1800, age 53: Kōkan presented his oil painting *Kisarazu* to the Itsukushima Shrine.
He held an exhibition of paintings at his house in Shibamon, Shinsenza.
Yoshio Kōsaku died, age 76.
Karahashi Sesai died, age 64.

1801, age 54: Kitayama Kangan died, age 34.

1802, age 55: Kimura Kenkadō died, age 66.

1803, age 56: Kōkan published *Gazu Saiyūdan* (Illustrated Account of a Western Journey).
Maeno Ryōtaku died, age 80.

1805, age 58: Kōkan published *Hinkai Zu* (Map of Navigation) and *Oranda Tsūhaku* (Dutch Navigation).
Wakasugi Isohachi died, age 46.

1806, age 59: Kōkan announced his retirement and held an exhibition of his paintings at the Yanagibashi Restaurant in Edo.
He visited Zeniya Gohei in Kanazawa, and verified as authentic the painting attributed to Rembrandt.

1808, age 61: Kōkan published *Ryōjusen Zusetsu* (Explanation of Adam's Peak), *Chitengi Ryakuzukai* (Illustrated Explanation of the Celestial Globe), and *Kopperu Temmon Zukai* (Illustrated Explanation of Copernican Astronomy).

1809, age 62: Kōkan published *Chitengi Shimō* (Enlightenment Concerning the Celestial Globe).
He presented his last votive offering, *Kintai Bridge,* to the Asakusa Shrine, Edo, and listed his other major paintings presented to shrines.
Gessen, priest of Itsukushima Shrine, died.

1810, age 63: Kōkan completed the manuscript *Dokushō Bōgen* (Self-laughter and Reckless Remarks).

1811, age 64: Kōkan completed the manuscript *Shumparō Hikki* (Notes by Shumparō).

1812, age 65: In April, Kōkan journeyed to Yoshino, Nara, Osaka, Suma, and Maiko Beach, and kept a diary entitled *Yoshino Kikō* (Account of a Journey to Yoshino). He arrived in Kyoto in May, returned to Edo in December.
On his painting *Mount Fuji from Kashiwabara, Suruga,* Kōkan wrote: "Winter, 1812. Painted in Kyoto by Kōkan Shiba Shun of Edo, age seventy-five."
Isaac Titsingh died, age 67.

1813, age 66: In August Kōkan became a disciple of the priest Seisetsu at Engaku-ji, Kamakura. He published his own obituary, giving his age as seventy-five.

1814, age 67: Kōkan completed the manuscripts *Mugon Dōjin Hikki* (Notes by Mugon Dōjin) and *Kummō Gakai Shū* (A Collection of Fables, Interpreted and Illustrated).
Kōkan's picture of a European basketmaker was published in *Keijō Gaen* (Kyoto Garden of Pictures).

1815, age 68: Kōkan completed his revised manuscript *Saiyū Nikki* (Diary of a Western Journey).
Sugita Gempaku completed *Rangaku Koto Hajime* (The Beginnings of Dutch Studies).

1816, age 69: Kōkan completed the manuscript *Tenchi Ridan* (Discussion on Astronomy and Geography).

1817, age 70: Sugita Gempaku died, age 84.
Ishikawa Tairō died, age 55.

1818, age 71: Kōkan died. He was buried at Jigen-ji, Edo. Later his grave was moved to Kōshinzuka Cemetery, Nishi-Sugamo, Tokyo.

APPENDIX II

WRITINGS AND CARTOGRAPHY OF SHIBA KŌKAN

1. *Yochi Zenzu* 輿地全圖 (Complete Map of the Earth). Edo: 2nd month, 1792 (Kansei 4). REPRODUCED: Kurita Mototsugu, *Nihon Kohan Chizu Shūsei,* Plate V.

2. *Yochi Ryakusetsu* 輿地略說 (Brief Explanation of the Earth). 1 vol. Edo: Bunkadō Zōhan, Autumn, 1792 (Kansei 4). REPRINTED: Nakai Sōtarō, *Shiba Kōkan,* 1–6.

3. *Chikyū Zenzu* 地球全圖 (Complete Map of the World). Edo: Spring, 1793 (Kansei 5). Second printing: 1796 (Kansei 8). REPRODUCED HERE: Plates 89 and 90.

4. *Chikyū Zenzu Ryakusetsu* 地球全圖略說 (Explanation of the Complete Map of the World). 1 vol. Edo: Shumparō Zōkoku, March, 1793 (Kansei 5). REPRINTED: Nakai, *Shiba Kōkan,* 7–18. Second edition with section added concerning countries of the world: 1797 (Kansei 9). Third edition (same as second): 1800 (Kansei 12). Fourth edition published posthumously. 3 vols. (Volume Three was not written by Kōkan.) REPRINTED: Nakai, *Shiba Kōkan,* 67–108.

5. *Saiyū Ryodan* 西遊旅譚 (Account of a Western Journey). 5 vols. Edo: Shumparō Zōkoku, Summer, 1794 (Kansei 6). Second edition entitled *Gazu Saiyūdan:* 1803. (See No. 13.) Third revised edition entitled *Saiyū Nikki:* 1815. (See No. 32.)

6. *Oranda Tensetsu* 和蘭天說 (Explanation of Dutch Astronomy). 1 vol. Edo: Shumparō Zōkoku, January, 1796 (Kansei 8). REPRINTED: Nakai, *Shiba Kōkan,* 19–54. *Kagakushi Kenkyū,* Vol. 4. Tokyo: Iwanami Shoten, 1963.

7. *Tenkyū Zu* 天球圖 (Planisphere). Edo: Shumparō Zōkoku, February, 1796 (Kansei 8). REPRODUCED HERE: Plates 9 and 10.

8. *Tenkyū Zenzu* 天球全圖 (Complete Illustrations of the Heavens). Edo: Shumparō Zōkoku, Autumn, 1796 (Kansei 8). REPRODUCED HERE: Plates 11–14, 98.

9. *Oranda Kokudan—Oranda Zokuwa* 和蘭國談・おらんだ俗話 (Tales and Anecdotes of Holland). 1 vol. Copied manuscript dated February, 1798 (Kansei 10). LOCATED: Kobe City Museum of Namban Art.

10. *Seiyōga Dan* 西洋畫談 (Discussion of Western Painting). Edo: Shumparō Zōkoku, August, 1799 (Kansei 11). REPRINTED: Hayakawa, *Nihon Zuihitsu Taisei,* Vol. VI, 805–12. Kususe Makoto, *Zuihitsu Bungaku Senshū,* Vol. II, 345–62. Sakazaki, *Nihon Gadan Taikan,* 114–20. Yoshikawa Hanshichi, *Hyakka Setsurin,* Vol. IV, 1074–78.

11. *Shumparō Gafu* 春波樓畫譜 (Illustrations by Shumparō). 3 vols. Lost manuscript intended for publication c. 1799 (Kansei 11). *Tenkyū Zenzu* was designed to comprise Volume Three.

12. Announcement of Painting Exhibition. July, 1800 (Kansei 12). LOCATED: Kobe City Museum of Namban Art.

13. *Gazu Saiyūdan* 畫圖西遊譚 (Illustrated Account of a Western Journey). 5 vols. Edo: Edo Shorin, September, 1803 (Kyōwa 3). REPRINTED: 1 vol. Kobe: Jugai Shobo, 1966.

14. *Hinkai Zu* 瀕海圖 (Map of Navigation). Edo: Shumparō Zōkoku, June, 1805 (Bunka 2). REPRODUCED HERE: Plate 93.

15. *Oranda Tsūhaku* 和蘭通舶 (Dutch Navigation). 2 vols. Edo: Shumparō Zōkoku, December, 1805 (Bunka 2). REPRINTED: Kususe, *Zuihitsu Bungaku Senshū,* Vol. VI, 341–86. Nakai, *Shiba Kōkan,* 109–60.

16. Announcement of Retirement. Spring,

1806 (Bunka 3). LOCATED: Kobe City Museum of Namban Art.

17. *Ryōjusen Zusetsu* 靈鷲山圖說 (Explanation of Adam's Peak). 1 vol. Edo: Sanensan Zōhan, February, 1808 (Bunka 5).

18. *Chitengi Ryakuzukai* 地轉儀略圖解 (Illustrated Explanation of the Celestial Globe). 1 vol. Edo: Shumparō Zōkoku, 1808 (Bunka 5). REPRINTED: Muraoka, *Tenchi Ridan,* Plates 18–20. Nakai, *Shiba Kōkan,* Plate 13.

19. *Kopperu Temmon Zukai* 刻白爾天文圖解 (Illustrated Explanation of Copernican Astronomy). Edo: Shumparō Zōkoku, December, 1808 (Bunka 5). REPRINTED: Nakai, *Shiba Kōkan,* 161–208.

20. *Chitengi Shimō* 地轉儀示蒙 (Enlightenment Concerning the Celestial Globe). 1 vol. Edo: Shumparō Zōkoku, 1809 (Bunka 6).

21. Announcement of Paintings. September, 1809 (Bunka 6). LOCATED: Kobe City Museum of Namban Art.

22. *Dokushō Bōgen* 獨笑妄言 (Self-laughter and Reckless Remarks). Unpublished manuscript completed in September, 1810 (Bunka 7). Copy owned by Gotō Shōichi, Osaka. REPRINTED: Arisaka Takamichi, "Dokushō Bōgen," *Historia,* No. 10 (1954). Another copy owned by Iwase Bunko, Nishio Shiritsu Library. REPRINTED: Hosono Masanobu, "Dokushō Bōgen," *Kikan Geijutsu,* No. 14 (1970).

23. *Shumparō Hikki* 春波樓筆記 (Notes by Shumparō). Unpublished manuscript completed in November, 1811 (Bunka 8). The original manuscript was lost in the earthquake of 1923; printed texts are based on a copy of the original by Ōtsuki Nyoden, owned by the Physical Science Department, Kyushu University, Fukuoka. REPRINTED: Hayakawa, *Nihon Zuihitsu Taisei,* Vol. I, 395–466. Yoshikawa, *Hyakka Setsurin,* Vol. I, 1119–87.

24. *Yoshino Kikō* 吉野紀行 (Account of a Journey to Yoshino). Unpublished manuscript written 1812 (Bunka 9). LOCATED: Mukyūkai Library. REPRINTED: Aimi Kōu, *Nihon Bijutsu Kyōkai Hōkoku,* No. 38.

25. Letter to Yamane Kazuma written July 9, 1813 (Bunka 10/6/12). REPRINTED: *Gakkō Kōyūkai,* Vol. III, No. 6 (March, 1905), 126–28.

26. *Jisei no Go* 辭世の語 (Words of Farewell). August, 1813 (Bunka 10). COPIES LOCATED: Kobe City Museum of Namban Art and Tenri Library. REPRINTED: Okamura, *Kōmō Bunka Shiwa,* 194. Nishimura, *Nihon Shoki Yōga no Kenkyū,* 351.

27. *Fugen Zenji Hōgo Mariuta* 不言禪師法語滿里歌 (A Buddhist Sermon Chanted to the Rhythm of a Child's Ball-bouncing Song, by Fugen Zenji). 1813 (Bunka 10). LOCATED: Kobe City Museum of Namban Art.

28. Letter to Yamane Kazuma written December 3, 1818 (Bunka 10/11/11). REPRINTED: *Gakkō Kōyūkai,* Vol. III, No. 8 (June, 1905), 178–81.

29. *Mugon Dōjin Hikki* 無言道人筆記 (Notes by Mugon Dōjin). Unpublished manuscript completed 1814 (Bunka 11). LOCATED: Tenri Library. REPRINTED: Muraoka Tsunetsugu, *Tenchi Ridan,* 1–146.

30. *Kummō Gakai Shū* 訓蒙畫解集 (A Collection of Fables, Interpreted and Illustrated). 1 vol. Unpublished manuscript completed August, 1814 (Bunka 11/7). LOCATED: National Library, Tokyo. PARTIALLY REPRINTED: Muraoka, *Tenchi Ridan,* Plates 6–12.

31. Letter to Yamane Kazuma written April 29, 1815 (Bunka 12/3/20). LOCATED: Tenri Library.

32. *Saiyū Nikki* 西遊日記 (Diary of a Western Journey). Unpublished manuscript completed April, 1815 (Bunka 12). LOCATED: Tokyo National Museum. REPRINTED: Kuroda, *Kōkan Saiyū Nikki.* Miyamoto et al. *Nihon Shominseikatsu Shiryō Shūsei,* Vol. II, 263–328. *Nihon Koten Zenshū,* Second Series, Vol. 42.

33. *Tenchi Ridan* 天地理譚 (Discussion of Astronomy and Geography). Unpublished manuscript completed April, 1816 (Bunka 13). COPIES LOCATED: Physics Department, Kyushu University, and Tenri Library. REPRINTED: Nakai, *Shiba Kōkan,* 209–53.

APPENDIX III

SEIYŌGA DAN (DISCUSSION OF WESTERN PAINTING)

BY SHIBA KŌKAN, 1799

1. THE DIAMETER of the world is more than seven thousand miles, and the sea route circumnavigating it is over twenty-four thousand miles. The land known as the West is in the region lying west of China and Japan. The most distant region of the West is called Europe. It is one of the great continents and contains several thousand countries the size of Japan. One of them, the Netherlands, is divided into seven districts, one of which is Holland.

The various countries of the West all have the same style of painting. Since this style was introduced to Japan by the Dutch, and since today there are numerous examples of Dutch art in Japan, we call all Western paintings "Dutch paintings." The technique employed in this art produces a true representation of reality, greatly different from the style that is used in Japan. Many persons in Japan—among them those who paint in the traditional Chinese or Japanese technique—consider Western-style painting absurd and have no desire to learn the Western method. Not only do they think it unworthy of study, but they feel that it has no artistic value and cannot be called painting at all! They seem to think that the artistic creations of the West are mere artisan's work. This is indeed an extremely foolish notion.

The Japanese and Chinese paintings that we refer to as *saiga,* or minutely painted pictures, actually come under the category of *saiku,* or artisan's work. Take, for example, the manner in which the Japanese draw hair and beards: every single strand of hair is drawn individually. The Western technique of drawing hair, however, is to suggest the hair in a few brush strokes, so that the resulting appearance is one of real hair, not a mere mass of lines. In ancient times, people were not concerned with the stress and character of the brush stroke. Fundamentally, a brush is a tool for drawing pictures. If one attempts to draw an ox without expressing the actual appearance of the ox, if one is concerned mainly with the impression given by the brush technique, then a mere spot of ink could just as well be called a picture of an ox.

For example, medical science cures illness with medicine. Relating this metaphorically to painting, let us call medical science the brush, illness the picture, and medicines the colors. The attempt of medical science to cure a specific illness with general medicine, or the attempt of the brush to correct a picture with color, is like not knowing exactly where the illness originates or just what is at fault in a painting. The primary aim of Western art is to create a spirit of reality, but Japanese and Chinese paintings, in failing to do this, become mere toys serving no use whatever.

By employing shading, Western artists can represent convex and concave surfaces, sun and shade, distance, depth, and shallowness. Their pictures are models of reality and thus can serve the same function as the written word, often more effectively. The syllables used in writing can only describe, but one realistically drawn picture is worth ten thousand words. For this reason Western books frequently use pictures to supplement descriptive texts, a striking contrast to the inutility of the Japanese and Chinese pictures, which serve no better function than that of a hobby to be performed at drinking parties.

The bones of mermaids are reputed to make a marvelous medicine. An old tale in a Dutch book tells of a mermaid who was caught just off the Indonesian island of

Amboina, which once belonged to Portugal and later to Holland.[1] The people of Amboina preserved the mermaid in embalming fluid and drew pictures of her, so that one could see both mermaid and illustrations. The drawings were done in color to convey her luster and shape, and they had an accompanying descriptive text. After some years the preserved mermaid lost her original appearance, so that a person today who desires to know what the mermaid once looked like must resort to the drawings made of her. Had the drawings not been executed in a realistic technique, they too would be virtually useless. (For further details concerning mermaids, see *Rokubutsu Shinshi* by Ōtsuki Gentaku.)[2]

2. Instead of using glue as we do to mix our pigments, Western artists use oil. This means that even if their paintings get wet they are not damaged. These pictures are commonly called oil paintings. Although many artists in Japan have copied this technique, few have ever attained a genuine knowledge. When I visited Nagasaki some years ago, a Hollander named Isaac Titsingh gave me a book on art entitled *Konst Schilderboek*. Perusing this work carried me into an intoxicating world. After a careful study of it, I finally attained a perfect command of its principles and can now draw whatever I wish with complete ease—landscapes, birds, flowers, men, or beasts.

Pictures that are intended to give information, because of the vast amount of accurate detail they contain, are far more effective than simple words of description. All things depicted in paintings—from the great wild goose down to the tiny sparrow, and even further to the components of eyes and beaks and legs—differ in shape and feeling. Even the color in plumage varies exceedingly. The written word in black and white cannot possibly recreate an accurate image of the true form. For this reason, the pictures drawn in Western countries are regarded even more highly than writing. Painting and writing both serve the nation; they are not devised merely for amusement.

3. Many Easterners consider Western art to be no more than "perspective pictures," but this belief is utterly fallacious for the reason I have stated previously: a picture that does not represent reality faithfully is not well executed. There is far more to realistic painting than the mere drawing of perspective. Eastern pictures have no accuracy of detail, and without such accuracy, a picture is not really a picture at all. To paint reality is to paint all objects—landscapes, birds, flowers, cows, sheep, trees, rocks, or insects—exactly as the original objects appear, thereby actually animating the drawing. No technique other than that of the West can achieve this feeling of reality. When a Western painter looks at the work of an Eastern artist, he surely must see it as the mere playing of a child, hardly worthy of the name "painting." But when an Oriental artist, who is used to living with his wretched paintings, has an opportunity to compare his work with the distinctly superior Western art, he stupidly considers the latter merely another school of art, calling it "perspective painting." Obviously, such categorizing represents an extreme misunderstanding of Western painting.

4. Western books contain pictures made by the copper-engraving process. They have, for example, botany books (something like our medical herb books) in which illustrations and words are equally important for description. Without illustrations it would be impossible to obtain a clear understanding of the plant's appearance. Similarly, in order to construct an unfamiliar article one must know its shape. What better way could there be to describe this than by means of a picture? Being realistic representations, the drawings of Western countries are executed according to the "three-face method" of shading.

The technique of bestowing color tonality in addition to shading, particularly in copper engraving, is a very difficult art. Therefore, early Western books published before the technique of copperplate engraving was sufficiently developed contain extremely poor illustrations, which only slightly resemble the genuine article. An example of this is the ancient Dutch book by Ambrosius Paré, which roughly corresponds to our books on medical herbs.[3] The inadequacy of these reproductions sometimes caused scholars of Dutch learning and others who were unaware of the misrepresentations to misjudge the engravings, making serious errors. Starting from the Dutch zoological encyclopedia by Johnston, the technique of making copperplates improved markedly, so that more recent publications reaching us from abroad all contain carefully detailed engravings, so realistic the pictures almost come alive.

Even though we often cannot read the descriptions written in the Dutch language, we still can get a thorough understanding of many of the things described merely by studying the pictures carefully. This fact alone proves the brilliance and superiority of Western art. Of course, the principles of Western art are quite impossible to comprehend unless one first has some notion of the principles of the art of Japan and China with which he can compare the Western technique.

The three-face method of shading in Western art must be studied carefully and understood thoroughly: 1) Keep pure white that part of the painting which is to depict objects in direct sunlight. 2) Paint in pale tones those objects on which the sun shines obliquely. 3) Paint in deep tones those objects that are shaded from the sun and are therefore dark. The effect of light and dark shadows is achieved in engraving by the use of parallel lines: when single parallel lines are used in close proximity, the tonality is light; when two sets of parallel lines are used crossing each other, the tone becomes dark.

When I was a young man, Hiraga Gennai told me that many years ago a Hollander arrived in Japan, bringing with him several hundred Dutch copperplate pictures. He offered them for sale; but the Japanese, too frivolous and superficial to realize what a rare and wonderful opportunity this was, declined his offer! They knew nothing of the technique involved, and this, in fact, was their first indication of the existence of copper engravings.

No one in Japan knew the proper method of making a copperplate. I therefore turned to the formula given in a book by a Hollander named "Boisu." I consulted with Ōtsuki Gentaku, who assisted me in translating the text so that I could manufacture copperplate pictures in Japan. In 1783, I produced the first engraving. Unfortunately, Asians are different in nature from Europeans, who have achieved such great skill in this art, and I could hardly hope to attain an equal perfection.

At the time of this writing I am more than fifty years old, and gradually my energy wanes. Though I have still much to learn, I should like to offer what slight knowledge I possess on the art of copperplate engraving to those whom it might interest. I therefore intend to publish another book, called *Oranda Kikō,* which will explain the engraving technique.

5. Western artists apply their theories to a technique of precise representation, and their works cannot be viewed in a frivolous manner. There is, in fact, a specific way to look at them. Perhaps to facilitate this, the pictures are usually framed and hung on a wall. Even when a painting is to be looked at casually, it should be hung directly in front of the observer. In the picture there is always a horizon line between sky and land. The viewer should move back five or six feet to a position where the horizon in the picture is level with his eyes. In this manner perspective is expressed in its truest form, clearly delineating the foreground from the background and setting off objects in space. Often a mirror is used in looking at small pictures, giving them an even greater appearance of depth and reality.[4]

6. Portraiture is an important art form in the West, where the faces of sages and political figures are recorded in copperplate engravings for the benefit of future generations. The portrayal of these men gives one as clear an understanding of their physiognomies as seeing the men themselves. Again, the contrast to Japanese and Chinese paint-

ings is striking, for without the technique of copying reality, the Eastern artist can paint only a subjective impression of an object or a face. The same man, if painted by two different Japanese artists, will appear to be two different men. Consequently, since the true form is not described, only a vague image appears. An image of grass and flowers that does not resemble the actual plants can hardly be called a picture of them.

7. The indigenous art technique of Japan and China cannot possibly reproduce reality. In drawing a spherical object, a Japanese artist will simply draw a circle and call it a sphere because he has no method for representing roundness. Being unable to deal with convexity, should he draw the front view of a man's face, there is no way of expressing the height of the nose! This difficulty is not due to the way in which the lines are drawn, but to the total disregard of shading in Japanese art. I shall discuss the drawing of Western pictures in greater detail in a later book, called *Seiyōga Den.*

FINIS

Works published by Shumparō Zōkoku:

1. Copperplate: *Tenkyū Zu* [Planisphere]
2. Copperplate: *Chikyū Zu* [Map of the World]
3. Copperplate pictures: Japanese and Dutch Landscapes
4. *Saiyū Ryodan* [Account of a Western Journey], 5 volumes

Soon to be published:

Shumparō Gafu [Illustrations by Shumparō], written simply and clearly in three parts:

1. *Seiyōga Den* [Commentary on Western Painting]. This volume will explain the geometric technique of using perspective in landscapes and in drawing buildings. Further, it will describe the realistic method of drawing human figures, birds, flowers, animals, and so forth, the technique of coloring, oil painting, use of the brush, and the three rules of shading. All will be fully illustrated: Japanese and Dutch landscapes, woodblocks, and copperplate etchings.

2. *Oranda Kikō* [Dutch Techniques]. Illustrations of various instruments used in measuring the heavens. A complete explanation of the technique of executing copperplate etchings. Explanations of many strange and marvelous instruments used in the world—inventions that would be extremely beneficial to Japan, such as windmills, water wheels, and so forth. All will be minutely illustrated.

3. *Temmon Chiri* [Astronomy and Geography]. The yearly revolutions of the heavens; true shapes of the sun, the moon, and the Five Planets; illustrations of Saturn, Jupiter, the tails of comets, warm and cold zones, snow, rain, lightning, earthquakes, tides, cold seasons, earth, seas, countries and peoples of the world, and products produced in different climates.

Paintings:

1. *Sōshū Shichirigahama.* Atagoyama Shrine, Edo.

2. *View of Shibaura from Teppōzu.* Jimmeigu Shrine, Shiba, Edo.

3. *Landscape of Sunshū Satta Fuji.* Kagura stage, Gion Shrine, Kyoto.

4. *Painting of a Hollander* and *View of Shichirigahama.* Ikutama Shrine, Osaka.

5. *Maikogahama, Hanshū.* Warei Shrine, Uwajima.

The above works are executed in the Western manner by Master Shiba Kōkan.

Listed by Shiba Kōkan's disciple. Autumn, Kansei 11 [1799].

APPENDIX IV

JAPANESE WRITINGS ON GEOGRAPHY ANTEDATING KŌKAN'S GEOGRAPHY TEXTS

Ka'i Tsūshōkō 華夷通商考 (Thoughts on Foreign Commerce). Nishikawa Joken 西川如見. 1695.

Sairan Igen 采覽異言 (Various Comments on New Events). Arai Hakuseki 新井白石. 1712.

Yonjūni Koku Jimbutsu Zusetsu 四十二國人物圖說 (Illustrated Explanations of Peoples of Forty-two Countries). Nishikawa Joken. 1714.

Oranda Chikyū Zusetsu 和蘭陀地球圖說 (Explanation of a Dutch Map of the World). Motoki Ryōei 本木良永. 1722.

Oranda Umikagami 和蘭海鏡 (Sea Mirror of Holland). Motoki Ryōei. 1781.

Orandabune Zusetsu 和蘭船圖說 (Explanatory Diagram of a Dutch Ship). Hayashi Shihei 林子平. 1782.

Bankoku Chikyū Zusetsu 萬國地球圖說 (Explanation of a Map of the Countries of the World). Nagakubo Sekisui 長久保赤水. 1782.

Akaezo Fūsetsukō 赤蝦夷風說考 (Rumors Concerning Kamchatka). Kudō Heisuke 工藤平助. 1783.

Sankoku Tsūran Zusetsu 三國通覽圖說 (Explanation of Three Countries). Hayashi Shihei. 1785.

Shinsei Chikyū Bankoku Zusetsu 新製地球萬國圖說 (Explanation of a Newly Made World Map). Katsuragawa Hoshū 桂川甫周. 1786.

Kōmō Zatsuwa 紅毛雜話 (Miscellany of Dutch Studies). Morishima Chūryō 森島中良. 1787. (Volume Three contains a section entitled "The Sea Routes from the Barbarian Countries to Japan.")

Taisei Yochi Zusetsu 泰西輿地圖說 (Explanatory Map of the World From the Western Countries). Kuchiki Masatsuna 朽木昌綱. 1788.

APPENDIX V

THE YEAR OF KŌKAN'S BIRTH

THE YEAR of Shiba Kōkan's birth is a disputed question among biographers because they are faced with contradictory evidence provided by Kōkan himself. Many authorities have stated he was born in 1738 and died in 1818, at the age of eighty (eighty-one by the former Japanese reckoning). I submit that the evidence points rather to 1747 as the year of his birth. It is appropriate to examine the factors behind both views, working backward from 1818 (Bunsei 1), the year of his death appearing on his gravestone.

Three indications support the traditional year 1738. In *Shumparō Hikki,* completed in 1811, Kōkan described himself as "over seventy,"[1] indicating he must have been at least seventy-seven when he died. On a painting dated 1812 (Pl. 84) he wrote that he was seventy-four. The following year, in *Mugon Dōjin Hikki,* he stated he was seventy-five.[2]

As much evidence favors 1747 as the year of his birth. In *Shumparō Hikki* Kōkan wrote that he was thirteen years old at the time of his father's death (1760).[3] In both *Seiyōga Dan* of 1799, and in a circular of 1800 announcing an exhibition of his paintings, he declared that he had passed his fiftieth year.[4] In 1805 he wrote in *Oranda Tsūhaku* that he would "soon be sixty years of age."[5] And in announcements of his retirement, distributed in 1806, he said: "This year I have turned sixty years old."[6]

Besides Kōkan's own statements, other evidence supports the 1747 birth date. Enkyō 4 (1747) is given as his birth in the first printed edition of *Ukiyo-e Ruikō.*[7] Especially convincing is a brief biography discovered by Hosono Masanobu written on the back of a listing of Kōkan's scientific etchings owned by the Seikadō Bunko.[8] The notation, written by Tōjō Kindai, states among other facts of Kōkan's life that he was born in Yotsuya, Edo, moved to Shiba Shinsenza, Udagawa Urakaidō, and died Bunsei 1, 11th month, 21st day (December 18, 1818) at the age of seventy-one (seventy-two by Japanese reckoning). The month (11th) contradicts that on Kōkan's gravestone (10th), but both day and year correspond. Tōjō Kindai, third son of the physician Tōjō Kyōtetsu, was born in Udagawa-cho, very near Kōkan's residence. The two families were certainly acquainted, and Kindai's firsthand knowledge would strongly suggest the reliability of his information. We may imagine that Kōkan, when already an old man, sought to enhance his venerability by adding nine years to his actual age. Most probably he was born in 1747 and died in 1818 at the age of seventy-one.

NOTES

Abbreviations used:

KSN: *Kōkan Saiyū Nikki,* ed. Kuroda Genji

NZT: *Nihon Zuihitsu Taikei,* 6 vols., comp. Hayakawa Junsaburō

SK: *Shiba Kōkan,* by Nakai Sōtarō

TR: *Tenchi Ridan,* ed. Muraoka Tsunetsugu

CHAPTER ONE

1. Shiba, *Shumparō Hikki,* in NZT, 1:412–13.
2. One of the most complete records is the *Nagasaki Semminden* (History of Early Nagasaki Artists), complied in 1731 by Ro Senri.
3. Kaempfer, 2:285, 357.
4. Shiba, *Shumparō Hikki,* NZT, 1:425.
5. An excellent discussion of the political and economic aspects of Tokugawa Japan is presented by Hall, chapters 1 and 2.

CHAPTER TWO

1. The dispute concerning the date of Kōkan's birth is discussed fully in Appendix V.
2. Samurai, farmer, artisan, and merchant. In his book *Oranda Tensetsu* (in SK, p. 53), Kōkan stated that he "grew up in the city"; his use of the word *shisei* implies the common, workingman's part of town.
3. The names he took after his marriage were Tsuchida Magodayū and Tsuchida Katsusaburō. His pen names and art names include Kungaku, Harushige, Shōtei Harushige, Shiba Kōkan, Shun, Shumparō, Rantei, Seiyō Dōjin, Tōgen, Mugon, Fugen Dōjin, and Mugon Dōjin.
4. Shiba, *Shumparō Hikki,* NZT, 1:411. Often represented in Japanese and Chinese painting, Daruma (Sanskrit: Bodhidharma) is the reputed founder of the Zen sect of Buddhism. Kōkan's text cites his ages as six and ten respectively. Specific ages throughout this book are given according to present-day calculation rather than the system prevalent in Kōkan's day, whereby a person was considered one year old at birth. Approximations in round numbers (e.g., "I am now over seventy") remain unchanged.
5. Shiba, *Shumparō Hikki,* NZT, 1:410.
6. The date of his father's death is recorded on Kōkan's gravestone at the Jigen-ji temple, Tokyo: 11th year of Hōreki, 2nd month, 22nd day (March 28, 1761). Dates in the text are converted to the solar calendar date, with footnotes giving the original lunar date by era, year, month, and day: e.g., Hōreki 11/2/22. In *Shumparō Hikki* (NZT, 1:413), Kokan wrote that he was only thirteen (solar calendar) when his father died, i.e., 1760.
7. The original *Shumparō Hikki* manuscript was lost in the earthquake of 1923, and all printed texts are from a copy made by Ōtsuki Nyoden. There is no way to ascertain, therefore, whether it was Kōkan or Nyoden who mistakenly transcribed the Kanō master's name.
8. The Yangtze and the Han rivers.
9. Shiba, *Shumparō Hikki,* NZT, 1:412. As for Shiba, besides being the Japanese pronunciation of the well-known Chinese surname Ssŭ-ma, Shiba was also the name of the section of Edo where Kōkan lived, a factor probably further prompting his choice.
10. The same restaurant at which the celebrated Edo novelist Takizawa Bakin (1767–1848) gave a sumptuous banquet in 1836 for more than eight hundred guests.
11. Shiba, *Shumparō Hikki,* NZT, 1:421. Although Kōkan here gave his age as thirty (Japanese reckoning), in the records of the Datè clan, *Tetsuzankō-jike Kirōku,* it is noted that the exhibition took place in 1781, making Kōkan thirty-four. The person Kōkan referred to as Fukagawa Shinwa was Mitsui Shinwa of Fukagawa, Edo. His son was Mitsui Shinkō.
12. Her Buddhist name, Kairen'in Myōge Nippō, is written on Kōkan's gravestone, and her death recorded: An'ei 10/1/26 (March 1, 1781).
13. Two well-known tales illustrate the character of Mencius's mother. When Mencius was born, his family lived near a graveyard, and the children at play often imitated the funeral ceremonies; Mencius's mother therefore moved to another area of town near a market. There, the children imitated the merchants, so she moved again to a university neighborhood, where children followed the ways of the scholars. The second story concerns her son's education. When Mencius returned from the university, his mother asked him what he had learned. He replied that schooling was useless, that one must learn naturally through self-education. His mother tore up the cloth she had been weaving and placed the torn fragments before her son saying: "If I were never to complete my weaving, of what use would these pieces be in making clothing?" Mencius realized his error and returned to school.

14. Matsuki Tantan (1674–1761).

15. Shiba, *Shumparō Hikki,* NZT, 1:413–14.

16. Ōtsuki Nyoden, p. 74. Nyoden compiled his chronology from records no longer extant kept by his grandfather Ōtsuki Gentaku.

17. Nishimura, *Nihon Shoki,* p. 320, quoting Sokei, *Ne Monogatari.*

18. Ibid.

19. Shiba, *Shumparō Hikki,* NZT, 1:414.

CHAPTER THREE

1. Sō Shiseki formed his name by changing the last character of Sō Shigan's name from *gan* (rock) to *seki* (stone). It is often supposed that Shiseki went to Nagasaki in 1758 and studied under Sō Shigan, but other events of his life indicate he studied with Kumashiro Yūhi before Shigan arrived. Shiseki's family name was Kusumoto, his early given name Kōhachirō, and his art name Kunkaku. Other pen names included Sekkei, Sekko, and Kasumi Tei.

2. Although signed Kōkan Kungaku, to my knowledge, this painting has never been published as one of Kōkan's works. While the vast range of extant Kōkan forgeries indicates that signature alone is insufficient evidence of authorship, the close correlation between this painting and one by Kōkan's known mentor, Sō Shiseki, provides additional support for assuming its authenticity.

3. *Tarashikomi,* a technique originated by Sōtatsu in the early seventeenth century, consists of laying down one color wash on another of a different tone while the first is still wet. The second color spreads, in large part displacing the first, and intermingling at the interfaces, thereby creating a third tone by the color fusion, and a shape formed without outline.

4. See footnote 7 below.

5. Reproductions of both paintings appear in Yonezawa Yoshiho and Yoshizawa Chu, *Japanese Painting in the Literati Style* (New York and Tokyo: Weatherhill, 1974), Pl. 157 and 158.

6. Wada Mikio, *Hikkō-en* (Tokyo: Shimbi Shoin, 1912). See Pl. 6, 14, 35, and 39.

7. The styles called *nanga* (southern painting) and *bunjinga* (literati painting) were never clearly distinguished by Japanese artists. Japanese *bunjinga,* moreover, was very different from Chinese Wên-jên-hua (literati painting); it incorporated elements and styles that would have shocked the more conservative Chinese. While Chinese artists utilized models reflecting in a more or less pure state systematic sets of aesthetic theory, the Japanese, in a characteristically pragmatic fashion, included a broad range of Chinese styles in their works without reference to preconceived theories. Ostensibly, Chinese Southern style was most admired, but the Japanese had no clear understanding of what comprised that style. In theory, they were opposed to Chinese Northern style, but in practice were quick to admire and accept any landscape painting of the Ming Dynasty, and to borrow elements from Shên Nan-p'in's bird-and-flower compositions, as well. The *bunjinga* artist Kuwayama Gyokushū went so far as to accept the Japanese *rimpa* tradition as Southern, primarily because it represented, in Japanese context, opposition to the academic Kanō school, an attitude comparable to Chinese Literati opposition to the Academy. Japanese admiration of Chinese styles was, then, more a matter of taste than of integrated philosophy, and *bunjinga* paintings displayed marked eclecticism.

CHAPTER FOUR

1. Shiba, *Shumparō Hikki,* NZT, 1:411–12.

2. Another explanation offered by Inoue Kazuo, pp. 150–51, and reiterated by Narazaki Muneshige in *The Japanese Print: Its Evolution and Essence* (Tokyo and Palo Alto: Kodansha International Ltd., 1966), p. 118, is that Harushige was first the student of Suzuki Harunobu, later becoming Sō Shiseki's understudy. There are no facts supporting this assumption, however, and it contradicts what Kōkan himself wrote in his diary. Arthur Waley's assertion that Shiba Kōkan was not Harushige, despite the evidence of the diary, is ingenious, but unconvincing. Aside from his failure to recognize the stylistic peculiarites of Harushige prints, Waley's argument rests solely upon his interpretation of the Japanese text, from which he draws hypothetical conclusions based on the difficulties involved in correctly reading the Japanese cursive script. See Waley, "Shiba Kōkan and Harushige Not Identical," *Burlington Magazine,* LII (April, 1928), pp. 178–83.

3. Five of the set are reproduced in *The Clarence Buckingham Collection of Japanese Prints* (Chicago: The Art Institute of Chicago, 1965), Vol. II, Pl. 101–5.

4. Komachi was a ninth-century poetess famous for her incredible beauty, formidable wit, ingenious poetry, cruelty to her innumerable lovers during her youth, and desolate wanderings in old age as a beggar recognized by no one. In the fourteenth century Kan'ami and his son Zeami, creators of the Nō drama, wrote a series of plays about her, collectively known as *Nana Komachi* (Seven Komachi Stories), one of which is *Kiyomizu Komachi.* Komachi provided a favorite theme for Kabuki and Jōruri theater during the eighteenth century, and ukiyo-e artists borrowed the title with its classical overtones for depicting seven beautiful women of Edo.

5. Concerning Harushige's prints, Binyon and Sexton wrote (p. 69): "If Shiba Kōkan was the author of all the prints signed Harushige, as presumably is the case, he was a singularly skillful imitator of Harunobu's manner. Some of the Harushige prints are beautiful and, so far as we can tell, show independent invention. Certain characteristics found in these prints—a long nose, and an exaggerated slenderness of figure—seem to mark some of the prints

signed Harunobu as forgeries by Kōkan. But this is a problem on which there will probably always be difference of opinion."

6. See footnote 4 above.

7. *Tsuki ya aranu / Haru ya mukashi no / Haru naranu / Wa ga mi hitotsu wa / Moto no mi ni shite.* (Is not the moon the same? / The spring / The spring of old? / Only this body of mine / Is the same body. . . .) Translation by Helen Craig McCullough in *Tales of Ise* (Stanford: Stanford University Press, 1968), 4:71.

8. In 1734, Shimada Dōkan of Edo published a book on perspective entitled *Kiku Gempō Chōken Bengi* (A Layman's Explanation of the Rules of Drawing with a Compass and Ruler). His work summarized the technique described in 1664 by Abraham Bosse in his Dutch text, based on yet another manual written in 1636 by the French geometrician Gerard Desargues. The Dutch book, preserved at the Matsuura Museum, Hirado, was published at Amsterdam, entitled *Algemeene Manier van de Hr. Desargues Tot de practijk de Perspectiven, gelijck tot die der Meet-kunde, met de kleyne Voet-maat* (Mr. Desargues's General Rules for Drawing Perspective, Using both Geometry and Precise Measurements).

CHAPTER FIVE

1. The earliest known engraving brought to Japan by the Jesuits is an illustration of the Virgin Mary and Child seated on a throne beside Saint Anne. The Latin inscription on the print mentions it as an indulgence issued under Pope Alexander VI in 1494 and indicates that it was owned by the seminary at Arie in 1596. The earliest extant engraving believed executed in Japan is a standing portrait of the Virgin and Child called the "Madonna of Seville," based on a mural of Nuestra Senora de Antiqua in Seville Cathedral, Spain. This print bears the Latin inscription stating that it was produced at the Jesuit seminary at Arie in 1597. After the closing of the Arie seminary in 1597, both engravings were removed from Japan; they were discovered in 1869 in Manila by Bishop Petitjean and sent to Pope Pius IX in Rome. The pope returned the pictures to Japan with Bishop Petitjean, who later built the Hall of the Twenty-six Martyrs of Ōura Church, Nagasaki. Both engravings are reproduced: Nagayama Tokihide, *Kirishitan Shiryō Shū*, (Nagasaki: Taigai Shiryō Hōkan Kankōkai, 1927), Pl. 73, 74; Nishimura, *Namban Bijutsu*, Pl. 117, 123; Okamoto Yoshitomo, *Namban Art of Japan* (New York and Tokyo: Weatherhill, 1972), Pl. 31, 30.

2. Shiba, *Seiyōga Dan*, NZT, 6:809. In referring to his works, Kōkan used the Japanese word *dōbanga* (copperplate pictures), a generic term including any process of printing with a copperplate—engraving, etching, mezzotint, etc. He did not use the term *fushoku dōban* (etching). In translating his statements here, the term "engraving" is used in its generic sense. Kōkan, in fact, made use of both etching and engraving techniques in his own work.

3. Shiba, *Shumparō Hikki*, NZT, 1: 411.

4. John Johnston was an eminent Polish physician and zoologist of Scottish descent. He wrote his text in Latin and published it in Frankfurt in four installments: the first in 1649 on fish and other sea creatures, the second in 1650 on birds, the third in 1652 on four-legged animals, and the final volume in 1653 on snakes and reptiles. The illustrator, Matthieu Mérian, had studied painting under Anthony van Dyck (1599–1641). In 1660, M. Grausius translated the work into Dutch and published it at Amsterdam in one volume. The Dutch edition was presented to the fourth Tokugawa shogun, Ietsuna, in 1663 by Hendrick Indijck, factory director of Nagasaki at that time. Probably it met the fate of most European books presented to the shogunate and was carefully stored away in a government warehouse for the next hundred years. Gennai, in any case, did not obtain his copy until 1761.

5. Some of Sō Shiseki's copies together with Mérian's engravings are reproduced in Okamura, Pl. 7–16.

6. Shiba, *Seiyōga Dan*, NZT, 6:808–9. For a complete translation, see Appendix III.

7. Shiba, *Seiyōga Hō*, part of *Oranda Tsūhaku*, SK, pp. 127–28.

8. In *Seiyōga Dan*, Kōkan confounded the author of the book with its title *Huishoudelijk*. . . referred to in Japan as Buis or Huis. Chomel's text was first published in 1709, entitled *Dictionnaire oeconomique, contenant divers moyens d'augmenter son bien, et de conserver sa santé*. It was reprinted several times in Europe, a fourth revised edition appearing in 1741 with a supplement added by M. Pierre Roger in which the etching technique was described in detail. In 1743 both text and supplement were translated into Dutch by Jan Lodewyk Schuer, published in two volumes under the full title *Huishoudelijk Woordenboek, Vervattende Veele middelen om zijn Goed Te Vermeerderen, en zijne Gezondheid Te Behouden* (Household Dictionary, Containing Many Means to Increase One's Knowledge and Improve One's Health). In 1778 it was again revised, enlarged, and republished by Jacques Alexandre de Chalmot (1730–1801), and called *Algemeen Huishoudelijk-, Natuur-, Zedekundigen Konst-Woordenboek, Vervattende veele middelen om zijn Goed Te Vermeerderen, en zijne Gezondheid Te Behouden* (Dictionary of General Economics, Nature, Moral Philosophy, and Art, Designed for the Improvement of Knowledge and Betterment of Health). Both the 1743 and 1778 editions were imported into Japan.

Ōtsuki Gentaku later collaborated with Takahashi Kageyasu and Baba Sadayoshi in translating Chomel's complete encyclopedia under the sponsorship of the Tokugawa government and called the translation *Kōsei Shimpen* (New Compilation for the Public Welfare). The translation, based on the Dutch revised edition of 1778, required thirty-five years to complete and was not published during the lifetimes of the translators. Three manuscript copies were made for the Tokugawa government; the first printed edition, finally appearing in 1937, was made from the second manuscript.

We know that Kōkan was also familiar with a Dutch text written in 1769 by Egbert Buys entitled *Nieuw en Volkomen Woordenboek van Konsten en Weetenschappen* (New and Complete Dictionary of the Arts and Sciences). Some scholars have claimed that Kōkan's use of the word Boisu was a reference to Buys's book; this text, however, does not adequately describe the etching method and provides only a brief summary of engraving. The conclusion that Kōkan obtained his information from the text by Chomel rather than from the dictionary by Buys is corroborated and thoroughly investigated by Sugano Yō in his article.

9. Gentaku, a native of Sendai, had excellent background training in the Dutch language. His first teachers were Maeno Ryōtaku and Sugita Gempaku, pioneer scholars in the study of the Dutch language and Western medicine. About 1770, Gentaku went to Nagasaki to perfect his studies under the tutelage of the interpreter Yoshio Kōsaku. Upon his return he published in 1783 a study of the Dutch language called *Rangaku Kaitei* (Ladder to Dutch Studies), which established him as a principal contributor to Western learning.

10. The principle of the camera obscura was known in the West from antiquity, but the first description of a picture-viewing contraption was given in 1558 by the Venetian Giovanni Battista della Porta (c. 1538–1615) in his four-volume work on natural science, *Magia Naturalis.* The first portable box-type camera obscura was constructed about 1665 by Robert Boyle (1627–91). Camera obscuras were of two types. One consisted of a convex lens placed near the top of an upright wood support, as seen in Pl. 34. The picture was laid on a flat surface, reflected in a mirror placed above it at a forty-five degree angle, and the reverse magnification of the reflected image viewed through the lens. The other was an enclosed box without a mirror; the picture stood perpendicular to one end and was viewed through a lens at the other. The latter contraption required that pictures be mounted on heavy board so that they would stand upright; the pictures were not seen in reverse through the lens. The first variety was known in Japan usually as *nozoki karakuri* (trick peepshow) and the second as *nozoki megane* (peep glasses), though the distinction was often disregarded and both types referred to as *nozoki megane.* Other names included *Oranda megane* (Dutch glasses), *shashin kagami* (mirror of reality), and the Dutch word *donker kamer* (dark chamber). Perspective pictures designed to be seen through a camera obscura were called *megane-e.*

11. The five Japanese landscapes referred to were probably the following. 1) *Mimeguri, Edo.* September, 1783. 2) *Ochanomizu, Edo.* April, 1784. 3) *Oyaji Teahouse at Hirō, Edo.* May, 1784. 4) *Shinobazu Lake, Ueno.* May, 1784. 5) *Enjoying the Evening Cool by the River.* Undated.

All these engravings, which are in the Kobe City Museum of Namban Art, bear titles and signatures in the margins.

The copy of a Western picture was either *A European Hospital* or *The Serpentine, Hyde Park, London.* Both, likewise in the Kobe City Museum of Namban Art, are undated but stylistically similar to the above five. Their titles are inscribed in the margins in reversed roman letters: "Serhentine" and "Zitenhuys," this last being Kōkan's spelling of the Dutch *ziekenhuis* (hospital).

There is also a third undated foreign landscape by Kōkan, in the same museum, depicting a lion in the left foreground. The picture has no title, is crudely executed, and color is added roughly, with little relation to the composition. The lion drawn by Odano Naotake for Morishima Chūryō's book *Kōmō Zatsuwa* of 1787 is nearly identical to the lion in this engraving.

12. Like Kōkan's engraving, this unsigned painting is in mirror image, probably intended as a *megane-e* for a camera obscura. A fourth depiction of the same vista by Ōta Nampo—the poet-artist who wrote the laudatory inscription on Kōkan's painting of Shichirigahama (Pl. 7)—is nearly identical to Naotake's *megane-e,* though the image is in the same order as Naotake's signed painting. Traditionally, the unsigned work has been attributed to the lord of Akita, Satake Shozan, but a study by Takehana and Naruse ascribes it to Odano Naotake based on its similarity to known works by that artist. Both works are discussed and reproduced in Takehana Rintarō and Naruse Fujio, Pl. I-a and II-a. Naotake's painting of Shinobazu and potted peonies is reproduced in Sakamoto, Sugase, and Naruse, *Genshoku Nihon no Bijutsu,* 25:102–3.

13. Matsudaira Sadanobu, p. 46.

14. Yamana Kakuzō wrote (p. 208) that Denzen was Kōkan's disciple, but no evidence supports this assertion.

15. Shiba, *Shumparō Hikki,* NZT, 1:422.

16. Shiba, *Seiyōga Dan,* NZT, 6:811. For a translation of the announcement, see Appendix III.

17. For example, Aōdō Denzen, Matsumoto Yasuoki, and Yasuda Raishū.

It is interesting to note that a few years after Kōkan rediscovered the engraving technique in Japan, copperplates were first executed in China under the auspices of Jesuit missionaries. In a letter to M. Delatour written in 1786, Pere Bourgeois wrote: "You can judge for yourself about the European buildings at Yüan Ming Yüan from the twenty engravings that I am sending you. These are the first attempts at engraving on copper done in China on the order and under the eyes of Emperor Ch'ien Lung." (See Louis François Delatour, *Essai sur l'architecture des*

Chinois, sur leur jardins, leur principes de médecine, et leurs moeurs et usages [Paris: Clousier, 1803], p. 215.)

CHAPTER SIX

1. "Three or four hundred sheets" was a rough estimate; the actual diary manuscript was 229 double-folded sheets. Kōkan selected only 30 of the 103 illustrations in *Saiyū Ryodan* for inclusion in *Saiyū Nikki,* but added 24 new ones.

2. Shiba, *Saiyū Nikki,* in KSN, p. 71 (Temmei 8/9/8).

3. Ibid., p. 191 (Kansei 1/4/13).

4. Ibid., p. 76 (Temmei 8/9/20).

5. Ibid., pp. 29–30 (Temmei 8/6/29).

6. Ibid., p. 62 (Temmei 8/8/18).

7. Ibid., p. 182 (Kansei 1/3/20). The advertisement section of *Saiyū Ryodan* also refers to "Eight Views of Edo," undoubtedly the same scenes shown to the prince. These engravings, judging from extant works, must have been: 1) *Mimeguri,* 1783, 2) *Ochanomizu,* 1784, 3) *Oyaji Teahouse,* 1784, 4) *Shinobazu Lake,* 1784, 5) *Enjoying the Evening Cool by the River,* c. 1784, 6) *Shichirigahama,* 1787, 7) *Ryōgoku Bridge,* 1787, and 8) *Mimeguri,* 1787.

Though the site of number six, Shichirigahama, is not actually in Edo, it is close enough for Kōkan to have included it in the group. Strictly speaking, there are only seven different scenes, for numbers one and eight both depict Mimeguri. A later book, *Oranda Tensetsu* (1796), however, refers to only seven prints in its advertisement section; this notice would seem to be Kōkan's admission that he had actually drawn only seven different landscapes. Another possible eighth engraving is the *View of Edo Bridge* mentioned in *Saiyū Nikki,* KSN, p. 29 (Temmei 8/6/29). There is, however, no extant picture of this scene; Kōkan could have meant simply Ryōgoku Bridge in Edo.

In selecting eight views, Kōkan was following a traditional practice said to have been originated by the eleventh-century Chinese artist Sung Ti, who painted the famous *Eight Views of Hsiao and Hsiang.*

The house of Kan'in no Miya was descended from Emperor Higashiyama (reigned 1687–1709), whose son, Prince Naohito, received the title Kan'in no Miya in 1718. Kan'in no Miya's grandson became Emperor Kōkaku in 1779 and reigned until 1817. Since Kōkan's engravings were shown to Prince Kan'in in 1788, the prince referred to is probably Emperor Kōkaku's father, Prince Kan'in no Miya Sukehito, son of Kan'in no Miya Naohito, and grandson of Emperor Higashiyama.

8. According to the journal kept by Tani Bunchō during his journey to Nagasaki at that time, Bunchō made the trip to Itsukushima with Shiba Kōkan. His account of the expedition coincides with Kōkan's even to the description of the weather and the inclusion of the same poem. It is unclear, therefore, with whom Kōkan actually traveled. For a discussion of the meeting between Kōkan and Bunchō based on Bunchō's diary, see Muramatsu Shōfū, *Honchō Gajin Den* (Biographies of Famous Japanese Artists; Tokyo: Chuō Kōronsha, 1940), 1:343–47; and Yorozu Tetsugōrō, *Bunchō* (Tokyo: Arusu Shuppansha, 1928), pp. 23–25.

9. Shiba, *Saiyū Nikki,* KSN, p. 75.

10. References to time are converted to the present-day system according to the explanation by Suzuki Takanobu in *Dai Hyakka Jiten,* ed. Kimura Kyūichi (Tokyo: Heibonsha, 1951), 19:63–66.

11. Shiba, *Saiyū Nikki,* KSN, pp. 89–90 (Temmei 8/10/3).

12. Kenkadō's residence was a mecca for many artists and scholars of his day. Kōkan visited his establishment both on his way to Nagasaki and on his return trip to Edo. During one of these visits he showed Kenkadō his engravings, and proudly reported: "When I showed him the copperplate picture of Ryōgoku Bridge that I myself had made, Kenkadō could scarcely believe that it had been produced in Japan." (Shiba, *Saiyū Nikki,* KSN, p. 62 [Temmei 8/8/18].)

An extant portrait of Kenkadō in the Osaka Museum was painted by Tani Bunchō. An accomplished artist in his own right, Kenkadō was also a well-known art collector and botanist. For a discussion of his life and accomplishments, see the article "Kimura Kenkadō," by Takanashi Mitsukazu, Aimi Kōu, and Maruyama Toshio in *Kamigata,* No. 146 (March, 1943), pp. 2–24.

13. Temmei 8/10/10–Temmei 8/11/14.

14. The Nagasaki office of Foreign or Chinese Art Inspector (*Kara-e Mekiki*) was established in 1697, with Watanabe Shūseki as first occupant of the post; it remained a government position until the end of the Tokugawa regime in 1868. The official was charged with a double duty: to establish the authenticity and determine the monetary value of pictures bought from China, and to make detailed drawings of articles imported by Chinese and Dutch traders—flowers, rare birds, animals, and all unusual receptacles and implements.

15. Shiba, *Saiyū Nikki,* KSN, p. 103 (Temmei 3/10/20).

16. Yoshio Kōsaku (1724–1800).

17. Shiba, *Saiyū Nikki,* KSN, pp. 106–10 (Temmei 8/10/25).

18. Ibid., pp. 111–13 (Temmei 8/10/27).

19. Hendrik Godfried Duurkoop was a Dutch captain of the East India Company who died at sea July 27, 1778, and was buried at Nagasaki on August 15. His grave can still be seen at Goshin-ji.

20. Shiba, *Saiyū Ryodan* (1794 edition), Part III, pp. 22–23.

21. Shiba, *Saiyū Nikki,* KSN, pp. 122–23 (Temmei 8/11/12).

22. Ibid., pp. 128–29 (Temmei 8/11/21).

23. From December 30, 1788, until January 29, 1789 (Temmei 8/12/4–Kansei 1/1/4).

24. This was probably a local belief; China could not be visible from Ikitsuki-shima.

25. Masutomi Matanosuke, son of Masutomi Matazaemon.

26. Shiba, *Saiyū Nikki,* KSN, pp. 137–38 (Temmei 8/12/5).

27. Shiba, *Saiyū Ryodan* (1794 edition), Part IV, pp. 14–15.

28. Kōkan also executed an oil painting on silk (54.6 × 80 cm. 21½ × 31½ in.) in 1794 based on this section of the scroll. Kimura Coll., Hyogo; reproduced: Sakamoto, Sugase, and Naruse, *Genshoku Nihon no Bijutsu,* 25:118.

29. The humpback whale (*zatō-kujira*), Rudolph's whale or sei whale (*iwashi-kujira*), right whale (*semi-kujira*), finback whale (*nagasu-kujira*), and grey whale (*ko-kujira*).

30. Another copy of the same book as well as the woodblocks used in printing it are owned by the Matsu-ura Museum, Hirado. This edition is dated Bunsei 12 (1829). Frank Hawley writes (p. 190) that the book was published in 1832. Obviously, Kōkan could not have seen either of these later editions.

31. See Kōkan's comments on this subject in his essay on Western art, Appendix III. It must be remembered that his knowledge of Western art was derived from Dutch technical manuals and scientific illustrations.

CHAPTER SEVEN

1. At the time they were painted, a variety of names designated these exotic creations: *abura-e* (oil pictures), *abura-enogu* (oil pigments), *gofun-e* (chalk pictures), *kōmōga* (red-hair paintings), *ranga* (Dutch paintings), *rōga* (wax paintings), *rōyuga* (wax-oil paintings), *seiga* (Western paintings), *yusai* (oil colors), and *Shiba-e.* The term *Shiba-e* probably originated in reference to the production of oil paintings in the Shiba section of Edo, and no doubt also reflected the fact that Shiba Kōkan lived there.

2. There is, of course, the often-reproduced *Portrait of a Western Beauty* painted by Gennai in oil, apparently derived from an anonymous oil portrait of a Dutch couple, both paintings owned by the Kobe City Museum of Namban Art. It would seem that the man of many talents also showed his virtuosity in this domain. On the basis of one poorly executed work, however, Gennai can hardly be considered an artist.

3. In an article published in Meiji 39 (1906) in *Kaiga Zōshi,* No. 232, Omitsu Sukekichi wrote that it had come down to him by word of mouth that Gennai taught Western art techniques to three Akita men: Omitsu Magotarō Katsutaka (Sukekichi's grandfather), Tashiro Shūsuke, and Odano Naokata (Naotake); and that the lord of Akita, Satake Shozan, eager to obtain the information directly from Gennai, sought him out and received special instruction.

4. Hirafuku, p. 9. A report preserved in the Akita Library verifies that Gennai was at Kakudate in 1773; entitled "Hiraga Gennai to Yoshida Rihei Akita ni Maneku Koto," it was written by two government officials of Akita, Ōta Idaifu and Oyama Rokuzaemon.

5. Naotake returned to Akita in December, 1777, but spent another year with Gennai in Edo from the winter of 1778 until the winter of 1779. See Takehana Rintarō and Naruse Fujio, p. 39.

6. Chōkai Genryū, who as a young man had married into a family in Akita and studied medicine in Edo, was a habitué of Gennai's establishment. In 1835, after his retirement, he wrote his memoirs of his years in Edo, mentioning that Odano Naotake taught Western painting to Shiba Kōkan, and commenting that Naotake, who died while still a young man, was no longer known. Genryū's text, called *Okina Hidarizonae,* is not extant, but sections of it were copied by Ikeda Gensai in *Okina Hidarizonae Nukigaki* (Excerpts from Okina Hidarizonae), and repeated in his major work of 139 volumes called *Kōsai Roku,* completed in 1845 and now located in the Kōkyū Library in Sakata, Yamagata prefecture. The relevant portion of the text is printed in the article by Takehana and Naruse, p. 41.

7. Shiba, *Seiyōga Dan,* NZT, 6:808.

8. Shiba, *Seiyōga Hō* in *Oranda Tsūhaku,* SK, p. 126.

9. The first Dutch edition of 1707 was entitled *Het Groot Schilderboek* (The Great Painter's Book). The edition Kōkan obtained was probably the reprint of 1712 entitled in full *Groot Schilderboek, Waar in de Schilderkonst In Al Haar Deelen Grondig werd onderweezen* (Great Painter's Book, Wherein Painting in All Its Branches Is Methodically Demonstrated); an appended section, dated 1713, is entitled *Grondlegginge Ter Teekenkonst* (Fundamental Rules of Drawing). In Japan the book was referred to both as *Groot Schilderboek* and as *Konst Schilderboek.*

10. Titsingh, captain of the Dutch East India trading company, first arrived in Japan August 15, 1779. Custom required that whenever a Dutch ship arrived, the captain of the Dutch factory was obliged to visit the capital at Edo the following spring to pay his respects to the shogun. Titsingh left Nagasaki on February 19, 1780, and arrived at Edo on March 25. Received by Shogun Ieharu on April 5, he left the capital on April 14, arriving back at Nagasaki on May 27. On November 6, 1780, he left Deshima for Batavia, the Dutch trading headquarters in Indonesia. He returned to Nagasaki on August 12 of the following year and made a second journey to the shogunal court in 1782, arriving at Edo on April 7, where he stayed until April 22. No Dutch ship arrived in Japan from Java during 1782, and Titsingh remained in Nagasaki as head of the Dutch trading company until November 6, 1783, when he again left for Batavia. He made a third and final journey to Japan in 1784, arriving at Deshima on August 18.

During this last sojourn in Japan, however, he made no trip to Edo and, on November 26 of the same year, left the country to become governor of the Dutch settlement in Chinsura, Bengal. See Titsingh's records, British Museum, Add. MSS., 18100.

11. Titsingh suggested to the Board of Directors in Holland that the director of the Deshima post be selected not merely for his commercial ability but for his educational attainments, as well. The Japanese, he claimed, were far more impressed by academic and scientific learning than by business acumen, and the company ultimately would benefit from improved personal relations. The company's reply: "It is a general rule in these parts to sacrifice to Mercury, but never to Pallas." (Boxer, "The Mandarin at Chinsura," pp. 3–4.)

12. Gennai's book, *Butsurui Hinshitsu* (Classifications and Different Materials), was published in 1763, and illustrated by Sō Shiseki. The sketchbook, although attributed to Satake Shozan, quite possibly is the work of Odano Naotake (Toyama, p. 159). It is divided into three sections: 1) *Gahō Kōryō* (Discussion of Painting), 2) *Gato Rikai* (Technical Explanation), and 3) *Seitan Bu* (Blue and Red Coloring). A printed copy of *Gahō Kōryō* appears in Sakazaki, pp. 71–74.

13. Morishima Chūryō, *Kōmō Zatsuwa*, p. 121. Ten of Morishima's *Schilderboek* illustrations depict anatomical drawings. Six others, labeled "from a different part of the same book," give the technique of drawing heads, hands, and feet by the use of lines drawn with a compass. The last two in the series, displaying engraving tools, were not copied from the *Schilderboek* but from Chomel's encyclopedia.

14. See Appendix III for a complete translation of *Seiyōga Dan*. A translation of *Seiyōga Hō* can be found in C. L. French, "Shiba Kōkan and the Beginnings of Western Art in Japan" (Master's thesis, Department of Chinese and Japanese, Columbia University, 1958), pp. 90–93.

15. In 1708, for example, Nishikawa Joken reported the importation of "various Dutch pictures" in his book *Ka'i Tsūshō Kō* (A Study of Chinese and Western Trade). Joken's complete list of imported articles is given by Boxer in *Jan Compagnie*, Appendix I, pp. 174–76.

16. The van Royen painting was one of five imported in response to Shogun Yoshimune's request of 1722 for Dutch paintings; four years later they were delivered by the Dutch captain Hendrik Durven. Yoshimune, one of the few rulers of Japan who actively encouraged the study of Dutch language and scholarship, was also a dilettante painter and demonstrated a taste for Western oils.

17. Nakayama Kōyō, p. 47.

18. The van Royen painting is no longer extant. Ishikawa Tairō's copy, owned by Isurugi Michiyuki, Tokyo, was executed after Tairō had spent five days studying the original; it was highly praised by Ōtsuki Gentaku in his book *Bansui Mansō* (Bansui's Miscellany), written in 1826 (*Bansui Mansō*, pp. 66–67). Bunchō's copy is owned by the Kobe City Museum of Namban Art. Reproductions of both paintings may be found in *Museum*, No. 227, Tokyo Kokuritsu Hakubutsukan Bijutsu Shi (February, 1970), pp. 8, 9.

19. Destroyed during World War II; illustrated in *Kokka*, No. 544 (March, 1936).

20. Satake Shozan, p. 73.

21. Shiba, *Seiyōga Dan*, NZT, 6:807; Appendix III, paragraph 2.

22. Honda Toshiaki, *Seiiki Monogatari*, translated by Donald Keene, in *Japanese Discovery of Europe: 1720–1798*, pp. 206–7.

23. Satō Chūryō, in the section entitled "Dutch Painting" (NZT, Vol. 2, Part III, pp. 69–72). Additional explanation describes the method of painting with oil on glass, wood, cloth, or paper; the process of mixing paint; and the techniques of perspective, shading, and coloring.

24. The chief foreign-art school, the Araki, founded by Araki Genkei, included Araki Gen'yū, Ishizaki Yūshi, Araki Jogen, and Kaburagi Baikei (1749–1803). Independent artists in Nagasaki, especially Wakasugi Isohachi and Kawahara Keiga, also gained recognition for their paintings in European style.

25. Part 1 was entitled *Seiyōga Den* (Commentary on Western Painting), and Part 2, *Oranda Kikō* (Dutch Techniques). See translation, Appendix III. Shiba, *Seiyōga Dan*, NZT, 6:811.

26. The first, dated July 9 (Bunka 10/6/12), states in the final paragraph: "Very soon my book *Oranda Kikō* will be printed at Yoshida Shimbē's printing shop west of Tominokōji on Sanjō Street, Kyoto. In this book I have drawn Mount Fuji and other famous Japanese landscapes using the realistic Dutch method, which I was the first to employ in Japan." The second, written December 3 (Bunka 10/11/11), repeats: "I finally have completed my original manuscript *Oranda Kikō*, and shall take it to the publisher very soon. I expect it will be published next year." (Shiba Kōkan, in "Shiba Kōkan no Shukan," *Gakkō Kōyūkai*, Vol. III, No. 6 [March, 1905], p. 128; and No. 8 [June, 1905], p. 180.)

27. The manuscript may still turn up, as did Kōkan's *Dokushō Bōgen*, believed to have been lost.

28. There are extant at least ten paintings of Daruma attributed to Shiba Kōkan and many others executed in the same style. One unsigned painting of Daruma very possibly by Kōkan is owned by the Museum of Fine Arts, Boston.

29. Shiba, *Saiyū Nikki*, KSN, pp. 21–22 (Temmei 8/6/24).

30. Ibid., pp. 43–44 (Temmei 8/8/5).

31. Reproductions of several paintings attributed to Nobukata or executed in his manner are in Nishimura, *Namban Bijutsu*, Pl. 102–13. See especially the portrait of an old man reading a book (Pl. 104) and the portrait of Nikkyō Shōnin, a Buddhist priest of

the Nichiren sect at the Seiren-ji temple (Pl. 107).

32. Kensu (Chinese: Chien-tzŭ), a Zen priest of Sung-dynasty China, was a common subject in both Chinese and Japanese art. Well-known Japanese paintings depicting him include a hanging scroll in the Tokyo National Museum by Kao, and a painting on *fusuma* doors in the Shinju-an, Daitoku-ji, by Hasegawa Tōhaku.

33. "Paap" might also be interpreted as "pope" or the Dutch slang term for "Roman Catholic."

34. Father Abraham (lay name Johann Ulrich Megerle) first published his book at Würzburg in 1699 and entitled it *Etwas für Alle, Das ist: Eine kurtze Beschreibung allerley Stands- Ambts- und Gewerbs-Personen, mit beygedruckter Sittlichen Lehre und Biblischen Concepten* (Something for All, That Is: A Short Description of Various Nobles, Officials, and Merchants, Accompanied by Moral Doctrines and Biblical Concepts). A second German edition, also printed at Würzburg, appeared in 1711. In 1717 the book was translated into Dutch by J. Le Long, published at Amsterdam, and entitled *Iets Voor Allen, zynde een Verhandeling en Verbeelding Van allerhande, Standen, Studien, Konsten, Wetenschappen, Handwerken enz: Waar in derfelver Oorfprong, Opkomft, Aardt, Eygenfchap, Deugdt, en Ondeugden, opeen Geeftige wyze beschreven werdt* (Something for Everyone, Being a Treatise and Representation of All Kinds of Things: Classes, Studies, Arts, Sciences, Crafts, etc., Whose Origins, Developments, Natures, Characteristics, Virtues, and Vices Are Described in a Spirited Manner). Revised editions in Dutch appeared in 1736 and 1759, each time with new plates added illustrating different professions, and others omitted. The prototype for Kōkan's painting of the Hollander (Pl. 63), for example, appears only in the Dutch edition of 1759, but is also included in the German edition of 1711. Many of the illustrations in these texts were taken from an earlier book of 1698 by Christoph Weigel entitled *Abbildung der Gemein-Nützlichen Haupt-Stände*. Locations of the texts used by the author are as follows: Weigel 1698, Princeton University; Abraham German edition of 1699 (reprint 1905), author's collection; German edition of 1711, Columbia University; Dutch edition of 1717, Columbia University; Dutch edition of 1736, Columbia University; Dutch edition of 1759, Harvard University.

35. Another interpretation, of equally obscure significance, might be "First Sunday in Japan," in which case "Zonders" should be "Zondag." The signatures in Chinese characters on these two paintings may have been added at a later date.

36. Naruse, "Shiba Kōkan no Gagyō ni tsuite," pp. 29–31.

37. See chapter six, p. 69. Shiba, *Saiyū Nikki*, KSN, p. 128.

38. Discovered by Naruse in Gotfridi, p. 254. A copy of this book is owned by the Memorial Library, University of Wisconsin.

39. Reproduced Ono, *Kōmō Zatsuwa*, pp. 274–75.

40. Shiba, *Seiyōga Dan*, NZT, 6:807–9.

41. "De tinnegieter, Zoekt 'n Zeltsden Schat Vant allerschoonste Vat."

42. The sketch is reproduced in Ono, *Edo no Yōgaka*, Pl. 79.

43. Another is reproduced in Nishimura, *Nihon Shoki*, plate section.

44. The book, housed in Waseda University Library, Tokyo, also contains the signature of Sugita Gempaku, and beside it the notation: "Age 29,016 days."

45. These artists went a step further by adopting Western names. Ishikawa Tairō used the name "Tafel Berg"; Kitayama Kangan (Handeiki), "Van Dyck"; and Kawahara Keiga (Toyosuke), "M. E. R. Tojosky."

46. Ōta Nampo, also known as Shokusanjin and Kyōkaen, was one of the so-called eighteen men about town (*jūhachi daitsū*), style setters of their time. His serious writings include *Ichiwa Ichigen*, a collection of anecdotes and comments on the social and official world of his day. He was also one of the leading figures in the *kyōka* school of humorous poetry.

47. Seizandō Biwamaro, a book dealer of Edo and a *kyōka* poet.

48. Another painting by Kōkan nearly identical in composition, though not a *doro-e*, is owned by Yabumoto Sōgorō, Osaka. Two works reproduced in Kyoto Hakubutsukan, *Meiji Izen*, Pl. 23 and 67, are also similar; only the position of Mount Fuji has been shifted slightly, and the two standing fishermen replaced by single seated figures. In 1787, Kōkan executed the scene in a copperplate engraving, now owned by the Kobe City Museum of Namban Art.

49. The painting, now in the Atami Museum, was formerly owned by the Hotta family of Shimōsa (present-day Chiba prefecture), as the inscription on the box containing the scroll indicates. The head of the family was interested in European studies and commissioned his retainer Tozuka Seikai (1799–1876) to study Dutch medicine.

50. Several undated depictions by Kōkan of Futamigaura are extant. One, owned by Geijutsu Daigaku, Ueno, is reproduced in Ono, *Edo no Yōgaka*, Pl. 77. Another is reproduced in Sakamoto, Sugase, and Naruse, Pl. 112.

51. Shiba, *Seiyōga Dan*, NZT, 6:807.

52. Shiba, *Shumparō Hikki*, NZT, 1:421.

53. Kansei 12/6. Circular of 1800; Kobe City Museum of Namban Art.

54. The Japanese word translated here as "water colors" is *sentanga*. The term in Chinese—*hsüantan*—referred to the technique of creating specific textural effects by the use of black ink and washes. *Hsüan* means to "sprinkle" or "drip" with well-watered ink and has connections with the "wrinkle" technique of painting; *tan* implies a process carried out with ink of a light value. Soper discusses the interpreta-

tions of this term in his article. Kōkan's use of the term *sentanga,* however, apparently was intended to refer to his own style combining Oriental and Western elements, or simply to his paintings executed in Japanese watercolor pigments, in contrast to his Western oils.

55. Circular of 1806 (Bunka 3); Kobe City Museum of Namban Art. Here, as in the previous announcement of 1800, Kōkan gives an accurate statement of his age. Age sixty, however, is the former Japanese reckoning; by Western count he was fifty-nine years old in 1806.

56. There are extant two nearly identical paintings of *Mount Fuji Viewed from Kashiwabara,* the one shown here and that in the collection of Yabumoto Sōshirō, Tokyo.

57. Views of Mount Fuji by Tani Bunchō and Hirose Daizan illustrate the pervasive influence of Western techniques in Japan at this time. It is interesting that Daizan, a *bunjinga* artist, and Bunchō, who often painted in the *bunjinga* manner, both displayed a technical competence comparable to Kōkan's in handling Western style. See the painting of Mount Fuji by Daizan, reproduced in *Kokka,* No. 578 (January, 1939), Pl. 6, and Bunchō's work on the same theme, *Bijutsu Kenkyū,* No. XLVII (November, 1935), Pl. 7.

58. A small reproduction of the painting, owned by Michigami Toshii, appears on p. 106 of his article.

59. It has been established that the painting was executed approximately three hundred years ago on European canvas with European oil paint and that the Japanese mounting is made of cloth three hundred years old. The painting, then, dates from the time of Rembrandt and is not a Japanese copy of a European work; all the owners, from Zeniya Gohei to the present Michigami Toshii, have been ascertained. Unquestionably, the inscription was written by Shiba Kōkan. There is no proof, of course, that Rembrandt executed the work. According to the eminent Rembrandt authority Dr. Seymour Slive, who has examined the painting, there is "no reason to support its attribution to Rembrandt. In my judgment, it has nothing in common with works painted by him, his pupils, or contemporary followers." (Personal correspondence, February 24, 1970.)

60. Hsi-hu (West Lake), a manmade pleasure lake in Hangchow, famous for its great beauty.

61. Circular of 1809. Kobe City Museum of Namban Art.

62. Shiba Kōkan, *Shumparō Hikki,* NZT, 1:422.

63. Shiba, *Gakkō Kōyūkai,* Vol. III, No. 6 (March, 1905), p. 128. Letter dated Bunka 10/6/12 (1813).

64. Ibid., No. 8 (June, 1905), p. 181. Letter dated Bunka 10/11/11.

65. The painting is reproduced in Kuroda, *Nagasaki-kei Yōga,* Pl. 52.

66. Haga Tōru, "The Formation of Realism in Meiji Painting: The Artistic Career of Takahashi Yuichi (1828–94)," unpublished manuscript (Tokyo University, January, 1966), Chapter IV.

CHAPTER EIGHT

1. A. E. E. McKenzie, *The Major Achievements of Science* (Cambridge: Cambridge University Press, 1960), 1:21.

2. Fukansai Fabian (Sakuma Sōtō), considered one of the pillars of the Jesuit order in Japan, ultimately became disillusioned with the Church system and the reluctance of his foreign superiors to ordain him. In 1607, he apostatized.

3. Sugita Gempaku, *Rangaku Koto Hajime,* Vol. I, Section 18, Wada Shinjirō, ed. (Tokyo: Tozai Igakusha, 1950), p. 52.

4. An excellent discussion of these events is presented by Keene, in *Japanese Discovery of Europe: 1720–1798,* pp. 27–31.

The foreign text was *Tabulae Anatomica,* written in 1647 by a German, Johan Adam Kulmus; it had been translated into Dutch in 1734 by Gerardus Dieten, and entitled *Ontleedkundige Tafelen.*

5. Ryōei's ancestors were from Hirado, where they served the local lord Matsu-ura. His grandfather became an interpreter in Nagasaki in 1664, a post later held by his father, and finally by Ryōei himself.

6. Ryōei entitled his book *Tenchi Nikyū Yōhō* (Directions for the Use of the Two Charts of the Heavens and Earth). The Dutch book was written by Willem Janszoon Blaeuw and published at Amsterdam in 1666. In making his translation, Ryōei used both the Dutch original and a Chinese version provided by his sponsor Matsumura Mototsuna, who assisted him in reading the Chinese. The book contained both Ptolemy's geocentric theory and Copernicus's heliocentric; Ryōei faithfully translated both, though in his commentary to the translation he stated that he supported the Copernican theory.

7. The book, entitled *Taiyō Kyūri Ryōkaisetsu* (An Explanation of Solar Physics), required a year and a half to complete. The original seven manuscripts have been collected and bound in two volumes and are now kept in the Nagasaki Library together with Ryōei's other translated works. The original book, written by George Adams in 1770, had been translated into Dutch under the title *Gronden der Sterrenkunde, gelegd in het Zonnestelzel bevatlijk gemaakt; in eene Beschrijving van't Maaksel en Gebruik der nieuwe Hemel-en Aard-Globen in't Engelsch beschreeven door George Adams, in't Nederduits vertaald en met aanmerkingen verrijkt door Jacob Ploos van Amsterdam* (Principles of Astronomy, Based on the Solar System: A Treatise Describing and Explaining the Construction and Use of New Celestial and Terrestrial Globes, Written in English by George Adams and Translated into Dutch with Annotations by Jacob Ploos of

Amsterdam). Ryōei appended to his translation his own comments and opinions, mentioning the difficulties encountered in translation, his use of Chinese characters rather than the Japanese syllabary for Dutch words, and the differences between solar and lunar calendars and between the geocentric and heliocentric theories.

8. Shiba, *Shumparō Hikki,* NZT, 1:434.

9. In 1911, the scholar Kitano Takaharu came across Motoki Ryōei's works in the course of his research on Nagasaki history.

10. Katayama Shōsai, *Sōkai Itteki Shū,* part 5, p. 73. Part I of this work explains the heliocentric theory using practically the same wording Kōkan used.

11. Shiba, *Shumparō Hikki,* NZT, 1:411. There is some doubt concerning the veracity of Kōkan's account.

12. Kōkan's illustration of Adam's Peak was copied from an engraving (Pl. 92 here) in *Oud en Nieuw Oost-Indiën,* written in 1726 by François Valentijn. He depicted the scene again on his world map *Chikyū Zenzu* (Pl. 91).

13. Shiba, *Saiyū Nikki,* KSN, pp. 50–51 (Temmei 8/8/11).

14. Shiba, *Chikyū Zenzu Ryakusetsu* (1793 ed.), p. 1 (or see SK, p. 71).

15. *Chikyū Zenzu Ryakusetsu,* Preface, pp. 1–3.

16. Gentaku had the Covens and Mortier map mounted as a hanging scroll in 1789, and above the map he noted that he had received it from the Dutch surgeon Stutzer in 1737. The date must be in error, for Gentaku was not yet born at that time. He wrote the date by the sexagenary cycle 丁已 rather than by era name and number; possibly it should have been written 丁未, which would make the year 1787. Kōkan, as noted, met Stutzer in Nagasaki in 1788. Until World War II, Gentaku's foreign map was housed in the Municipal Library in Sendai; it was lost when the library was destroyed.

17. Chinese characters were generally pronounced in an approximation of contemporary Chinese pronunciation rather than in the Japanese *kan'on* or *go'on* systems.

18. Shiba, *Yochi Ryakusetsu,* SK, pp. 5–6.

19. Shiba, *Chikyū Zenzu Ryakusetsu* (1793 ed.), p. 12 (or see SK, p. 70). Ba Shin'yō was a *bunjinga* painter, as well as a scholar of geography and astronomy; his son was the artist Kitayama Kangan. He began the restoration of the terrestrial and celestial globes in 1791 and presented the completed work to the government in 1795. See Kaikoku Hyakunen Kinen Bunka Jigyōkai Hen, *Sakoku Jidai,* pp. 36–38.

20. Gentaku, in a letter written the second month of Kansei 5 (1793) to Horiuchi Rintetsu, a medical doctor in Yonezawa (Yamagata prefecture), stated: "Kōkan's world map will be completed this winter it seems. If you wish to have a copy you should write directly to him." The same month Kōkan also wrote to Rintetsu promising to send him a copy of his map "when it is completed." A second letter from Kōkan dated the following month announced: "I am sending you a copy of my world map." The letters were discovered by Katagiri Kazuo in a collection of *rangakusha* letters owned by Horiuchi Jun'ichi and are published in Katagiri's article "Shiba Kōkan no Shin Shokan," pp. 101–10.

21. Ibid., p. 102.

22. Kōkan apparently owned the book, for his contemporary Katayama Shōsai wrote: "Some time ago I visited Shiba Kōkan's house and examined the world map contained in the Dutch book by Valentijn." Katayama, *Sōkai Itteki Shū,* 4:28. See footnote 12 above.

23. Aōdō Denzen, for example, executed a world map in 1810 under the direction of Takahashi Kageyasu, a scholar of European science who collaborated with Ōtsuki Gentaku in translating Chomel's *Encyclopedia.* In 1846, a world map drawn by Nagai Seigai was engraved by Yasuda Raishū.

24. Shiba, *Yochi Ryakusetsu,* SK, p. 5.

25. The book was the *Nieuw en Volkomen Woordenboek van Konsten In Weetenschappen* (New and Complete Dictionary of the Arts and Sciences) written by Egbert Buys in 1769. Kōkan produced his own copperplate engraving of an orrery (Pl. 98) copied from Buys's illustration.

26. Josui (Matsubara Uchū) was an engraver and scholar of world geography and astronomy. A world map executed by him entitled *Bankoku Yochi Zenzu* (Complete Map of the World) is preserved in the library of Waseda University, Tokyo.

27. Shiba, *Chikyū Zenzu Ryakusetsu* (1793 ed.), pp. 9–10 (or see SK, p. 77).

28. Ibid. (1797 ed.), p. 15 (or see SK, p. 85). A similar description of England was written in 1798 by Honda Toshiaki, who may have obtained his information from Kōkan. See the translation in Keene, *Japanese Discovery of Europe: 1720–1798,* pp. 116–17.

29. A list of the more important works dealing with geography and related topics in circulation before 1792 is given in Appendix IV.

30. Shiba, *Oranda Tsūhaku,* SK, p. 111. The map Kōkan copied must have been a Dutch map used for navigation.

31. Katsuragawa's work was entitled *Shinsei Chikyū Bankoku Zusetsu* (New Explanation of the Countries of the World). A copy of the original manuscript is owned by Akioka Takejirō, Setagaya-ku, Tokyo. The printed text appears in *Kōmō Zatsuwa,* pp. 1–34.

32. Shiba, *Oranda Tsūhaku,* SK, pp. 117–18.

33. The last three sections of Volume One have no relation to world geography, and probably were not originally intended to form a part of *Oranda Tsūhaku.* One is *Seiyōga Hō* (Principles of Western Painting), the second *Dōbanga* (Copperplate Engraving), and the third *Tenshō Chiri* (Astronomical Phenomena and Geography). The content of the first two is the same as *Seiyōga Dan.* These three

sections were probably written to constitute part of the ill-fated *Shumparō Gafu.*

34. Miura Baien, p. 182.

35. Shiba, *Oranda Tsūhaku,* SK, pp. 135–36.

36. Honda Toshiaki's letter to Tachihara Suiken in Honjō, p. 380.

37. Honda Toshiaki also described the Colossus. See Keene, *Japanese Discovery of Europe: 1720–1798,* p. 207.

38. Gotfridi, p. 254.

39. Reproduced Morishima Chūryō, *Bankoku Shinwa,* Section 4, pp. 274–75.

40. Kōkan probably derived his information from Nishikawa Joken's *Yonjūni Koku* (in Ono, *Kōmō Zatsuwa,* p. 372). A later book, *Kaigai Jimbutsu Shū* (Collection of Pictures of Foreign Peoples) published in 1854 also has an illustration of the "midgets of Novaya Zemlya." The book was written by Yamamura Shōei and Nagada Nankei and was based on Nishikawa's book. (In Ono, *Kōmō Zatsuwa,* opposite p. 381.)

41. Czarina Elizaveta Alekseyevna (Louisa Maria Augusta of Baden), married Czar Alexander on October 9, 1793.

42. He did not. The Rezanov envoy had not originated from official Russian policy, although this was not known to the Japanese. The Russian ship was en route around the world with the intent of developing trade with India and Southeast Asia. The mission of Rezanov was subsidiary, designed merely to provide a stopping place for a fur-trading company.

43. Shiba, *Shumparō Hikki,* NZT, 1:451.

44. A map of Ceylon and southern India, a coconut palm from Coromandel, a betel palm, natives of Coromandel, a map of part of Southeast Asia, and a view of a Buddhist temple in Canton.

45. Shiba, *Ryōjusen Zusetsu,* p. 7.

46. Shiba, *Oranda Tensetsu,* SK, p. 23.

47. A zodiacal chart Kōkan may have had an opportunity to see during his Nagasaki journey is owned by the Matsu-ura Museum in Hirado. It is contained in an atlas by Petri Schenck, printed at Amsterdam in 1700. This chart, however, is more detailed than either Blaeu's or Kōkan's.

48. The zodiacal constellations are referred to as twelve *kyū,* the lunar constellations as twenty-eight *shuku.*

49. The map is reproduced in Kaikoku Hyakunen Kinen Bunka Jigyōkai Hen, *Sakoku Jidai,* p. 233.

50. Honda Toshiaki, p. 213.

51. Shiba, *Oranda Tensetsu,* SK, p. 25.

52. Matteo Ricci's Chinese names were Li Matou and Hsi-t'ai.

53. Shiba, *Tenchi Ridan,* SK, pp. 217–18. Kōkan's assertion of Matteo Ricci's false claim to Western citizenship is reiterated in his *Shumparō Hikki* (NZT, 1:433–34), where he mentions that he learned this from Arai Hakuseki's book *Sairan Igen.* Arai Hakuseki wrote that he received the information from a Hollander in Japan. (Arai Hakuseki, original book undated, Vol. 5, Appendix, p. 1.) Goa, of course, was a trading port controlled by the Portuguese.

54. Many of Ricci's scientific teachings were also recorded by the Chinese scholars Hsü Kuang-chi'i (1562–1633) and Li Chih-tsao (1569–1630), but it is unlikely that Kōkan saw their books or that they even reached Japan.

55. According to Kuroda, it was Nishikawa Joken who published the Japanese edition in 1730, but Joken was dead by the time of the book's publication. See Kuroda Genji, "Shiba Kōkan no Shizen Kagakuteki Gyōseki ni tsuite," p. 53. Joken, however, worked together with his son Nishikawa Seikyū in editing the Chinese book.

56. The Nagasaki interpreter Motoki Ryōei also had access to the *T'ien-ching Huo-wên,* referred to in his book *Taiyō Kyūri Ryōkaisetsu,* NZT, 8:355.

57. The following were the more important commentaries:

Tenkyō Wakumon Hakki (Demonstration of the *Tenkyō Wakumon*), Matsunaga Ryōhitsu. Manuscript, 1735.

Tenkyō Wakumon Seigi (Veracity of the *Tenkyō Wakumon*), Tsuchimikado Yasukuni. Manuscript, 1737.

Tenkyō Wakumon Chūkai (Commentary on the *Tenkyō Wakumon*), Irie Osamu. Published, 1750.

Temmonkeii Kokujikai (Explanation in Native Script of the Longitude and Latitude of the Heavens), Hara Nagatsune. Published, 1770.

Tenkyō Wakumon Chūkai (Commentary on the *Tenkyō Wakumon*), Nishimura Enri. Nine copy books, 1771.

Kōsei Tenkyō Wakumon (Collated Edition of the *Tenkyō Wakumon*), Shibukawa Yūken. Revised manuscript, 1852.

58. Shiba, *Oranda Tensetsu,* SK, illus. 13 and 14.

59. Ibid., pp. 34–35. Earth's equatorial circumference is actually 24,902.45 miles. Copernicus, using the same image to arrive at the opposite conclusion, wrote: "It is but as the saying of Aeneas in Virgil: 'We sail forth from the harbor, and lands and cities retire.' As the ship floats along in the calm, all external things seem to have the motion that is really that of the ship, while those within the ship feel that they and all its contents are at rest." (*On the Revolutions of the Celestial Orbs,* 1543.)

60. Shiba, *Oranda Tensetsu,* SK, p. 35.

61. This picture was copied from an illustration in the encyclopedia by Egbert Buys.

62. Shiba, *Kopperu Temmon Zukai,* SK, p. 167.

63. Ibid., p. 169.

64. Kepler's name never appears in any of Kōkan's texts. For Copernicus he used the Chinese characters 刻白爾 (Kopperu), the same characters used by other Japanese authors. In China, however, these characters were used for Kepler (K'o Pai-erh), whereas Copernicus was written 歌白泥 (Ko Pai-ni). Kōkan apparently considered the two men the same

person. His contemporary, Katayama Shōsai, wrote in his book on astronomy that "Kepler" was simply another name for Copernicus. (Katayama, *Sōkai Itteki Shū*, part 5, p. 72.)

65. Shiba, *Tenchi Ridan,* SK, p. 238.
66. Shiba, *Shumparō Hikki,* NZT, 1:457–58.
67. Yamazaki, p. 558.
68. Shiba, *Tenchi Ridan,* SK, p. 251.
69. Katayama, *Hokusō Zatsuwa*, p. 373.
70. The *chitengi* diagram of the heavens made in 1808.
71. A character in the Chinese fourteenth-century novel *Romance of the Three Kingdoms.* At a state banquet, Ch'in Fu gave a discourse on "astronomy," proving that heaven had a head, ears, feet, and a surname. (Lo Kuan-chung, *Romance of the Three Kingdoms,* trans. C. H. Brewitt-Taylor [Tokyo: Tuttle, 1959], 2:269.)
72. Shiba, *Shumparō Hikki,* NZT, 1:449–50.
73. Nobuhiro was an economist, philosopher, and Dutch scholar from a family of physicians in Dewa.
74. By the lunar calendar, Kansei 6/11/11.
75. As noted earlier, Kōkan referred to Matsubara Uchū in *Chikyū Zenzu Ryakusetsu* as the constructor of an orrery. A picture drawn at the first New Year's party in 1794 depicting the scholars seated round a table, as well as the playbill and symbol chart of 1796 and the sumo program of 1799 are illustrated in Okamura, Pl. 2–6. The originals are in Waseda University Library, Tokyo.
76. Shiba, *Shumparō Hikki,* NZT, 1:411.
77. Entitled *Enroku* (Notes on Tobacco), published in 1796. It is contained in Volume 2 of *Bansui Sonkyō* (Echoes of Bansui).
78. Entsū wrote his book in refutation of the *rangakusha*'s claim that Buddhism was lacking in scientific accuracy. Before publishing his book, Entsū devoted thirty years to the study of the Indian calendar.
79. According to Buddhist teachings, Sumeru (Japanese: Shumi-sen), home of the gods, is a mountain square in shape located in the center of the world, in the area of Tibet.
80. Shiba, *Shumparō Hikki,* NZT, 1:415.
81. Ōnishi Hajime, "Shiba Kōkan no Sekaikan," *Kokumin no Tomo,* Supplement No. 233 (August, 1894), p. 52. Ōnishi Hajime (1864–99) was a scholar of idealistic philosophy during the Meiji era.
82. Ayuzawa, "Taisei Chirigaku," p. 56.

CHAPTER NINE

1. Shiba, *Shumparō Hikki,* NZT, 1:457.
2. Ibid., p. 408.
3. Ibid. Also, Shiba, *Mugon Dōjin Hikki,* TR, p. 120.
4. Shiba, *Mugon Dōjin Hikki,* TR, p. 87.
5. Shiba, *Dokushō Bōgen,* in *Historia,* p. 101.
6. See chapter 8n79.
7. Shiba, *Tenchi Ridan,* SK, p. 220.
8. Shiba, *Shumparō Hikki,* NZT, 1:434.
9. Ibid., p. 402.
10. Ibid., p. 405.
11. Shiba, excerpt from the discussion of an orrery, *Tenkyū Zenzu,* Kobe City Museum of Namban Art.
12. Shiba, *Mugon Dōjin Hikki,* TR, p. 87.
13. See, for example, *Dokushō Bōgen,* in *Historia,* p. 94.
14. The painting, in color on paper, measuring 93.7 × 27.5 cm., is in the Waseda University Library, Tokyo.
15. Saigyō (lay name Satō Norikiyo), the famous twelfth-century itinerant Buddhist priest-poet.
16. Shiba, *Dokushō Bōgen,* in *Historia,* p. 93.
17. Ibid., pp. 95–96.
18. Shiba, *Shumparō Hikki,* NZT, 1:457, 465.
19. Karl R. Popper, *The Open Society and Its Enemies* (New York: Harper Torch Books, Harper and Row, 1963), 1:12–14.
20. Hiraga Gennai, pp. 247–49.
21. Tominaga Nakamoto, *Shutsujō Gogo,* cited by Nakamura Yukihoko in *Nihon Koten Bungaku Taikei* (Tokyo: Iwanami Shoten), 55:440.
22. Huai-nan Tzŭ, 1:5. The first paragraph of the above translation is in *Sources of Chinese Tradition,* ed. Wm. Theodore de Bary, p. 209.
23. Shiba, *Shumparō Hikki,* NZT, 1:452. One person who did understand was the celebrated novelist Natsume Sōseki, who wrote to the poet Masaoka Shiki: "Recently I have been reading Shiba Kōkan's *Shumparō Hikki* and have found in it so many statements and ideas that I wish I myself had written. I feel that I share his feelings and am happy to find that I have a like-minded friend from the past." (Letter of August 3, 1891. In Natsume, 12:18.)
24. Shiba, *Shumparō Hikki,* NZT, 1:462–63.
25. Ibid., p. 414.
26. Shiba, *Dokushō Bōgen,* in *Historia,* p. 94.
27. Shiba, *Shumparō Hikki,* NZT, 1:407.
28. Ibid., pp. 397–98.
29. Ibid., p. 429. See also p. 413.
30. Ibid., p. 429.
31. See ibid., pp. 428, 445, 447.
32. Keene, *Japanese Discovery of Europe: 1720–1798,* p. 79.
33. Shiba, *Shumparō Hikki,* NZT, 1:447.
34. Ibid., p. 463.
35. Ibid., p. 395.
36. Shiba, *Mugon Dōjin Hikki,* TR, p. 104.
37. Matsudaira Sadanobu.
38. Shiba, *Shumparō Hikki,* NZT, 1:450–51.
39. As early as 1798 Kōkan wrote that he planned eventually to settle permanently in Kyoto. (*Saiyū Nikki,* KSN, p. 181.) He had even considered moving there while still in his thirties after the death of his mother. (*Shumparō Hikki,* NZT, 1:413.)
40. The *Yoshino Kikō* manuscript is on twenty-four sheets with ten illustrations.

41. Shiba, *Mugon Dōjin Hikki,* TR, p. 64.

42. The Ibun-kai, founded in Kyoto about 1810 for medical doctors, literary men, artists, and other scholars. Here Kōkan participated in learned discussions and expounded on Western astronomy, geography, and painting. He mentioned the society to Yamane Kazuma in a letter of July 9, 1813 (Bunka 10/6/12), published in *Gakkō Kōyūkai,* Vol. III, No. 6 (March, 1905), pp. 126–28.

43. Shiba, *Saiyū Nikki,* KSN, p. 59.

44. Shiba, *Mugon Dōjin Hikki,* TR, p. 28.

45. Ibid., pp. 70–71.

46. Ibid., pp. 63, 71–74.

47. Shiba, "Shiba Kōkan no Shukan," *Gakkō Kōyūkai,* Vol. III, No. 6 (March, 1905), pp. 126–28. Letter written Bunka 10/6/12.

48. Liang-huang served at the court of Emperor Hsüan Tsung (Ming Huang Ti; reigned 712–756). His poem appears in *Ch'üan T'ang Shih* (Complete Poetic Works of the T'ang Dynasty), compiled under imperial auspices by P'eng Chiu-ting, Yang Chung-na, and others between 1706 and 1708. 12 vols. (Peking: Chung Huo, 1960 reprint of the 1708 edition), Vol. III, p. 2116. Kōkan included Liang-huang's poem in both *Shumparō Hikki* (NZT, 1:435–36) and *Mugon Dōjin Hikki* (TR, pp. 79–80).

49. The rooster was a popular motif on Chinese porcelains of the Ch'ien Lung period (1736–96). The crane, another Chinese symbol, is found in Japanese art as early as the Nara period on objects in the Shōsō-in; it became a part of the repertory of the textile designers and ceramics makers and was used by Kōrin (1658–1716) as a major theme.

50. The name Fugen first appears in *Shumparo Hikki* (NZT, 1:399) together with the date May 9, 1811 (Bunka 8/3/28).

51. He took the characters *tō* and *gen* from the phrase "Tōri fugen ji sei kei." The proverb is found in the *Shih Chi,* Ssŭ-ma Ch'ien's dynastic history of China.

52. Owned by the Kobe City Museum of Namban Art.

53. Kōkan was actually sixty-six. One copy of this announcement is owned by the Kobe City Museum of Namban Art, another by Tenri Library.

54. Shiba, *Mugon Dōjin Hikki,* TR, pp. 28–29.

55. Takemoto, p. 44.

56. The elephant was imported to Japan in June, 1813; the same month, Ishizaki Yūshi executed a painting of it, reproduced in Kuroda, *Nagasaki-kei Yōga,* Pl. 1. Previously, in August, 1597, an elephant, "never before seen in Japan," had been presented to Hideyoshi by a Spanish embassy from Manila.

57. Bunka 10/11/11. *Gakkō Kōyūkai,* Vol. III, No. 8 (June, 1905), 178–81.

58. The original manuscript, in two volumes, has on the cover the title *Tenchi Ridan* (Discussion of Astronomy and Geography); *Mugon Dōjin Hikki,* which appears on the first manuscript page, would seem the more appropriate title.

59. Kōkan wrote: "The book *Isoho Monogatari* is a translation of a European work that I discovered in the library of the lord of Kii. When I examined the book, I found that it was written entirely in allegories . . . translated into Japanese more than two hundred years ago. . . . It is extremely difficult to read, even for someone who has studied Dutch learning. Important to note, however, is that Western learning has been pursued in our country now for more than two hundred years." (*Shumparō Hikki,* NZT, 1:446–47.)

60. The main body of the text contains ninety-three sketches and fables, followed by an appendix containing an additional twenty-five. Most also appear in *Mugon Dōjin Hikki.* The date of the completion of *Kummō Gakai Shū* is verified by the listing in *Shinsen Yōgaku Nempyō* (p. 99), compiled by Ōtsuki Nyoden from the records kept by his grandfather, Ōtsuki Gentaku. Though never published, the original manuscript is extant, housed in the Tokyo National Library.

61. Bunka 12/3/20.

62. Bunsei 1/10/21. Muraoka, *Tenchi Ridan,* Appendix, p. 89. SK, p. 47. Kōkan may have died one month later, Bunsei 1/11/21 (December 18, 1818). See Appendix V here.

APPENDIX III

1. Amboina is the southernmost island of the Moluccas in the East Indies.

2. *Rokubutsu Shinshi,* first published in 1786, also contains an illustration of a mermaid copied by Shiba Kōkan from Valentijn's *Oud en Nieuw Oost-Indiën.* Ōtsuki, *Rokubutsu Shinshi,* pp. 21–22.

3. The Dutch translation of Paré's book was entitled *De Chirurgie en de Opera van alle de Werken van Mr. Ambrosius Paré* (Surgery and Operation Practices from All the Works of Mr. Ambrosius Paré). It was translated from the original French by Carolus Battus in 1649. Ambroise Paré was a leading French surgeon, the originator of modern dissection.

4. Kōkan is referring here to the camera obscura.

APPENDIX V

1. Shiba, *Shumparō Hikki,* NZT, 1:410.

2. Shiba, *Mugon Dōjin Hikki,* TR, p. 75.

3. Shiba, *Shumparō Hikki,* NZT, 1:413.

4. Shiba, *Seiyōga Dan,* NZT, 6:809. Circular of 1800 (*hikifuda*), Kobe City Museum of Namban Art.

5. Shiba, *Oranda Tsūhaku,* SK, p. 128.

6. Circular of 1806, Kobe City Museum of Namban Art.

7. Homma Mitsunori, p. 43. Early manuscript editions of *Ukiyo-e Ruikō* compiled in the late 1790s by Santō Kyōden (1761–1816) contain only Kōkan's name with no mention of his birth or death dates.

8. Discussed by Hosono Masanobu in "Shiba Kōkan no Seinen ni tsuite," pp. 18–24.

BIBLIOGRAPHY

Abe Jirō 阿部次郎. *Tokugawa Jidai no Geijutsu to Shakai* 徳川時代の藝術と社會. Tokyo: Kaizōsha, 1931.

Abraham a Sancta Clara, Pater. *Etwas für Alle, Das ist: Eine kurtze Beschreibung allerley Stands- Ambts- und Gewerbs-Personen, mit beygedruckter Sittlichen Lehre und Biblischen Concepten.* Würzburg, 1699 and 1711.

———. *Iets Voor Allen, zynde een Verhandeling en Verbeelding Van allerhande, Standen, Studien, Konsten, Wetenschappen, Handwerken enz: Waar in derfelver Oorfprong, Opkomft, Aardt, Eygenfchap, Deugdt, en Ondeugden, opeen Geeftige wyze beschreven werdt.* Trans. J. Le Long. Amsterdam, 1717, 1736, and 1759.

Arai Hakuseki 新井白石. *Sairan Igen* 采覽異言. 5 vols. Tokyo: Suzuki Suishun, 1881.

Araki Shumma 荒木俊馬. *Nihon Rekigakushi Gaisetsu* 日本暦学史概說. Tokyo: Kōseisha, 1960.

Arisaka Takamichi 有坂隆道. "Shiba Kōkan Cho, Dokushō Bōgen ni tsuite" 司馬江漢著, 独笑妄言について. *Historia* ヒストリア, No. 10 (November, 1954), 87–104.

Asaoka Kōtei 朝岡興貞. *Koga Bikō* 古畫備考. 4 vols. Tokyo: Kōbunkan, 1903.

Ayusawa Shintarō 鮎澤信太郎. *Sakoku Jidai no Sekai Chirigaku* 鎖國時代の世界地理學. Tokyo: Nichidaidō Shoten, 1943.

———. "Taisei Chirigaku ni okeru Shiba Kōkan no Keimō Undō" 泰西地理學に於ける司馬江漢の啓蒙運動. *Rekishi Chiri* 歷史地理, Vol. 72, No. 3 (September, 1938), 49–62.

Bellah, Robert N. *Tokugawa Religion.* Glencoe, Illinois: Free Press, 1957.

Binyon, Laurence, and Sexton, J. J. O'Brien. *Japanese Colour Prints.* London: Faber and Faber, Ltd., 1960.

Blacker, Carmen. *The Japanese Enlightenment: A Study of the Writings of Fukuzawa Yukichi.* Cambridge: Harvard University Press, 1964.

Boxer, C. R. *Christian Century in Japan 1549–1650.* Berkeley and Los Angeles: University of California Press, 1951.

———. *Jan Compagnie in Japan 1600–1850.* The Hague: Martinus Nijhoff, 1950.

———. "The Mandarin at Chinsura; Isaac Titsingh in Bengal, 1785–1792." *Koninklijke Vereeniging Indisch Instituut* (Royal Institute for the Indies), Mededeling No. LXXXIV, Afdeling Volkenkunde No. 32 (1949), 1–28.

Buys, Egbert. *Nieuw en Volkomen Woordenboek van Konsten en Weetenschappen.* Amsterdam, 1769.

Chomel, Noël. *Algemeen Huishoudelijk-, Natuur-, Zedekundig-en Konst-Woordenboek, Vervattende veele middelen om zijn Goed Te Vermeerderen, en zijne Gezondheid Te Behouden.* Revised by Jacques Alexandre de Chalmot. Amsterdam, 1778.

———. *Huishoudelijk Woordenboek, Vervattende Veele middelen om zijn Goed Te Vermeerderen, en zijne Gezondheid Te Behouden.* Trans. Jan Lodewyk Schuer. Amsterdam, 1743.

de Bary, Wm. Theodore, ed. *Sources of Chinese Tradition.* New York: Columbia University Press, 1963.

———, ed. *Sources of Japanese Tradition.* New York: Columbia University Press, 1958.

de Lairesse, Gerard. *Groot Schilderboek, Waar in de Schilderkonst In Al Haar Deelen Grondig werd onderweezen.* Amsterdam, 1712.

———. *Het Groot Schilderboek.* Amsterdam, 1707.

Feenstra Kuiper, J. *Japan en de Buitenwereld in de Achttiende Eeuw.* The Hague: M. Nijhoff, 1921.

Fujii Shin 藤井信. "Rangakusha no Shisō Naiyō ni tsuite" 蘭學者の思想內容について. *Rekishigaku Kenkyū* 歷史學硏究, Vol. I, No. 5 (March, 1934), 346–65.

Fujioka Sakutarō 藤岡作太郎. *Kinsei Kaigashi* 近世繪畫史. Osaka: Sōgensha, 1941.

Goodman, Grant Kohn. *The Dutch Impact on*

Japan (1640–1853). Monographies de T'oung Pao, Vol. V. Leiden: E. J. Brill, 1967.

Gotfridi, Joh. Lud. *Historische Chronyck*. Trans. Jacob van Meurs. Amsterdam, 1660.

Haga Tōru. "The Formation of Realism in Meiji Painting: The Artistic Career of Takahashi Yuichi (1828–94)." Unpublished manuscript, Tokyo University, January, 1966.

——— 芳賀徹. "Gajin Shiba Kōkan no Sekai: Sono Dōbanga to 'Saiyū Nikki'" 画人司馬江漢の世界—その銅版画と「西遊日記」 in *Nihon Kindaika to sono Kokusaiteki Kankyō* 日本近代化とその国際的環境. Tokyo: Tōkyō Daigaku Kyōyō Gakubu, Nihon Kindaika Kenkyū Kai, 1968.

———. "Shiba Kōkan 'Saiyū Nikki' no Sekai" 司馬江漢「西遊日記」の世界 *Kenkyū Hōkoku* 研究報告, No. 172 (July, 1965), 1–11.

———. "Takahashi Yuichi to Shiba Kōkan" 高橋由一と司馬江漢 *Kenkyū Hōkoku* 研究報告, No. 147 (July, 1963), 1–14.

Hall, John Whitney. *Tanuma Okitsugu, 1719–1788: Forerunner of Modern Japan*. Cambridge: Harvard University Press, 1955.

Hawley, Frank. *Miscellanea Japonica II: Whales and Whaling in Japan*. Kyoto: Kawakita Printing Company, 1958.

Hayakawa Junsaburō 早川純三郎, comp. *Bummei Genryū Sōsho* 文明源流叢書, 3 vols. Tokyo: Kokusho Kankōkai, 1914. Reprinted 1940.

———, comp. *Nihon Zuihitsu Taisei* 日本随筆大成. 41 vols. Tokyo: Yoshikawa Kōbunkan, 1927.

Hayashi Tsuruichi. "A List of Some Dutch Astronomical Works Imported into Japan from Holland," *Nieuw Archief voor Wiskunde,* 2nd Series, Vol. 7, 1907.

Hirafuku Hyakusui 平福百穂, ed. *Nihon Yōga Shokō* 日本洋畫曙光. Tokyo: Iwanami Shoten, 1929.

Hiraga Gennai 平賀源內. *Hōhi Ron* 放屁論 (1777), in *Nihon Koten Bungaku Taikei* 日本古典文学大系, Vol. 55. Tokyo: Iwanami Shoten, 1961, 228–55.

Homma Mitsunori 本間光則, ed. *Shin Zōho Ukiyo-e Ruikō Gesakusha Ryakuden* 新增補浮世繪類考戲作者略傳. Tokyo: Suwara Tetsuji, 1889.

Honda Toshiaki 本多利明. *Seiiki Monogatari* 西域物語, Vol. 20 of *Nihon Keizai Sōsho* 日本經濟叢書. Tokyo: Keimeisha, 1915.

Honjō Eijirō 本庄榮治郎, ed. *Honda Toshiaki Shū* 本多利明集. Vol. 8 of *Kinsei Shakai Keizai Gakusetsu Taikei* 近世社會經濟學說大系. Tokyo: Seibundō Shikosha, 1935.

Hosono Masanobu 細野正信. "Dokushō Bōgen" 独笑妄言. *Kikan Geijutsu* 季刊芸術, No. 14 (1970).

———. "Shiba Kōkan no Seinen ni tsuite" 司馬江漢の生年について. *Museum,* No. 230, Tokyo Kokuritsu Hakubutsukan Bijutsu Shi (May, 1970), 18–24.

Huai-nan Tzŭ 淮南子. *Huai-nan Tzŭ T'ien Wên Hsün* 淮南子天文訓. 2 vols. Hopei: Ch'ung Wên Shu Chu, 1877.

Ikenaga Hajime 池長孟. *Hōsai Banka Taihōkan* 邦彩蠻華大寶鑑. 2 vols. Osaka: Sōgensha, 1932.

———. *Namban Bijutsu Sōmokuroku* 南蛮美術総目録. Kobe: Shiritsu Kobe Bijutsukan, 1955.

———. *Taigai Kankei Bijutsu Shiryō Nempyō* 對外關係美術史料年表. Kobe: Ikenaga Bijutsukan, 1940.

Imai Itaru 今井溱. *Clavius to Kenkon Bensetsu* Clavius と乾坤弁說. Nihon Temmon Kenkyū Kai, Vol. 1, No. 4, 1957.

———. *Maruchin no Kyūrisho* マルチンの究理書. Nihon Temmon Kenkyū Kai, Vol. 2, No. 3, 1960.

Inoue Kazuo 井上和雄. *Ukiyo-e Shi Den* 浮世繪師傳. Tokyo: Watanabe Hangaten, 1931.

Irita Seizō 入田整三, ed. *Hiraga Gennai Zenshū* 平賀源內全集, 2 vols. Tokyo: Chūbunkan Shoten, 1935.

Ishii Hakutei 石井柏亭. *Nihon ni okeru Yōfūga no Enkaku* 日本に於ける洋風畫の沿革. Tokyo: Iwanami Shoten, 1932.

Itazawa Takeo 板澤武雄. "Kinsei ni okeru Chidōsetsu no Tenkai to Sono Handō" 近世に於ける地動說の展開とその反動. *Shigaku Zasshi* 史學雜誌, Vol. 52, No. 1 (January, 1941), 1–30.

———. *Nichiran Bunka Kōshōshi no Kenkyū* 日蘭文化交涉史の研究, Tokyo: Kōbunkan, 1959.

———. *Nihon to Oranda* 日本とオランダ. Tokyo: Shibundō, 1955.

———. "Rangaku to Jugaku to no Kōshō oyobi Bakufu no Tai Rangaku Seisaku" 蘭學と儒學との交涉及び幕府の對蘭學政策, in *Kinsei Nihon no Jugaku* 近世日本の儒學, comp. Fukushima Kashizō. Tokyo: Iwanami Shoten, 1941, 639–71.

Johnston, John. *Naeukeurige Beschryving van de Natuur der Viervoetige Dieren, Vissen en Bloedlooze Water-Dieren, Vogelen, Kronkel-Dieren,*

Slangen en Draken. Trans. M. Grausius. Amsterdam, 1660.

Kaempfer, Engelbert. *Kaempfer's History of Japan*. Trans. J. G. Scheuchzer. 3 vols. New York: Macmillan, 1906.

Kaikoku Hyakunen Kinen Bunka Jigyōkai Hen 開国百年記念文化事業会編. *Sakoku Jidai: Nihonjin no Kaigai Chishiki* 鎖国時代一日本人の海外知識. Tokyo: Kangensha, 1953.

Katagiri Kazuo 片桐一男. "Shiba Kōkan no Shin Shokan: Dōban 'Chikyū Zenzu' no Seisaku Jijō o Kataru" 司馬江漢の新書翰一銅版「地球全図」の製作事情を語る. *Ko Bijutsu* 古美術, No. 30 (June, 1970), 101–10.

———. "Yōfū Gaka Ishikawa Tairō to Edo no Rangaku Kai" 洋風画家石川大浪と江戸の蘭学界. *Museum,* Nos. 227 & 228, Tokyo Kokuritsu Hakubutsukan Bijutsu Shi (February & March, 1970), 4–17; 16–28.

Katayama Shōsai 片山松齋. *Hokusō Zatsuwa* 北窓雜話 (1826), in *Hyakka Zuihitsu* 百家随筆, comp. Hayakawa Junzaburō 早川純三郎. Vol. III, Tokyo: Kokusho Kankōkai, 1918.

———. *Sōkai Itteki Shū* 滄海一滴集. Edo: Seisendō, 1821.

Katsuragawa Hoshū 桂川甫周 (trans.) and Ōtsuki Gentaku 大槻玄澤 (ed.). *Shinsei Chikyū Bankoku Zusetsu* 新製地球萬國圖說 (1786), in *Kōmō Zatsuwa* 紅毛雜話, ed. Ono Tadashige, Tokyo: Sōrinsha, 1943, 1–34.

Keene, Donald. "Hirata Atsutane and Western Learning," *T'oung Pao*. XLII, Livr. 5 (May, 1954), 353–80.

———. *The Japanese Discovery of Europe: Honda Toshiaki and Other Discoverers 1720–1798*. New York: Grove Press, 1954.

———. *The Japanese Discovery of Europe, 1720–1830*. Revised Edition. Stanford, California: Stanford University Press, 1969.

Koga Jūjirō 古賀十二郎. *Nagasaki Kaiga Zenshi* 長崎繪畫全史. Tokyo: Hokkō Shobō, 1944.

———. *Seiyō Ijutsu Denraishi* 西洋醫術傳來史. Tokyo: Nisshin Shoin, 1942.

Kokkasha 國華社. *Kokka* 國華:
No. 219 (August, 1908), 50–54.
Takanawa Zu 高輪圖, Ōigawa Zu 大井川圖
No. 336 (May, 1918), 378–79.
Sansui Zu 山水圖
No. 385 (June, 1922), 432–37.
Hogei Gakan 捕鯨畫卷
No. 544 (March, 1936), 88, 91.
Kanazawa Sekkei Zu 金澤雪景圖
No. 570 (May, 1938), 130–37.
Fugaku Embō Zu 富嶽遠望圖
No. 667 (October, 1947), 374–75.
Sunshū Yoshiwara Eki Zu 駿州吉原驛圖
No. 726 (September, 1952), 274–77.
Fūzoku Zu 風俗圖
No. 838 (January, 1962), 33–36.
Yanagi ni Kawasemi Zu 柳に翡翠圖
Yanagi ni Yamabato Zu 柳に山鳩圖

Kokuritsu Kagaku Hakubutsukan 国立科学博物館. *Edo Jidai no Kagaku* 江戸時代の科学. Tokyo: Meisho Kankōkai, 1969.

Koyama Fujio 小山冨士夫. "Shiba Kōkan Sometsuke Kikyū Zu Sara" 司馬江漢染付気球図皿. *Geijutsu Shinchō* 芸術新潮. No. 7 (July, 1970), 122–23.

Krieger, C. C. *The Infiltration of European Civilization in Japan During the 18th Century*. Leiden: E. J. Brill, 1940.

Kurita Mototsugu 栗田元次. *Nihon Kohan Chizu Shūsei* 日本古版地圖集成. Tokyo: Hakata Seishōdō, 1932.

Kuroda Genji 黒田源次. "Kōkan: Chūki no Sakuhin to Sono Garon" 江漢一中期の作品とその画論. *Ukiyo-e* 浮世絵, No. 18 (July, 1965), 50–64.

———. "Kōkan 'Harushige' no Gisaku Kenkyū" 江漢「春重」の偽作研究. *Ukiyo-e* 浮世絵, No. 15 (April, 1965), 10–20.

———. "Kōkan no Nenrei to Seikatsu Kō" 江漢の年齢と生活考. *Ukiyo-e* 浮世絵, No. 19 (August, 1965), 43–59.

———. *Nagasaki-kei Yōga* 長崎系洋畫. Tokyo: Sōgensha, 1932.

———. "Saiyū Nikki ni Arawareta Kōkan no Sakuhin" 西遊日記にあらわれた江漢の作品. *Ukiyo-e* 浮世絵, No. 17 (June, 1965), 38–49.

———. *Seiyō no Eikyō o Uketaru Nihonga* 西洋の影響を受けたる日本畫. Kyoto: Chūgai Shuppan Kabushiki Kaisha, 1924.

———. "Shiba Kōkan no Shizen Kagakuteki Gyōseki ni tsuite" 司馬江漢の自然科学的業蹟について. *Bijutsushi* 美術史, No. 6 (June, 1952), 49–62.

———. "Shiba Kōkan no Sōki Abura-e" 司馬江漢の早期油絵. *Ukiyo-e* 浮世絵, No. 16 (May, 1965), 8–18.

———, ed. *Kōkan Saiyū Nikki* 江漢西遊日記. Tokyo: Sakamoto Shoten, 1927.

Kyoto Hakubutsukan 京都博物館. *Meiji Izen Yōga Ruishū* 明治以前洋畫類集. Kyoto: Kyoto Hakubutsukan, 1925.

———. *Nagasaki-ha Shasei Nansō Meigasen*

長崎派寫生南宋名畫選. Kyoto: Benridō, 1939.
———. *Nihon Kinsei Meiga Taikan* 日本近世名畫大鑑. 2 vols. Kyoto: Nakajima Taiseikaku, 1941.

Matsudaira Sadanobu 松平定信. *Taikan Zakki* 退閑雑記. Tokyo: Kokkōsha, 1892.

Michigami Toshii 道上寿一. "Watashi no Remburanto: Mangetsu no Zu" わたしのレンブラント「満月の図」. *Geijutsu Shinchō* 芸術新潮, No. 181 (January, 1965), 102–9.

Miura Baien 三浦梅園. *Kizanroku* 歸山錄, in *Nihon Tetsugaku Zensho* 日本哲學全書, Vol. 8, Tokyo: Daiichi Shobō, 1936.

Mochizuki Nobunaga 望月信亨, comp. *Bukkyō Daijiten* 仏教大辞典. 8 vols. Tokyo: Sekai Seiten Kankō Kyōkai, 1960.

Mody, N. H. N. *A Collection of Nagasaki Colour Prints and Paintings*. 2 vols. London: Kegan Paul, Trench, Trubner & Co., Ltd., 1939. Reprinted (in 1 vol.). Tokyo: Charles E. Tuttle, Co., 1969.

Morishima Chūryō 森島中良. *Bankoku Shinwa* 萬國新話, in *Kōmō Zatsuwa* 紅毛雑話, ed. Ono Tadashige, Tokyo: Sōrinsha, 1943, 175–278.
———. *Kōmō Zatsuwa* 紅毛雑話, ed. Ono Tadashige, Tokyo: Sōrinsha, 1943, 35–174.

Motoki Ryōei 本木良永. *Taiyō Kyūri Ryōkaisetsu* 太陽窮理了解說, in *Nihon Tetsugaku Zensho* 日本哲學全書, Vol. 8, Tokyo: Daiichi Shobō, 1936.

Muraoka Tsunetsugu 村岡典嗣. *Nihon Bunka Shi Gaisetsu* 日本文化史概說. Tokyo: Iwanami Shoten, 1938.
———, ed. *Tenchi Ridan* 天地理談. Tokyo: Oka Shoin, 1930.

Nakai Sōtarō 中井宗太郎. *Shiba Kōkan* 司馬江漢. Tokyo: Atoriesha, 1942.

Nakayama Kōyō 中山高陽. *Gadan Keijo* 畫譚鷄肋. Edo: Shōun Sambō, 1797.

Nakayama, Shigeru. *A History of Japanese Astronomy: Chinese Background and Western Impact*. Cambridge, Massachusetts: Harvard University Press, 1969.

Naruse Fujio 成瀬不二雄. "Akita Ranga no Sakufūteki Kentō" 秋田蘭画の作風的検討. *Yamato Bunka* 大和文華, No. 49 (November, 1968), 35–62.
———. "Shiba Kōkan Hitsu: Sōka Zu" 司馬江漢筆草花図. *Yamato Bunka* 大和文華, No. 49 (November, 1968), 64–67.
———. "Shiba Kōkan no Gagyō ni tsuite" 司馬江漢の画業について. *Yamato Bunka* 大和文華, No. 52 (August, 1970), 9–45.

Natsume Jun'ichi 夏目純一, ed. *Sōseki Zenshū* 漱石全集. 19 vols. Tokyo: Iwanami Shoten, 1935–37.

Needham, Joseph. *Science and Civilization in China*. Cambridge: Cambridge University Press, 1959.

Nishikawa Joken 西川如見. *Ka'i Tsūshō Kō* 華夷通商考, in *Nihon Keizai Sōsho* 日本經濟叢書, Vol. 5, Tokyo: Nihon Keizai Sōsho Kankōkai, 1914.
———. *Yonjūni Koku Jimbutsu Zusetsu* 四十二國人物圖說 in *Kōmō Zatsuwa* 紅毛雑話, ed. Ono Tadashige, Tokyo: Sōrinsha, 1943, 278–375.

Nishimura Tei 西村貞. *Namban Bijutsu* 南蛮美術. Tokyo: Kōdansha, 1958.
———. *Nihon Dōban Gashi* 日本銅版畫史. Tokyo: Shomotsu Tembōsha, 1941.
———. *Nihon Shoki Yōga no Kenkyū* 日本初期洋畫の研究. Kyoto: Zenkoku Shobō, 1945.

Norman, E. H. "Andō Shōeki and the Anatomy of Japanese Feudalism," *Transactions of the Asiatic Society of Japan*, 3rd Series, Vol. 2, 1949.

Numata Jirō 沼田次郎. *Yōgaku Denrai no Rekishi* 洋学伝来の歴史. Tokyo: Shibundō, 1960.

Ogata Tomio 緒方富雄, ed. *Rangaku to Nihon Bunka* 蘭学と日本文化 Tokyo: Tokyo Daigaku Shuppankai, 1971.

Okamura Chibiki 岡村千曳. *Kōmō Bunka Shiwa* 紅毛文化史話. Tokyo: Sōgensha, 1953.

Ōnishi Hajime 大西祝. "Shiba Kōkan no Sekaikan" 司馬江漢の世界觀. *Kokumin no Tomo* 國民の友, No. 233 (August, 1894), 35–52.

Ono Tadashige 小野忠重. *Doro-e to Garasu-e* 泥絵とガラス絵. Tokyo: Asoka Shobō, 1954.
———. *Edo no Yōgaka* 江戸の洋画家. Tokyo: Sansaisha, 1968.
———. "Shiba Kōkan: Kanryū Suikin Zu" 司馬江漢―寒柳水禽図. *Ko Bijutsu* 古美術, No. 28 (December, 1969), 111–14.
———, ed. *Kōmō Zatsuwa* 紅毛雑話. Tokyo: Sōrinsha, 1943.

Ōtsuki Fumihiko 大槻文彦. "Edo Jidai no Rangaku" 江戸時代の蘭學 in *Edo Jidai Shiron* 江戸時代史論, Nihon Rekishi Chiri Gakkai. Tokyo: Jin'yūsha, 1915, 461–98.

Ōtsuki Gentaku 大槻玄澤. *Bansui Mansō* 磐水漫草, in *Bansui Sonkyō* 磐水存響, comp. Ōtsuki Shigeo, Vol. 2, Tokyo: Tsukiji Kappan Seizōsho, 1912, 1–128.

———. *Ransetsu Benwaku* 蘭說辯惑, in *Bummei Genryū Sōsho* 文明源流叢書, ed. Hayakawa Junsaburō, Tokyo: Taizansha, 1940, 487–518.

———. *Rokubutsu Shinshi* 六物新誌. Osaka: Naniwa Kenkadō, 1795.

Ōtsuki Nyoden 大槻如電. *Shinsen Yōgaku Nempyō* 新撰洋學年表. Tokyo: Rokugōkan, 1927.

Ozawa Toshio 小澤敏夫. *Nagasaki Nempyō* 長崎年表. Nagasaki: Guroria Shobō, 1935.

Rangaku Shiryō Kenkyūkai 蘭学資料研究会. *Yōgaku Koto Hajime Ten* 洋学ことはじめ展. Tokyo: Rangaku Shiryō Kenkyūkai, 1954.

Sadamatsu Shūzō 貞松修藏, ed. *Kōsei Shimpen* 厚生新篇. Shizuoka: Aoi Bunko, 1937.

Saitō Gekkin 齊藤月岑, comp. *Zōtei Bukō Nempyō* 増訂武江年表. Tokyo: Kokusho Kankōkai, 1925.

Sakamoto Mitsuru 坂本満, Sugase Tadashi 菅瀬正, and Naruse Fujio 成瀬不二雄. *Genshoku Nihon no Bijutsu* 原色日本の美術, Vol. 25: *Namban Bijutsu to Yōfūga* 南蛮美術と洋風画. Tokyo: Shōgakukan, 1970.

Sakazaki Tan 坂崎坦, comp. *Nihon Gadan Taikan* 日本畫談大觀. Tokyo: Mejiro Shoin, 1917.

Satake Shozan 佐竹曙山. *Gahō Kōryō* 畫法綱領, in *Nihon Gadan Taikan* 日本畫談大觀, comp. Sakazaki Tan, Tokyo: Mejiro Shoin, 1917, 71–74.

Sansom, G. B. *The Western World and Japan*. New York: Alfred A. Knopf, 1950.

Satō Chūryō 佐藤中陵. *Chūryō Manroku* 中陵漫録 (1826), in *Nihon Zuihitsu Taikei* 日本隨筆大系, comp. Hayakawa Junsaburō, Vol. 2. Tokyo: Nihon Zuihitsu Taisei Kankōkai, 1929.

Satō Nobuhiro 佐藤信淵. *Rangaku Daidōhen* 蘭學大道編. Nagasaki: Kotōkan, undated. (In Waseda University Library, Tokyo.)

Sawamura Sentarō 澤村專太郎. "Nihon ni okeru Shoki no Yōga" 日本に於ける初期の洋畫, in *Kaikoku Bunka* 開國文化, comp. Ōmichi Hirō, Tokyo: Asahi Shimbunsha, 1929.

Shiba Kōkan 司馬江漢. See Appendix II.

Shimmura Izuru 新村出. *Namban Ki* 南蠻記. Tokyo: Tōadō Shobō, 1915.

———. *Namban Kōki* 南蠻廣記. Tokyo: Iwanami Shoten, 1925.

———. *Namban Sarasa* 南蠻更紗. Tokyo: Kaizōsha, 1924.

———. *Shiden Sōkō* 史傳叢考. Tokyo: Rakurō Shoin, 1934.

———. *Shimmura Izura Senshū* 新村出選集. Tokyo: Kōtori Shorin, 1943.

———. *Tenseki Sōdan* 典籍叢談. Tokyo: Oka Shoin, 1925.

———. *Tenseki Zakkō* 典籍雑考. Tokyo: Tsukushi Shobō, 1944.

Shimonaka Yasaburō 下中彌三郎. *Dai Jimmei Jiten* 大人名事典. 5 vols. Tokyo: Heibonsha, 1957.

Soper, Alexander C. "Some Technical Terms in the Early Literature of Chinese Painting," *Harvard Journal of Asiatic Studies*. Vol. XI, Nos. 1 & 2 (June, 1948), 163–73.

Sugano Yō 菅野陽. "Shiba Kōkan Sōsei no Fushoku Dōbanga Gihō no Genten ni tsuite" 司馬江漢創製の腐蝕銅版画技法の原典について. In two parts. *Bijutsu Kenkyū* 美術研究. Nos. 265–266 (September and November, 1969), 81–102; 127–46.

Sugase Tadashi 菅瀬正. "Shiba Kōkan Shōron" 司馬江漢小論. *Yamato Bunka* 大和文華, No. 52 (August, 1970), 1–8.

Szczesniak, Boleslaw. "The Penetration of the Copernican Theory into Feudal Japan," *Journal of the Royal Asiatic Society* (Great Britain and Ireland). London (April, 1944), 52–61.

Takahashi Shin'ichi 高橋磌一. "Yōgaron" 洋畫論, in *Nihon Rekishi Zensho* 日本歴史全書, Vol. 20. Tokyo: Mikasa Shobō, 1939.

Takanashi Kōshi 高梨光司, Aimi Kōu 相見香雨, and Maruyama Toshio 丸山季夫. "Kimura Kenkadō" 木村蒹葭堂. *Kamigata* 上方, No. 146 (March, 1943), 2–24.

Takehana Rintarō 武塙林太郎 and Naruse Fujio 成瀬不二夫. "Odano Naotake to Shiba Kōkan no Kankei ni tsuite" 小田野直武と司馬江漢の関係について, *Bijutsushi* 美術史 70, Vol. 18, No. 2 (September, 1968), 33–51.

Takemoto Sekitei 竹本石亭. *Sekitei Gadan* 石亭畫談. Tokyo: Zuga Kankōkai, 1918.

Tokyo Kokuritsu Bunkazai Kenkyūsho Bijutsubu 東京國立文化財研究所美術部. *Nihon Bijutsu Nenkan* 日本美術年鑑. Tokyo: Ōkurashō Insatsukyoku, 1936.

Tominaga Nakamoto 富永仲基. *Shutsujō Gogo* 出定後語 (1744), in *Nihon Shisō Tōsō Shiryō* 日本思想闘諍史料, comp. Washio Junkei, Vol. 3. Tokyo: Tōhō Shoin, 1930.

Toyama Usaburō 外山卯三郎. *Nihon Shoki Yōgashi Kō* 日本初期洋畫史考. Tokyo: Kensetsusha, 1932.

Tsuji Zennosuke 辻善之助. *Tanuma Jidai* 田沼時代. Tokyo: Nihon Gakujutsu Fukyūkai, 1936.

Valentijn, François. *Oud en Nieuw Oost-Indiën*. 5 vols. Amsterdam: Gerard Onder de Linden, 1726.

Waley, Arthur. "Shiba Kōkan, 1737–1818," *The Secret History of the Mongols*. London: George Allen & Unwin Ltd., 1963, 108–27.

Watanabe Kurasuke 渡辺庫輔. *Kiyō Ronkō* 崎陽論攷. Nagasaki (?), 1964.

Waterhouse, D. B. *Harunobu and His Age: The Development of Colour Printing in Japan*. London: Grosvenor Press, 1964.

Yabuuchi Kiyoshi 藪内清. *Edo Jidai ni okeru Seiyō Temmongaku no Eikyō* 江戸時代における西洋天文学の影響. Tokyo: Sōgensha, 1960.

———. *Edo Jidai no Kagaku Kikai* 江戸時代の科学器械. Tokyo: Kōseisho Kōseikaku, 1964.

Yamamura Shōei 山村昌永 and Nagada Nankei 永田南溪. *Kaigai Jimbutsu Shū* 海外人物輯 (1854), in *Kōmō Zatsuwa* 紅毛雑話, ed. Ono Tadashige, Tokyo: Sōrinsha, 1943, 377–402.

Yamana Kakuzō 山名格藏. *Nihon no Ukiyo-e Shi* 日本の浮世繪師. Tokyo: Daiichi Shobō, 1930.

Yamazaki Naokata 山崎直方. "Shiba Kōkan" 司馬江漢, *Chishitsugaku Zasshi* 地質學雜誌, Vol. 1, No. 11 (July, 1894), 556–61.

Yanagi Ryō 柳亮. "Shiba Kōkan, Yōga, Dōbanga, soshite Rigaku no Senkusha" 司馬江漢, 洋画, 銅版画, そして理学の先駆者. *Bijutsu Techō* 美術手帖, No. 141 (May, 1958), 97–111.

Yashiro Yukio 矢代幸雄, ed. *Yōga no Senkakusha Shiba Kōkan Ten* 洋画の先覚者司馬江漢展. Nara: Yamato Bunkakan, 1969.

Yoshida Shimbē 吉田新兵衛. *Keijō Gaen* 京城畫苑. Kyoto: Yoshida Shimbē, 1814.

Yu I 游藝. *T'ien-ching Huo-wên* 天經或問. Edo: Kōzanbō, undated.

Yuasa Mitsutomo 湯浅光朝, ed. *Kagaku Bunkashi Nempyō* 科学文化史年表. Tokyo: Chūō Kōronsha, 1957.

INDEX

Japanese are generally listed under their common names, which are not necessarily their family names. References to Notes are given only where they indicate matters of special interest or importance. They are written with the page number followed by the number of the note; 185 n 7, for example, refers to page 185, note 7. Numbers in italics refer to the plates.

STUDIES OF THE EAST ASIAN INSTITUTE

The Ladder of Success in Imperial China, by Ping-ti Ho. New York: Columbia University Press, 1962.

The Chinese Inflation, 1937–1949, by Shun-hsin Chou. New York: Columbia University Press, 1963.

Reformer in Modern China: Chang Chien, 1853–1926, by Samuel Chu. New York: Columbia University Press, 1965.

Research in Japanese Sources: A Guide, by Herschel Webb with the assistance of Marleigh Ryan. New York: Columbia University Press, 1965.

Society and Education in Japan, by Herbert Passin. New York: Bureau of Publications, Teachers College, Columbia University, 1965.

Agricultural Production and Economic Development in Japan, 1873–1922, by James I. Nakamura. Princeton: Princeton University Press, 1966.

Japan's First Modern Novel: Ukigumo of Futabatei Shimei, by Marleigh Ryan. New York: Columbia University Press, 1967.

The Korean Communist Movement, 1918–1948, by Dae-Sook Suh. Princeton: Princeton University Press, 1967.

The First Vietnam Crisis, by Melvin Gurtov. New York: Columbia University Press, 1967.

Cadres, Bureaucracy, and Political Power in Communist China, by A. Doak Barnett. New York: Columbia University Press, 1967.

The Japanese Imperial Institution in the Tokugawa Period, by Herschel Webb. New York: Columbia University Press, 1968.

Higher Education and Business Recruitment in Japan, by Koya Azumi. New York: Teachers College Press, Columbia University, 1969.

The Communists and Chinese Peasant Rebellions: A Study in the Rewriting of Chinese History, by James P. Harrison, Jr. New York: Atheneum, 1969.

How the Conservatives Rule Japan, by Nathaniel B. Thayer. Princeton: Princeton University Press, 1969.

Aspects of Chinese Education, edited by C. T. Hu. New York: Teachers College Press, Columbia University, 1970.

Documents of Korean Communism, 1918–1948, by Dae-Sook Suh. Princeton: Princeton University Press, 1970.

Japanese Education: A Bibliography of Materials in the English Language, by Herbert Passin. New York: Teachers College Press, Columbia University, 1970.

Economic Development and the Labor Market in Japan, by Koji Taira. New York: Columbia University Press, 1970.

The Japanese Oligarchy and the Russo-Japanese War, by Shumpei Okamoto. New York: Columbia University Press, 1970.

Imperial Restoration in Medieval Japan, by H. Paul Varley. New York: Columbia University Press, 1971.

Japan's Postwar Defense Policy, 1947–1968, by Martin E. Weinstein. New York: Columbia University Press, 1971.

Election Campaigning Japanese Style, by Gerald L. Curtis. New York: Columbia University Press, 1971.

China and Russia: The "Great Game," by O. Edmund Clubb. New York: Columbia University Press, 1971.

Money and Monetary Policy in Communist China, by Katharine Huang Hsiao. New York: Columbia University Press, 1971.

The District Magistrate in Late Imperial China, by John R. Watt. New York: Columbia University Press, 1972.

Law and Policy in China's Foreign Relations: A Study of Attitudes and Practice, by James C. Hsiung. New York: Columbia University Press, 1972.

Pearl Harbor as History: Japanese-American Relations, 1931–1941, edited by Dorothy Borg and Shumpei Okamoto, with the assistance of Dale K. A. Finlayson. New York: Columbia University Press, 1973.

Japanese Culture: A Short History, by H. Paul Varley. New York: Praeger, 1973.

Doctors in Politics: The Political Life of the Japan Medical Association, by William E. Steslicke. New York: Praeger, 1973.

Japan's Foreign Policy, 1868–1941: A Research Guide, edited by James William Morley. New York: Columbia University Press, 1973.

The Japan Teachers Union: A Radical Interest Group in Japanese Politics, by Donald Ray Thurston. Princeton: Princeton University Press, 1973.

Palace and Politics in Prewar Japan, by David Anson Titus. New York: Columbia University Press, 1974.

The Idea of China: Essays in Geographic Myth and Theory, by Andrew March. Devon, England: David and Charles, 1974.

The "weathermark" identifies this book as a production of John Weatherhill, Inc., publishers of fine books on Asia and the Pacific. Supervising editor: Rebecca Davis. Book design and typography: Dana Levy. Layout of illustrations: Rebecca Davis. Production supervisor: Mitsuo Okado. Composition: Samhwa Printing Co., Seoul. Color plate engraving and printing: Nissha Printing Co., Kyoto. Monochrome platemaking and printing and text printing: Kinmei Printing Co., Tokyo. Binding: Okamoto Binderies, Tokyo. The typeface used is Baskerville, with Japanese characters in hand-set Mincho, and with hand-set Bernhard Modern for display.